SUBJECT TO CHANGE

SUBJECT TO CHANGE

Guerrilla Television Revisited

Deirdre Boyle

New York   Oxford
OXFORD UNIVERSITY PRESS
1997

Oxford University Press

Oxford   New York
Athens   Auckland   Bangkok   Bogota   Bombay   Buenos Aires
Calcutta   Cape Town   Dar es Salaam   Delhi   Florence   Hong Kong
Istanbul   Karachi   Kuala Lumpur   Madras   Madrid   Melbourne
Mexico City   Nairobi   Paris   Singapore   Taipei   Tokyo   Toronto

and associated companies in
Berlin   Ibadan

Copyright © 1997 by Deirdre Boyle

Published by Oxford University Press, Inc.
198 Madison Avenue, New York, New York 10016

Oxford is a registered trademark of Oxford University Press

Library of Congress Cataloging-in-Publication Data
Boyle, Deirdre.
   Subject to change : guerrilla television revisited / Deirdre Boyle.
     p. cm.
   Includes bibliographical references and index.
   ISBN 0-19-504334-0; 0-19-511054-4 (pbk.)
    1. Video recordings—Political aspects. 2. Documentary television
programs. 3. TVTV (Production company)—History. 4. Public-access
television—United States. 5. Public television—United States.
I. Title.
PN1992.945.B68 1996
791.45'0973'09046—dc20   96-33448

9 8 7 6 5 4 3 2 1

Printed in the United States of America
on acid-free paper

Preface

Any historian can write the history of a conventional movement, but to write the history of a hip movement, to know when to laugh and when not to, to be able to distinguish—most difficult of tasks— straightforward literal language from the hyperbole that is hip's special trait, to see the logic in the foolery, to evoke some of the joyfulness of a hip rebellion, to remember always that standards of conventional politics don't apply to movements devoted to oppositional politics—to do all this one needs not only a suitable background but also to have in some measure overcome that background.

—Paul Berman, *The New Republic*

So much of what you had counted on as a solid wall of convictions now seems on bad nights, or in sickness, or just weakness, no longer made of much that can be leaned against. It is then that one can barely place oneself in time. All that you would swear had been can only be found again if you have the energy to dig hard enough, and that is hard on the feet and the back, and sometimes you are frightened that near an edge is nothing.

—Lillian Hellman, *Maybe, A Story*

The stories people tell have a way of taking care of them. If stories come to you, care for them. And learn to give them away where they are needed. Sometimes a person needs a story more than food to stay alive. That is why we put these stories in each other's memory.

—Barry Lopez, *Crow and Weasel*

I began work on this book in 1983 as an attempt to understand not only what had happened to the guerrilla television of the 1970s but what had happened to the "Now" generation, my generation. Facing the realities of the '80s was tough for someone whose world view had been shaped by the civil rights and antiwar movements and molded by the anti-establishment beliefs of youth who fervently believed they could change the world. Despite the ravages of a long and distant war in Vietnam and continuing social inequities at home, my generation possessed an optimism and belief in social progress that still takes my breath away. I wanted to know what had happened to that expansiveness, that creative trust in the future, the arrogant and perhaps adolescent belief that we could re-make the world.

To find answers to these questions, I chose video as my focus and point of departure. It was an obvious choice for me. I was a charter member of the first television generation, raised on "Howdy Doody" and "Playhouse 90," on "The Honeymooners" and "Omnibus." Television had been my window on the world: I had watched John Kennedy's first press conferences on television, and there I joined millions who followed his funeral cortege down Pennsylvania Avenue. I had even appeared on a local children's program, invited to speak out in the show's "Gripe Session" about the injustice of demanding that "children should be seen and not heard." I later realized the "Wonderama" producers found my social critique funny, but at the age of 12 I was too busy enjoying the thrill of being in front of the camera, wielding the power of a mass medium to shape public opinion. Making television, I discovered, was a lot more exhilarating than just watching it. And it seemed just as natural too. So when portable video first became widely available in the early '70s, allowing baby boomers access to the tools to make their own brand of television, I was lugging and plugging a portapak and eager to join a new movement, an alternative television movement.

I learned video production from members of the Videofreex, one of video's pioneering groups, but I never joined any production collective. It was a question of timing. I entered the scene late, and my first encounter with video coincided with a technological revolution that was propelling video away from its funkier, low-tech, black-and-white beginnings into a more sophisticated, expensive, and technologically daunting era of three-quarter-inch production. The collective spirit of early video was giving way to a more individualistic style and method of production. Faced with the expense of video, I abandoned thoughts of becoming a producer and decided to write about video instead. Video had yet to produce critics and historians of the caliber of Pauline Kael and Erik Barnouw. Perhaps there was still room to make my mark. I began writing about video in 1976 and followed it from the high idealism of guerrilla video through the slick prosperity of MTV and the home video boom (when video became a household word and meant "Jane Fonda's Workout" or Hollywood movies on tape), changes that left me puzzled about video's future and my own.

With generous support from the New York State Council on the Arts and a Guggenheim Fellowship I embarked on a year-long research odyssey that took me to San Francisco; Los Angeles; New Orleans; Minneapolis; Whitesburg, Kentucky; Washington, D.C.; and Boston. I looked at hundreds of tapes and talked with more than 100 video pioneers. I swung between great excitement during my trips and extreme depression on my return. I was overwhelmed by the stories people confided in me. Although the individual stories differed there was a consistent theme to all: early daring efforts to create a new kind of television were met first with often spectacular success but, for a variety of reasons, invariably led to the demise of the innovative enterprise and the disillusionment of many participants. Although some succeeded at adapting to the changing demands of the time, many did not.

For the next ten years I worked in fits and starts, trying to tell the story of guerrilla television. I had gathered enough material to write several books, it seemed, but I felt I lacked the emotional detachment and mental stamina to address it all. I wrestled with the question of what the book was about—a study of alternative video or a study of the living people who made it. During this time I succeeded in organizing several retrospectives of documentary video and published several essays based on my research. I was fortunate in being given fellowships to write at many artist colonies, where I did my best and most concentrated writing. As time passed I discovered that the once eager interest in video history was being overtaken by a stinging backlash that condemned what had been written as "mythologies" that reinforced the "canon." In addition to the formidable challenge of writing history, I now had to grapple with outright hostility to the very effort. What had attracted me to alternative video in the first place—an arena that was undefined, open to invention and interpretation—had become a minefield. By the late '80s, without the cover of a prevailing theory—postmodern, post-Freudian, post-Marxist—I felt doubly naked and vulnerable. I recalled one of my favorite lines from Pauline Kael, writing in response to the academic takeover of film criticism by auteurist theory in the '60s: "A critic with a single theory is like a gardener who uses a lawnmower on everything that grows." The lawnmowers were on the ascendant again.

Then a series of events in my personal life intervened to complicate the process further. As all the supports in my world began to fall out from under me, I returned to work on the guerrilla television story. What had begun ten years earlier as intellectual curiosity about the ways creative people negotiate change, how they managed to be true to themselves and adapt to changing conditions, letting go of the past and moving on, became a deeply personal quest. Like those who had clung to a vision of alternative television beyond a time that readily supported it, I had clung to my story about them, unable to let go and move on myself. It was only when I faced failure—my own at not being able to write about it all, and guerrilla television's at not being able to create a viable alternative to commercial television—that I felt free to finish the work.

My quandary in the '80s over what had happened to my generation's optimism and creative energy has been magnified a hundredfold by life in the '90s. Faith in the future, which seemed so natural to youth in the late '60s, is conspicuously lacking today if my graduate students are any indication. They are smart, talented, and deeply sensitive, but instead of a boundless belief in themselves and in their ability to affect the world, many are plagued by depression, hopelessness, and doubt. The infrastructure created in the '60s to support budding talent and public channels for art and information is rapidly being dismantled as arts budgets are slashed and public institutions become privatized, driven by market forces, or forced to close down altogether. Young people today are understandably afraid they will not be able to find work or the financial and moral support needed to make their own critical and creative work.

If my experience is any example, failure is not what it appears to be and the end is really only the beginning. So rather than presenting the story of guerrilla television as a chronicle of failure, I offer it instead as a cautionary tale with a guardedly hopeful sequel. That sequel depends on nurturing hope in the future and in youth's ability to initiate change. Change alone, as video guerrillas discovered the hard way, is not enough. By learning from the mistakes of an earlier effort at democraticizing the media, the possibility of creating a more viable model today or tomorrow may be found. Not only hope but patience, fortitude, and perseverance need fostering; they are essential virtues if one is to work through all the obstacles the status quo erects against change and power sharing. These may be among the most important moral values we survivors of the '60s and '70s can pass on.

There's a joke among independent filmmakers that the credits usually run longer than the production. A proper effort at acknowledging all who helped me in researching and writing this book would surely rival the text in length. For brevity's sake, I will simply express my appreciation to the following.

I am grateful to the New York State Council on the Arts and the John Simon Guggenheim Memorial Foundation, which provided grants for the research of this book; to the Port Washington Public Library, which served as fiscal sponsor for my NYSCA grant; to Yaddo, the MacDowell Colony for the Arts, Blue Mountain Center, the Virginia Center for the Creative Arts, and UCross Foundation, for wonderful and productive writing residencies.

To the following individuals and their organizations at the time, many thanks: Mary Judge, Tom Tanselle, Joel Connaroe, Peter Kardon, and Diane Diamond, John Simon Guggenheim Memorial Foundation; Lillian Katz and Vivienne Lipsitz, Port Washington Public Library; Barbara London and Mary Lee Bandy, the Museum of Modern Art; Barbara Humphreys, Library of Congress; Bob Beck, Stephen Vitiello, and Lori Zippay, Electronic Arts Intermix; Susan Heske, Michael Curran, and Peter Haratonik, the New School for Social Research; Carol Brandenburg and Deborah Liebling, WNET/ TV Lab; Arthur Tsuchiya, New York State Council on the Arts; D.J. Stern, Woodstock Public Library; Buzz Hartshorn, International Center of Photography; and Sam McElfresh, American Federation of the Arts.

Thanks to those who opened their homes to me and cheered me on during various stages of the book: Bill Viola, Kira Perov, Rhea Rubin, Larry Berman, Don Roberts, Marilyn Rehnberg, Dee Davis, Mimi Pickering, Jo Carson, Jack Churchill, Karen and Jack Jennings, Burwell Ware, Karen Kern, Marie Gould, Louis Alvarez, Deborah Lefkowitz, Parry Teasdale, Carol Vontobel, Chris Donnell, and Ellen Nadel. Special thanks go to my graduate assistants—Beverly Robinson, Susan Murray, Akram Zataari, Johanna Hibbard, and Alex LeDuc—and to all who read and commented on the manuscript in various stages of completion: Steve Calvert, Rangan Chakravarty, Mary Cunnane, Ralph Engelman, Mary Judge, Deanna Kamiel, Alex LeDuc, Barbara London, Allen Rucker, and Andrei Zagdansky. To other friends who encouraged me and helped in various ways during this process, my heartfelt thanks: Violet Greenstein, Mary Grein, Catherine Egan, Alice Bissell, Heather Mac Donald, Helen McDonald, Susan Weiley, Wai Luk Lo, Marilyn Hillman, Mariarosy Cal-

leri, Cathy Cullen, Chris Donnell, and everyone else. Without the love
and support of my father, this book would never have been completed.

Most important, to all the many people who took time out of their
lives to speak freely and candidly about their video past, I owe an
enormous debt of gratitude. If your story is untold here, know that
it is part of the inspiration behind this work. Thanks to Peter Adair,
Lynn Adler, Jon Alpert, Louis Alvarez, Ellen Anthony, Wendy Appel,
Fred Barzyk, Skip Blumberg, Tom Borrup, Peter Bradley, Carol
Brandenburg, David Brown, Tobe Carey, Ted Carpenter, Nancy
Cain, Jo Carson, Tom Christy, Maxi Cohen, Connie Coleman, David
Cort, Victoria Costello, Dennis Darmek, Dee Davis, Jim Day, Nick
DeMartino, Janet Densmore, Mickey Dickoff, Loni Ding, Blaine
Dunlop, Linda Duraco, Bonnie Engel, Joan Engel, Mary Feldstein,
Kit Galloway, John Giancola, Gayle Gibbons, Davidson Gigliotti, Joan
Giummo, Sharon Goldenberg, Paul Goldsmith, Marie Gould, Mar-
garet Gregg, Julie Gustafson, DeeDee Halleck, Barbara Haspiel, Mi-
chael Hazard, Perrin Ireland, Jane Jensen, Deanna Kamiel, Judi
Keleman, Doug Kellner, Joanne Kelly, Karen Kern, Larry Kirkman,
Howard Klein, Andy Kolker, Lucy Kostelanetz, Stephen Kulczycki,
Eddie Kurtz, Chip Lord, David Loxton, Mary Lucier, Ron McCoy,
Laurie McDonald, Susan Milano, James Morris, Jim Mulligan, Peter
O'Neil, Marty Newell, Stevenson Palfi, Michelle Parkerson, Mimi
Pickering, Greg Pratt, Kath Quinn, Sherrie Rabinowitz, Karen Ra-
nucci, Dan Reeves, John Reilly, Allen Rucker, Geraldo Saldo, Ira
Schneider, Kathy Seltzer, Michael Shamberg, Jody Sibert, Neil Sie-
ling, Lydia Sillman, Fred Simon, Tom Sims, Thea Sklover, Arlen
Slobodow, Ray Smith, Karen Snyder, Elon Soltes, Adam Steg, Bill
Stephens, George Stoney, Skip Sweeney, Bonnie Syzmanski, Parry
Teasdale, Rick Tejada-Flores, Mary Tiseo, Keiko Tsuno, Edin Velez,
Ann Volkes, Carol Vontobel, Gail Waldron, Burwell Ware, Morrie
Warshawski, Don West, Megan Williams, Ann Woodward, and Tom
Zafian.

I thank my editors, Sheldon Meyer, Andrew Albanese, and Lisa
Stallings, of Oxford University Press, copyeditor Barry Katzen, copy-
writer Phil Hanrahan, and my friend, Erik Barnouw, who introduced
me to Oxford and offered moral support and inspiration. Without
John Culkin and the Center for Understanding Media, I would never
have embarked on this strange career: I honor his memory with this
work. A special thanks to Andrew Albanese who, like the Biblical
Job, suffered much; your merit is great and your kindness deeply
appreciated. A very special thanks to Allen Rucker, who keeps

alive the TVTV flame; without his enthusiasm, kindness, and bound-less assistance, this book would not have been possible. And finally I wish to thank all my students, past, present, and to come: this book is for you.

New York, New York D.B.
March 1995

Introduction

What is "guerrilla television"? The term may conjure up American hostages looking haggard and coerced in clumsily produced ransom tapes or propaganda diatribes, what the mass media often characterize as hostile takeovers of the airwaves by Third World provocateurs. Some may think of tapes produced in former Eastern Bloc countries, the Philippines, or maybe Central America, tapes designed to rally morale during a labor strike, document the death of a patriot, or launch a people's revolution with the seizure of government broadcast studios and transmitters. Still others may think of the historic camcorder tapes of police beatings that galvanized viewers around the world, raising issues of racism, institutional abuse, and the legitimacy of citizen video to serve as a weapon and a witness.

Whether typified as media terrorism or as amateur video, whether seen as a boon or a threat to democracy, guerrilla television has been a part of our information landscape since the mid-'60s when the arrival of lightweight, affordable consumer video equipment made it possible for ordinary people to make their own television. In today's multichannel television maze, it is difficult to imagine how different things were twenty years ago when three broadcasting corporations controlled all of American television and the only power viewers seemed to have over television was the power to turn it off.

Guerrilla television was part of the larger alternative media tide that swept across the country during the '60s, affecting radio, newspapers, magazines, and publishing, as well as the fine and performing arts. Just as the invention of movable type in the fifteenth century made books portable and private, video technology did the same for the televised image; and just as the development of offset printing launched the alternative press movement in the '60s, video's advent launched an alternative television movement in the '70s.

In 1971 the movement got a name and a manifesto with the publication of *Guerrilla Television* by Michael Shamberg and the Raindance Corporation. The book outlined a technological radicalism claiming that commercial television, with its mass audiences, was a conditioning agent rather than a source of enlightenment. Video offered the means to "decentralize" television so that a Whitmanesque democracy of ideas, opinions, and cultural expressions—made both by and for the people—could then be "narrowcast" to targeted audiences. Molded by the insights of theorists like Marshall McLuhan and Buckminster Fuller, influenced by the style of New Journalism practiced by Tom Wolfe and Hunter Thompson, and inspired by the content of the agonizing issues of the day, video guerrillas plotted a utopian program to change the structure of information in America.

At first, guerrilla television aimed at creating a distinct, parallel system to broadcast TV but, when that dream proved difficult to realize, it turned into a reform movement to "remake" television into something new, vital, peculiarly electronic, and responsive to the needs and expectations of a generation raised on the medium. In the process, guerrilla television became entwined within the system it claimed could not be reformed, propelled from cable to public to network television and eventually devoured by the parent that spawned it.

Subject to Change is not an encyclopedic history of the alternative video movement in the United States, but rather a more modest story about some of the most influential video collectives of the late '60s and '70s and their uneasy relationship to American television. The story of how guerrilla television came into being, blossomed, and then faded by the end of the '70s points to the larger story of an era, a new technology, a new documentary form, and a generation of talented young people all of whom proved subject to change.

The book opens by looking at the early underground video scene and its efforts at differentiating video from television and then explores how guerrilla television's more radical aspirations repeatedly were shipwrecked by the siren call of broadcasting. Interweaving the stories of three very different video collectives of the '70s, the book focuses on the fortunes of TVTV, Broadside TV, and University Community Video.

Top Value Television, better known as TVTV, was the best-known and most controversial guerrilla television group of the decade. Founded by Michael Shamberg, author of *Guerrilla Television,* TVTV came into being to cover the 1972 Presidential Nominating Conventions for cable television, and their brash hour-long tapes turned the worlds of both independent media and network television on their heads. TVTV's funky brand of documentary video—part satire, part "you are there" immediacy, part Andy Hardy "Hey gang, let's do a show"—breathed new life into notions of television documentary. *Washington Post* TV critic Tom Shales was so struck by TVTV's work that he wrote in 1975:

> Forces are at work in television to make "documentary" a nonpejorative term. It won't be easy. But in the vanguard of what may in fact be a revolution, a Los Angeles group called TVTV (formerly Top Value Television) is producing documentaries so remarkable and bright they threaten to make obsolete the mass of clichés it has taken other TV documentary producers years to accumulate.

Within a concentrated period of four years, TVTV produced nearly 15 hours of innovative video, forging a style that, though often criticized, was hailed as the documentary's new wave. Selecting sacred cows as sacrificial victims to their satire, TVTV tackled power-seekers in the world of politics (*Four More Years, Gerald Ford's America*), religion (*Lord of the Universe*), sports (*Superbowl*), and entertainment (*TVTV Looks at the Oscars*).

TVTV was an exception to the rule, concentrating on innovative programs rather than community service. Most guerrilla video activism during the '70s came from geographically specific, community-based groups whose work, though less publicized and more narrowly viewed than TVTV's opus, more closely followed the ideal of using the video medium for social change. Profiles of two prominent but very different community video organizations active in the '70s—University Community Video (UCV) in Minneapolis, Minnesota, and Broadside TV in Whitesburg, Kentucky—offer a contrast to TVTV and reveal divergent models of guerrilla video activity.

Broadside TV was an unusual experiment in local-origination programming for cable invented by Ted Carpenter, a Canadian-born visionary who glimpsed the possibility of using video to create an alternative information network for Appalachian highlanders. Seizing on federal regulations that mandated cable companies provide local programming to subscribers, Carpenter created the electronic equivalent of a community newspaper. University Community Video was a highly successful collaboration between Minneapolis community activists and university video journalists that for a brief but exciting time produced "Changing Channels," an award-winning series of video documentaries aired on local public television. Why TVTV, UCV, and Broadside TV flourished and then foundered is the heart of this story.

Subject to Change concludes with an examination of the larger forces operating in society that made creating an alternative system

to commercial television virtually impossible. It suggests, given the
resurgence of video activism today, that many of the lessons of the
portapak era have been learned and transcended by a younger generation determined to avoid the pitfalls that derailed pioneers.

This little-known chapter in the history of American television—
the story of the first TV generation's dream of remaking television
and their frustrated attempts at democratizing the medium—has implications for the future of free speech and public discourse in the
United States today. Promised that the Information Superhighway
will take us to a utopia where electronic democracy will be ours, we
may want to consider what happened to the last pilgrims to venture
down that rocky road.

Contents

SUBJECT TO CHANGE

Television in the U.S. often resembles a drowsy giant, sluggishly repeating itself in both form and content season after season. But out on TV's fringe, where the viewers thus far are few, a group of bold experimenters are engaged in nothing less than an attempt to transform the medium. During the past few years, television has developed a significant avant-garde, a pioneering corps to match the press's underground, the cinema's *vérité*, the theater's off-off-Broadway. Though its members are still largely unknown, they are actively creating imaginative new programs and TV "environments"— not for prime time, but for educational stations, closed-circuit systems in remote lofts and art galleries and, with fingers crossed, even for the major networks.

—*Newsweek*, Douglas Davis, February 9, 1970

Every fury on earth has been absorbed in time. . . . Official acceptance is the one unmistakable symptom that salvation is beaten again, and is the one surest sign of fatal misunderstanding, and is the kiss of Judas.

—*Let Us Now Praise Famous Men*, James Agee

I.

Underground Video

For children growing up in the '50s, television was a family member. The tiny screen buried in the big wooden box offered kinship with familiar figures who seemed as much a part of kids' everyday lives as parents, siblings, and neighborhood playmates. Nightly viewing of Disney's "The Mickey Mouse Club" was a ritual in American television households where children sang along with the club anthem and joined vicariously in the adventures of Karen and Cubby and Sharon and Dave. Other shows also reinforced this feeling of membership in an enduring group, such as "Andy's Gang," which weekly drew kids eager to hear Andy Devine's raspy and slightly raunchy command, "Pluck your magic twanger, Froggy!"

The Baby Boomers grew up with television, developing a love–hate relationship with it and a sense of possessiveness about it that, some might argue, was Oedipal in its complexity. As they came of age in the late '60s, television achieved its own independence in the form of the first portable video recorders. It made sense that a generation linked together by their television memories and nurtured by the communal spirit of television clubs should form their own video gangs to make their own television, once the tools were available.

Corporate control of television had been secured in the post–World War I years as government nationalization of the telecommunications industries was opposed in the government controlled versus free enterprise debate. Television was developed as an extension of radio, effectively consolidating the power of the broadcasting industry by limiting television's role in American society to what the radio networks felt they could produce and control. As broadcast historian Garth Jowett has observed:

> Despite the official rhetoric about the enormous educational and informational potential of the medium, the institutions which were capable of developing this role for television (universities, schools, churches, gov-

ernment agencies, trade unions and private localized citizen's groups) were never able to penetrate successfully or alter the dominant discourse which took for granted that television was going to be essentially "visual radio" with some content aspects of the motion picture industry grafted on to it.[1]

That television was a different cultural form was almost totally ignored until the early '70s, when the advent of new technologies— notably video—began to liberate the medium from existing restrictions.[2] Video offered the first TV generation a means to challenge the authority of the "boob tube," to replace television's banal entertainment and negative images of youthful protest and rebellion with the counterculture's[3] values and a fresh, new televisual reality. Fueled by adolescent rebellion and utopian dreams, video promised an alternative to the slickly civilized, commercially corrupt, and aesthetically bankrupt world of Television.

Between 1965 and 1968, video served as a way of documenting the happenings[4] of the late '60s and as a means of exploring the system consciousness that new technology and popular communications theories promised. Experimental production centers at public TV stations were founded at this time to encourage artistic exploration of television. But the 1968 debut of the battery-operated Sony CV video portapak (and an industry agreement to standardize half-inch video technology, thus eliminating the hodge-podge of incompatible formats) made video equipment truly portable,[5] widely available, and relatively affordable, ushering in a new era of documentary video work.

One version of the birth of portable video begins on an October day in 1965 when Korean-born artist Nam June Paik purchased one of the first portable video cameras and recorders at the Liberty Music Store in New York City. Hopping in a cab and pointing his half-inch, black-and-white video camera out the window, as the story goes, he recorded the arrival of Pope Paul VI in New York on his way to address the United Nations. That evening Paik played his tape at the Café au Go Go in Greenwich Village and circulated a video manifesto declaring this new electronic medium would revolutionize art and information:

> As collage technic replaced oil-paint, the cathode ray tube will replace the canvass [*sic*]. It is the historical necessity, if there is a historical necessity in history, that a new decade of electronic television should follow to the past decade of electronic music.[6]

Seventy years earlier the Lumière brothers had shown their first films, also documentaries, in a café in Paris. Paik's gesture suggested a subtle acknowledgement of video's relationship to its motion picture heritage, while emphatically asserting video's intention to supercede in the realms of art and television.

Paik's self-styled role as the "George Washington of Video" has been attacked by critics[7] who take issue with the privileging of video art over video activism in the histories that have been written. Although Paik's interests arose out of the Fluxus Movement in art rather than the documentary tradition in film and television, during video's Wonder Bread years people could and did try everything, from avant-garde art experiments to homely documentaries, with no distinction drawn between "art" and "activism" until the '70s.

At first, video pioneers discovered one another when hanging out on city street corners with their portapaks, banding together in small groups with frequent realignments. In the wake of the bloody protests of the 1968 Democratic Convention in Chicago—with the whole world watching the death-in on network TV—groups gathered together pooling equipment, energy, and ideas to facilitate production and advance video as a tool for social and cultural change. They were, in the words of alternative media historian David Armstrong, "a generation at home with technology, the Bomb and the cathode-ray tube, primed to make imaginative use of the communications media to convey its message of change."[8]

New York City was a major hub of early video activity. The first group to emerge called itself "Commediation"—a contraction of community, media, and mediation. Founded by David Cort, Ken Marsh, Frank Gillette, and Howard Gutstadt, Commediation lasted a scant three months in late 1968 and produced, as far as anyone can recall, very little except for a documentary on the famous school decentralization crisis in New York City, centering on the Oceanhill–Brownsville school district. More important perhaps than its output, Commediation marked the beginning of collective video action.

David Cort was one of the most flamboyant members of the video underground. Trained in the theater of Pirandello, Artaud, and Grotowski, Cort used his background to help students with learning disabilities, which led him to a job at the Brooklyn Children's Museum in 1967. Amazed that a museum on the fringes of Bedford–Stuyvesant attracted no black children, he applied for federal money through the Office for Economic Opportunity to create "Operation Discovery," an anti-poverty outreach program. He was soon joined by Ken Marsh, who had some background in documentary filmmaking, having worked as an assistant film editor for American cinema vérité pioneer Robert Drew. Eric Siegel, a self-taught electronics wizard, introduced them to broadcast-quality video equipment.[9]

Cort was intrigued by video. "I was overwhelmed by the lightness of the portable video camera, the intimacy of it, the way you could talk from behind the camera to people, and they could talk to you." He recognized that video could involve people by making them active participants in the "video environment" rather than passive viewers of network TV fare. He saw video's potential to offer people a variety of viewpoints rather than the official, objective one promoted by Walter Cronkite's "And that's the way it is."[10]

Cort—with his wild laughter, unruly black hair, long beard, and nervous energy—looked and acted more like a hippie than a museum programmer. He reveled in the role of countercultural pied piper leading black youths into the museum's pristine halls, and it came as no surprise when he was thrown out of his job. Undaunted, he set up a community organization, believing blacks should be running their own program. After securing additional funding from the Rockefeller Brothers to buy half-inch video equipment for the kids and locating a mother's group to run the organization, Cort and Marsh left the project to the community. Commediation was a natural progression.

Frank Gillette was a painter of monochromist minimal paintings. He was preoccupied with communications, philosophy, and futurology when he met Paul Ryan on a street in the East Village in 1968. Gillette, with his long blond hair, Vandyke beard, and lean body, looked like a latter-day Wild Bill Hickok in search of his own Wild West Show. Coolly intellectual, Gillette found his equal in the cerebral Ryan, a conscientious objector to the Vietnam war and Marshall McLuhan's research assistant at Fordham University. Ryan had left studying for the priesthood, received a degree in English, and become interested in figuring out whether McLuhan's theories were correct. If so, he should be able to decode this new medium McLuhan had not touched. Ryan had Fordham's video equipment for the summer. It was June 1968, and for three months Ryan loaned Gillette studio cameras, portable cameras, playback decks and monitors, minimal editing equipment, and about $300 in videotape.

The first tape Gillette produced was a five-and-a-half hour documentary of street life on St. Marks' Place in New York's East Village. He spent three weeks in front of Gem's Spa, a newspaper-and-candy store that served as unofficial headquarters of the Eastern hippie community at the time, consuming countless egg creams and marshmallow candies while interviewing the locals. The important element for Gillette was that he was not imposing his structure on people; instead, he was letting people "give their raps on videotape." Gillette then experimented through the Village Project with video's effect on kids on "bad trips"—teenagers burnt-out on LSD. He had them use the camera as a means of expression, turning it on him and themselves. This was a radical notion at the time, since videotape's use in most psychiatric facilities was to record interviews objectively and extract information from patients. Control was never in the hands of the patients. The video "feedback" the teenagers got from their own tapes seemed to help these kids, who were already alienated from their psychiatrists. "They dug it," Gillette reported at the time.[11]

Howie Gutstadt, a painter and friend of Ken Marsh, ran into Gillette out taping one day and went back to Brooklyn to tell Ken and David Cort about him. The video underground was still small and friendly, eager to find someone new on the scene with equipment and introduce him (later her) to the fold. And so, in the fall of 1968, Cort, Gillette, Marsh, and Gutstadt formed Commediation, a tentative association that unravelled before the end of the year as mercurial artistic temperaments—and oversized egos—interfered with continued collective effort. None were derailed in their enthusiasm for video, however. In short order they would regroup in different constellations to launch new video dreams.

David Cort acquired his own equipment and went out shooting each day in Washington Square Park, developing a feeling of naturalness with the camera. Like many others in the video underground, Cort saw video as a "cyborgian" extension of himself. It was important to be able to move effortlessly with the camera and recording deck. Some pioneers worked with surveillance cameras, "freehanding" a camera without a viewfinder and creating dizzyingly different-looking videotapes. Although Cort began to experiment with razor-blade editing, the object was to shoot it well the first time, without relying on editing. It was process, not product, that the late '60s celebrated.

The immediate playback that portable video afforded after 1968 was tremendously important to Cort and his peers. It meant that tapemakers could see for themselves along with their subjects whatever had just been taped. Unlike film, which requires processing in a lab, recorded video is instantaneous. Years before, at the beginning of the century, documentary film pioneer Robert Flaherty had trained his Eskimo companions to develop and print film stock, precisely focusing light through a narrow slit cut in an igloo wall onto the film being printed. The purpose of this elaborate process, conducted under the most grueling circumstances, enabled Flaherty to share the on-going film with them, reinforcing their sense of active participation in a great undertaking. Video totally eliminated the arduousness of such playback processes; immediate video "feedback" was so effortless that it became a basic component of much documentary work, sensibly exploited to establish rapport and create a dialogue—or "interactive information loop"—with whomever one was taping.

The search for interesting subjects did not require videomakers to venture as far afield as Flaherty had. Many tapes made by early portapakers frequently fell under the heading of "street tapes," although not all street tapes were made on the street, living rooms and bedrooms being popular locations. But the intense social, political, and cultural flux of the late '60s provided comedy and drama right at the corner. Hanging out on New York's Lower East Side and rapping with the street people—drug-tripping hippies, sexually liberated young women, erstwhile revolutionaries, cross-country wanderers, bums, winos, and other characters—provided great spontaneous material found literally on one's doorstep.

Early in 1969 Frank Gillette met Ira Schneider at a party. Schneider started out as a doctoral student in physiological psychology, then got interested in filmmaking, producing a number of experimental films. He had been working on a film during the summer of 1968 that proved a disaster because the cameraman, an inveterate zoomer, had produced uneditable footage. After four months of depression, Schneider emerged thinking "television." That's when he met Gillette. Half-inch video, which allowed one person to go out and produce synchronous sound and images, seemed an ideal medium for the work Schneider was interested in making. He also discovered the quasimystical dimension of video produced by the flickering glow of electrons constantly being scanned and reconfigured on the television screen: "It fosters a life quality which . . . didn't always get on film." In exchange for the immediacy, portability, and independence video afforded, its makers had to compromise on image definition. The abstract, often murky black-and-white image was far removed from the rich textures and color palette of film. And when compared to broadcast TV, at the point of image reception on a home TV set, half-inch video's 220 lines of resolution was unmistakably inferior to broadcast's 320. Still, for Schneider and many others, the technological trade-off was worth it for the range of new possibilities video did provide.

Schneider grabbed a knapsack full of money, some videotape

equipment, a car, forty pounds of salt pork, some cans of baked beans, and headed out with Frank Gillette for Antioch College in Yellow Springs, Ohio. Provisions for their journey sounded more like supplies for a wagon-train expedition out West than food for two university grads off on a lark. The language hints at their state of mind and growing self-image as heroic trailblazers of video's virgin territory. They had been invited for a month-long stay to lecture and involve students in both studio and portable video work. They had their students experiment with what happens in front of a camera by creating games that played with the limits of perception and technology. Students would be told they could not communicate with each other unless they communicated through the camera. They could do anything they wanted, but it had to be through the medium. The duo also became involved in what was happening in town—producing tapes about the strike at a bookbindery and the daily lives of farmers intersecting at the local doughnut bakery. There were tapes of a jug band and even a vain effort at making a skin flick. (It would be several years before the women's movement would alter the sexism masquerading as liberation in evidence at this time.)

This mix of experimental and documentary work produced at Antioch was true of much of the work made then. Paul Ryan worked with a poverty project in Brooklyn in 1968, producing a documentary on Resurrection City, the makeshift village of the Poor People's Campaign led by Reverend Martin Luther King, Jr. The following year, Ryan set up a project in Newburgh, New York, using Ford Foundation money to turn high school kids onto video. In one of the first public access experiments in the United States, their tapes were transmitted locally into most Newburgh homes over the community antennae television system (what is now known as cable TV). At the same time, Ryan was also creating experimental video art environments that would soon begin appearing in art museums, galleries, and video theaters.

In the spring of 1969, an event transformed the then-underground video scene into an aboveground phenomenon. Frank Gillette received a phone call from Howard Wise, a gallery owner on posh 57th Street in Manhattan. Wise had exhibited a kinetic light show in 1967 that included video; he had become fascinated with the new form and conceived the idea of mounting the first American exhibition devoted solely to video. He invited 12 video artists—including Nam June Paik, Eric Siegel, Paul Ryan, and Frank Gillette—to produce something for "TV as a Creative Medium," which opened in May 1969.[12] Ryan's piece was *Everyman's Moebius Strip*, an interactive work involving a camera and a tape delay loop. Frank Gillette and Ira Schneider collaborated on *Wipe Cycle*, a television mural composed of a bank of nine TV monitors playing back live and delayed feedback images of gallery-goers stepping off the elevator mixed in with images from broadcast television as well as prerecorded tapes. The bathtub sequences from the aborted porno tape at Antioch were recycled for use here. It was an attempt to "demonstrate you're as much a piece of information as tomorrow morning's headlines," Gillette reported in an interview at the time. Schneider described *Wipe Cycle* as

> a live feedback system that enables a viewer standing in his environment to see himself not only NOW in time and space, but also 8 seconds ago and 16 seconds ago, and these are in juxtaposition and in flux. In addition he sees standard broadcast images which come on at periods alternating with his live image, and also two programmed shows which are collage-like, ranging from a shot of the earth from outer space to cows grazing to 57th St. Somehow there's a juxtaposition between the now of the person, the individual, with other elements of information about the Universe and America, and so the general reaction seems to have been a somewhat objectifying experience, and also a somewhat integrating experience in terms of one's place in the Universe.[13]

"TV as a Creative Medium" was a pivotal event for the video underground, attracting considerable public attention to the new medium while serving as a catalyst around which the video community coalesced. The show functioned as information central for practitioners and would-be videomakers who until then had operated in relative obscurity; many individuals who would play major roles in the video scene met there for the first time.

Filmmaker John Reilly came to "TV as a Creative Medium" and met Frank Gillette and Ira Schneider. Within a few months, ex-filmmakers Reilly and Schneider created "TeleVisionary Associates," an organization devoted to the exhibition of videotapes and video environments. The rapid proliferation of video organizations begun at this time was due in part to a fascination with the idea that for a few hundred dollars you could form your own corporation and be an officer.

Michael Shamberg, a young journalist for *Time*, also went to see the Wise gallery show. He heard about video from Frank Gillette, whom he had met through an old college friend. Shamberg was already a veteran observer of the underground scene, having covered the 1968 Democratic convention for a Chicago newspaper. He immediately picked up on video's exciting potential. It was like a lightbulb going off in his head: he could use the equipment to get the same information across without having to work anonymously for *Time*. While writing a story on "TV as a Creative Medium," Shamberg started hanging out with Gillette and Ryan.

It was Frank Gillette who conceived the idea of creating a hip think-tank that would be the countercultural equivalent of the Rand Corporation. As Shamberg once explained, "His idea was Raindance. R&D for research and development—Rand, Rain-Dance. I made up the explanation, he made up the name. Also Raindance is ecologically sound anticipatory design." But at first, R&D amounted to research and dinner; grand schemes were hatched over meals in Gillette's loft and then argued in night-long bull sessions. Women were allowed to serve the tea and granola bars but were asked to give up their chairs to the "guys" when seating ran short.[14]

Raindance intimate Marco Vassi captured what it was like to be a part of this early video scene:[15]

> We sit stoned and dig each other's worldview. We rap and eat and fuck and watch tape. And for us, it's about the same as it has always been: just living fully, openly, honest to the what *is*. Tape adds a dimension. . . . watch one of Frank's dada experiments, and feel your mind be turned to silly putty. Watch habit-dulled objects come alive in ways that make your hair stand on end, and know that your perception of reality has been radically altered. Through tape.
>
> The tube is heavy. Electrons whip through vacuum and fall in waves on a sensitized screen, where the human animal reads them as patterns, as *meaning*. Just like in real life, where the stuff of existence bops about, doing its subatomic thing, and lo and behold, vortices of consciousness appear to ham their way across the screen. No illusion of movement, as in film. What you see is the stuff of energy doing its dance, and the dance seems strangely familiar.[15]

They were university-bred intellectuals in awe of video, excitedly inventing new uses for it and spinning a radical rhetoric that announced their intentions, not merely for the future of video but for Planet Earth. Philosophically, their ideas sprang from the theoretical brows of Marshall McLuhan, Norbert Wiener, Pierre Teilhard de Chardin, Buckminster Fuller, and Gregory Bateson, among others.

A French priest–paleontologist–philosopher may seem an unlikely guru figure for the video underground, but *The Phenomenon of Man* by Teilhard de Chardin was ideally suited to video visionaries' search for a hopeful vision of change. "The history of the living world can be summarized as the elaboration of ever more perfect eyes within a cosmos in which there is always something more to be seen," he wrote.

"To see or to perish is the very condition laid down upon everything that makes up the universe."[16] To video freaks discovering life through the lens of a videofinder, Teilhard's focus on seeing—and making others see—coincided with their own apocalyptic sense of purpose.

The Jesuit scientist–philosopher elaborated a theory of the evolution of life producing more varied, more intense, and more highly organized mental activity or awareness. Once the critical moment of consciousness is reached, evolution becomes a psychosocial process based on the cumulative transmission of experience. Video theorists would read a role for themselves in Teilhard's universe as disseminators of "video data banks" of experience. Ever higher degrees of organization and new patterns of cooperation would lead to the ultimate good of global unity. Love, good will, and cooperation; personal integration and internal harmony; and increasing knowledge lay at the end of this evolutionary/spiritual quest. The irresistible altruism of Teilhard's vision inspired video freaks out to expand consciousness as well as religious Christians in search of God. Some of the best motives of the video underground reflected this cosmic vision.

R. Buckminster Fuller—"Bucky" to his young admirers—offered yet another utopian evolutionary vision in his 1969 book, *Operating Manual for Spaceship Earth*. Fuller stressed the importance of appropriate technology in his blueprint for survival, offering advice on how to "convert man's spin-dive toward oblivion into an intellectually mastered power pullout into safe and level flight of physical and metaphysical success, whereafter he may turn his Spaceship Earth's occupancy into a universe exploring advantage."[17] In the wake of *2001: A Space Odyssey*, this was music to the ears of video cyborgs. Unfortunately, Fuller's communications style, indulgently referred to as technical–verbal agglutinations, had an often devastating impact on the lucidity of early video writing. Still the cosmic vision and utopian dreams that he and other futurist philosophers offered became the touchstone of much video writing.

No theorist was more influential in shaping the video underground's mission than Marshall McLuhan, whose seminal study, *Understanding Media: The Extensions of Man*, appeared in 1964. According to McLuhan, the electric media, notably television, had decentralized modern life, turning the vast globe into a village retribalizing the human race. He celebrated the "totally radical, pervasive, and decentralized" electric media, believing their nonlinear, discontinuous mosaic of information involved viewers in depth and called forth a creative response. "The aspirations of our time for wholeness, empathy, and depth of awareness are a natural adjunct of electric technology," he boldly proclaimed.[18]

McLuhan's optimism about television and its dynamic impact not just on communications but on contemporary consciousness was seized by the first generation raised on television, who found in his theories a euphoric explanation of themselves and their changing times. "The TV child expects involvement and doesn't want a specialist job in the future," he told them. "He does want a role and a deep commitment to his society."[19] Seeing themselves thus glorified in McLuhan's vision as heros of a new electric age, these charter members of the first TV generation responded with their own expanded, radicalized, and decidedly more decentralized version of television.

2.

Subject to Change

The summer of 1969 was extraordinarily eventful. In July American astronauts were the first men to walk on the moon, and video pioneers watched the fuzzy black-and-white video of the lunar landing, finding exciting confirmation of Buckminster Fuller's theory that we are evolving through our technology. Michael Shamberg, who watched the broadcasts along with millions around the globe, experienced a great epiphany.

> Our mind is doing things that our body can't accommodate, so it's coming out in the form of the technology. So we are in fact evolving through the technology. And we've got to come to some relationship with the technology. The relationship isn't to embrace it wholeheartedly nor to reject it, but to understand it, to understand that . . . technology is ecology; finding that overspecialization of technology leads you to death. What can you do with an electric can opener? On the other hand, video is generalized technology and has a high variety of uses.[1]

In August, underground videomakers got a chance to show what some of those other uses were at a music festival held in a small town in upstate New York. Woodstock was about to change the future of the video underground and the fortunes of its innovators.

David Cort had been drawn into the political events of 1969 by Yippie leader Abbie Hoffman, an old college friend from Brandeis University. With his Boston broad A's, wicked sense of humor, Madison Avenue glibness, and extravagant mop of dark curls, Hoffman was one of the video underground's most mediagenic stars, and Cort was often on hand with his portapak, covering a Hoffman speech in New Haven or an SDS rally at City College. Cort covered both anti- and pro-war demonstrations—events at Columbia and New York Universities as well as the Construction Workers' Loyalty Day parade. So when the summer of 1969 came, he followed the action and headed to Woodstock.

Thanks to Hoffman, Cort managed to get electricity and a good location, and Hoffman checked in now and then to see that he was okay. Ira Schneider stopped by, as did a fellow named Parry Teasdale who was shooting tape with a surveillance video camera. Teasdale and Cort became friends immediately. Cort, who was older than most of the people at Woodstock, became responsible for charging everyone's batteries, playing back tapes, and producing survival information programs. Since no one had calculated the vast numbers who would descend on the town of Bethel (where the Woodstock Festival actually happened), provisions had not been made for many basic services. Cort produced "First Aid #1" and "First Aid #2" to help people handle the most prevalent problems, from sun burn to drug overdose, but perhaps the most vital tape made at Woodstock was "Latrines," a how-to tape shown in various strategic places around the encampment.

Cort met many people at Woodstock, but the person who would change his life and the future of the video underground was a fellow named Lou Brill. Brill worked in the mailroom at CBS and talked real fast. "I know someone who can just do everything for you, and open all kinds of doors," he told Cort. The boast hardly seemed legitimate to Cort, but he gave Brill his address and told him to come around to his place when he got back to New York. Brill then called up Don West, who was assistant to Frank Stanton, president of CBS. He begged West to come to Woodstock. "There's grass, and there's girls—you get down here," he insisted. West resisted Brill's entreaty that he charter a helicopter, a decision he later regretted. Instead, he told Brill he would see him in New York.

After Woodstock, Parry Teasdale moved into the Rivington Street loft Cort shared with his girlfriend, Curtis Ratcliff. Since three is a group, Cort decided it was time to create a new video entity: the Videofreex. Intrigued by the idea Brill had planted, they decided to take matters into their own hands and arranged an appointment to show their Woodstock tapes to Don Hewitt, producer of CBS's "60 Minutes." Hewitt was more impressed with Cort's age than his tapes. "You're just a kid," Hewitt told Cort, who replied, "I'm *not* a kid. I'm 35 years old!" Incredulous, Hewitt insisted he couldn't be and the two men argued over Cort's age as the tapes got lost in the verbal mayhem. When Lou Brill later knocked on the Videofreex door—having at last persuaded Don West to see the tapes—they had reason to doubt the seriousness of any CBS executive.

Don West was a veteran journalist for *Television* magazine who had become restless and eager to have a hand in the decisions of network TV. He wangled the job of Stanton's assistant, and after a month on the job came up with an idea for a journalistic series for Sunday nights titled "The Real World." West kept the idea quiet for three years until the spring of 1969.

"The Smothers Brothers Comedy Hour" was up for renewal. It was the most controversial entertainment show on the air at the time, and outside pressure was being exerted to cancel it.[2] Mike Dann, head of CBS network programming, came to Don West asking for help from the 35th floor, home of the corporate executives. West had discussed his "Real World" series with Dann periodically and considered Dann a friend. He agreed to help Dann and made a pitch to save the comedy show. It was renewed, although West suspected his efforts had little to do with the decision, but within three weeks, the Smothers Brothers were off the air. West was deeply disappointed because he felt it was the most important program on the air.

"If we want to prove that CBS indeed remains committed to contemporary relevancy, we've got to come up with a show," West resolved. He went to Mike Dann and announced, "I'm going to do my show." To his surprise, Dann agreed. West realized that no one knew what being assistant to the president really meant—people thought he really had some power. He had never used that power before, but he was determined to do so now.

West had no experience as a producer and had more in common with Don Quixote than Don Hewitt. He didn't even know what it was he wanted to do. But he went to Stanton, informed him that Dann had said he could produce his own show, and got leave to take as much time as needed.

He started by assembling a group of talented television people: Stan White, an art director; Bob Livingston, a studio director; and Bernie Solens, owner of Chicago's "Second City" company. Next he hired three writers. West was buoyed by his belief that in order to invent, one needs an essential naiveté to keep oneself going, to do things that under normal circumstances one would never think of attempting. By the first of August they had written a script for the first 10 minutes. "Oh my god, what have we done?," he gasped. "We have sat here on the 34th floor of CBS saying we were going to create—or discover—or present *the real world*, and all we've done is a television show. It's funny, and the jokes and situations are humorous, and it's even further out than the Smothers Brothers would have been, but it's *not* the real world." Because he did not know what else to do, West told his staff: "I'm going to burn it down and go away." He took off for vacation, where Lou Brill's excited phone call finally reached him.

When West returned to New York, Brill dragged him down to Rivington Street on a Saturday morning. Cort thought West was a very straight cat who kept smiling in a weird kind of way. For a lark, Cort invited West to come out shooting with them. West agreed to make an appointment for another day, then asked David to show him the Woodstock tapes. West was astonished by the raw energy he saw in those tapes, a kind of energy he had never seen before in television. He realized that was what he wanted for his program. He excitedly began telling the Videofreex about his idea for a television show. A few days later he returned and went out shooting with them, mainly following them around rather than handling the video equipment. The next day he returned with a check for three hundred dollars and a historic deal. The quid pro quo was this: if the Videofreex would tape for West, he would have their equipment optimized. West got engineers from CBS to work on their equipment—and did much more than that before they were through. He had decided to burn down not only his concept, his 10 minutes of script, but the very medium of television. Inspired by hippies digging latrines, he set out on his own crusade to rebuild television, using black-and-white, half-inch video instead of a shovel.

West named his production company SQM and renamed the show "The Now Project." His collaboration with the video underground began innocently enough. Cort recalled West's request was simple and loose: "Just do whatever you want, but put something together for me." Thus began a free-form process that involved the Videofreex traveling around the country to find out what was happening in America in 1969. The homegrown concept was equally homely in its execution. West used his own station wagon, his own money, and often his own children to lug and plug equipment.

Davidson Gigliotti, a sculptor who was eager to experiment with video, encountered David Cort around this time, standing in a line at the bank with his camera slung around his neck en route to the repair shop. Gigliotti introduced himself and Cort invited him to stop by the loft. Gigliotti effected many guises during his years in the world of video, but in the early days he appeared to be someone "in the lower depths, escaping from the upper depths." More directly stated, he was a mess: he looked like something out of a cartoon strip with flies buzzing around his head. Gigliotti's announcement that he was going to buy his own equipment met with general disbelief. When he returned with his own video rig, however, Parry's and Curtis's opinion of him altered, and he was more or less accepted, especially since he was a fine carpenter who volunteered to build them their first portable console.

When Don West's startling offer was made, Gigliotti was not officially a Freex, although he vividly recalled their excitement: "They were jumping around, hopping from one foot to the other, and rubbing their little hands together with glee." They were also very secretive about "The Now Project," refusing to tell Gigliotti anything. Through the underground grapevine, he found out that Don West was hiring people to shoot video. Gigliotti called West, made an appointment, and was hired on the spot. Like the others, he developed his own assignment and was sent to Washington to cover riots and demonstrations. He fancied himself as a war correspondent, shooting in the dark through tear gas, eagerly fashioning for himself the role of a romantic, devil-may-care adventurer. West gave him money for tape and paid his way to the capital; but when Gigliotti returned, the tape was blank. Since he couldn't play back the tape in his camera's viewfinder, he had no way of knowing his equipment was not recording. It was horrible, the worst thing that could happen in video then, except maybe dropping your camera in water.

Gradually it began to dawn on Cort that nearly everyone in the video underground was working for Don West. In all, roughly 60 people worked on "The Now Project," including filmmakers, TV professionals, and members of the video underground. Eventually lines of cooperation were drawn up and equipment started to be traded back and forth. Everyone was amazed by West's vision that he could make television that would appeal to youth with a capital Y. As far as Cort could tell, Don West thought he was ordained by God to do a presentation for a pilot for CBS *and* make a million dollars. With his grand vision of subverting conventional television and his unprecedented support for these countercultural videomakers, West appeared to them as slightly daft. But West's impractical idealism was rock-solid sanity when compared with the madness of one of his crews.

Not everyone West discovered was as innocent as he. On a trip to Boston he came across a commune near Roxbury known as Fort Hill. It was led by Mel Lymon, a counterculture hero who made his reputation by playing "Amazing Grace" on the harmonica at the end of the Newport Folk Festival, when everyone was going home in disgust because Bob Dylan had appeared on stage with an electronic guitar. Lyman's unamplified protest against this decadence won him a cult following which he managed to parlay into a dangerously fascistic commune that included, among its many dubious activities, videotaping. Unfortunately, West's naiveté did not penetrate the violence and repression lurking beneath Fort Hill's peace-loving hippie commune facade. The mature CBS executive and father of seven was taken in by Lyman's charisma. West blithely introduced Fort Hill's cameraman George Pepper to the Freex, and he stayed with them for most of the three months of production. During this time Pepper carried a revolver and otherwise terrified the Freex, one of whom was convinced he was the devil incarnate.

Despite the video minions clamoring for money and tape, West concentrated his attention on the Videofreex. In October he sent them to Chicago, where they covered the May Day demonstration and made some fine tapes with Jerry Rubin and Abbie Hoffman, who were then among the much-publicized defendants in the famous Chicago 7 trial.[3] There were also tapes of William Kunstler, Leonard Wineglass, and Tom Hayden. When Hayden learned the tapes were for CBS, he demanded they be erased. At first the Freex refused, arguing that Hayden had agreed. Once Hayden explained his fears that CBS might keep the tapes and use them against him, the Freex relented and erased what they had shot because it was a politically correct thing to do. At the same time, they also taped a historic interview with Illinois' Black Panther leader Fred Hampton—notable because it was the last interview he gave before his murder in a police raid.[4] Among the many ironies of this experience was the contrast the Freex discovered between the Yippies and the Panthers: the Yippies were invariably holed up in the worst slums whereas the Panthers were always found in posh houses. The Panther Party was organized revolution, the Yippies were disorganized pranksters.

The journalist in West vibrated when he learned about the Hampton interview, but the Freex refused to show it to him. The trip to Chicago had been a radicalizing one. Perhaps Tom Hayden's paranoia had rubbed off onto them, but also the reins of control were slipping out of West's grip and into the hands of the Freex, who had now begun to view West as "the enemy." Even before Hampton's death in December, the Freex were afraid West would turn the tape over to the FBI. Their paranoia was not without reason. Making the tape had been dangerous: the Panthers were being harassed by the police, and everyone knew they were capable of fighting back. A young man who had gone with the Freex to meet Hampton was later accosted at the airport by the Chicago police. Fortunately, the Freex had their own van and drove out of town without incident. So when West requested the tapes, they bluntly asked what he would do if the FBI demanded them. West honestly replied he would let the FBI have them. (It was not until December, when they had gone up to the country house West rented for the edit, that they relented and finally let West see the Hampton tape.)

The Freex next set off for California, where they exchanged radical politics for hot tub enlightenment. David, Curtis, Parry and an engineer they discovered named Chuck Kennedy flew to Los Angeles and were met by a friend in an RV. They climbed aboard and cruised up the California coast for a three-week all-expense-paid odyssey.

First they visited rock star Frank Zappa, who was interested in working with them although his agent put a stop to it. As far as the Freex could tell, no one had ever approached Zappa before about doing video. Next they stopped briefly at Esalen and Big Sur. Instead of announcing they were from CBS and shooting a documentary, they decided to play it cool and introduce themselves by saying, "Let us step into your life for a while. Let's see if it can work." Although the philosophy sounded groovy, in fact they wound up being intrusive and disruptive. They put away their equipment and decided to simply "be there." Maybe it was the hours spent in the hot tubs instead of taping, but by the time they reached Pacific Alternative School in Palo Alto, they were loose, laid back, and ready to do their thing. They invited people to come in, participate, be free. The tapes reflected this; they had no focus. Parry Teasdale remembers them as looking like Charles Collingwood on quaaludes. No one did any interviewing because the philosophy was to break down the barriers between the people behind the cameras and those in front, a disastrous theory championed by David Cort.

Back in New York, West was experimenting with studio video. He constructed a set at Global Village, John Reilly's new video organization. The idea was to have Bob Livingston direct live music groups on tape. West had conceived a loose, magazine format that blended video documentary with entertainment television. It was a concept that would later pervade television as soft-feature documentary shows. Since "The Now Project" was designed to replace "The Smothers Brothers Show" in its nine o'clock Sunday night time slot, humor and music were integral to the otherwise amorphous plan. West envisioned an MC and a presenter who would casually introduce each tape; an old man, a young guy, and a girl were the pilot's stock characters. He had novelist Kurt Vonnegut in mind as the senior figure: West wanted him to read a passage about the war from *Slaughterhouse–Five*. But Vonnegut, whose literary star was burning brightly, refused to work at scale. He tried bargaining with West, suggesting he would do the show if West would get him his own program. West gave up on the idea and, with it, the studio at Global Village and its plastic set, unwittingly abandoning the last link to anything remotely resembling television in 1969.

While he was still thinking of a three-character pilot, West heard Nancy Cain on a witty radio program on WBAI and thought she would be excellent as "the girl." He called her up and offered her a job. Cain had previous show business experience as a singer and proved to be an attractive, sharp-witted woman who knew her own mind, a distinct asset to the otherwise leaderless group. She was assigned as liaison to the Freex. At first she was loyal to West, but gradually her allegiance shifted to the Freex, who were doing more interesting things than her boss.

Cain's best friend and roommate, a former school teacher named Carol Vontobel, also became involved. She was hired to take care of Don West's books and promptly fell in love with Parry Teasdale. Nancy and Carol next introduced the Freex to Skip Blumberg, a draft-deferred teacher with some graduate credits toward an MBA. Blumberg, a long-haired, amiable kid who was marvelous at managing money, was very welcome because the Freex badly needed help in coping with their increasingly complicated financial affairs. West was giving them what seemed like a fortune to rent equipment and cover their day-to-day expenses. (By the end of December, West had spent somewhere between $80,000 and $100,000 on his dream.) The Freex were worried that someone at CBS would find out what West was doing with the money and put an end to it. But the money continued to flow—even as far as Sweden, to fly Eric Siegel back to California so he could devise a way of colorizing their black and white tapes. By the end, West was giving the Freex everything they demanded, dipping into his own money to cover expenses. Cash flowed so freely that Cort wryly speculated they could have had dancing girls if they had asked. Actually, most of the money went for equipment, which established the Freex's long-standing reputation as the most technologically sophisticated video group in the underground.

In return for West's largesse, the Freex frequently behaved like spoiled brats. Once, when the security guards followed a Videofreek who was drunk and riding the CBS elevators, he blew smoke in their faces. Their arrogance was kindled by the knowledge that they were connected to the very top. The Freex expected fantastic things to happen and were encouraged in this magical thinking by Don West, who set a lofty example. The Freex let West in on the video process but sagely refused to show him much of the tapes, knowing it was in the process that the magic lay. The tapes were horrible by professional standards, and the Freex knew it, keeping the truth from West as long as they could. They were cursed with having discovered the zoom lens, and their equipment, even when optimized by CBS engineers, was still primitive as were their skills. Whenever West asked to see tapes, they would object, claiming: "They have to be edited." "Well, let's edit them," West would reply. "We're into our shooting heads now. First we do the shooting, then we do the editing." West went along with it all. He thought as long as he said yes to the Freex, the project would continue. The idealistic, impractical, inexperienced producer was afraid to say no and impose his judgment "prematurely."

West's handpicked television crew did not go along with this rampant unprofessionalism. Bernie Solens was the first to go. When Stan White heard of Vonnegut's demand, he told West he wanted out. Finally Bob Livingston jumped ship. He had had it with the Freex, who greeted his TV standards and demands for a script with their forceful anarchy. As far as the Freex were concerned, Livingston was television, the enemy. Livingston wrote West a long, ardent letter telling him he was blowing the biggest chance anyone had ever been given in American television by working this way. But West did not agree: he did not want to tiptoe in, securing a small beachhead in the war to revolutionize television; he wanted to overwhelm the network with a frontal assault. And he did.

Since West had promised to deliver a live pilot on December 17, he felt wedded to the date despite the fact that they were not even close to being ready. Because of a brewing union dispute, West decided prudence demanded he get the Freex away from CBS and out of the city to edit. He rented a country estate in East Durham, New York, and everyone trooped upstate for three weeks of editing and carefree living. They trashed the house, virtually destroying its furnishings. The owner was a collector of Civil War memorabilia, and the Freex paraded about in uniforms and otherwise made merry. Alcohol and drugs were in plentiful supply; guests came and went. Amid the carnival atmosphere David and Parry did manage to edit, condensing 40 hours of tape into 53 minutes. Eric Siegel had a room at the back where he worked on his colorizer. Somehow, they produced six segments that would later be interspersed with live music, and the show was given a new title: "Subject to Change."

The Freex shared West's desire for a revolutionary format, but their conception was far more radical than his. They wanted to be so revolutionary that their format would destroy everything in front of and behind it, so that television as it was then known would never work again. They fully accepted their tape would be unacceptable, but not bad. Although they were working for a commercial TV network, the Freex never thought of their program as television. And so it came as no surprise to them that the grand showing on December 17 turned out to be a "happening," not a television show.

Doug Davis, *Newsweek*'s art reporter, had been following West and the Freex for several months while writing a story on avant-garde television. Davis thought "Subject to Change" was one of the greatest happenings he had witnessed in his career as a '60s art reporter. It was only later that West, who had been flattered by Davis's interest, realized that Davis was not a television critic.

Chased by snowstorms and bitter temperatures, the Freex vacated the ravaged house in East Durham, leaving behind their master tapes as well as numerous black plastic garbage bags buried in a snow bank for spring excavation, and hurried back to New York to meet their deadline. By now they had acquired, with CBS funds, a loft at 98 Prince Street, which they began rapidly converting into a studio. Davidson Gigliotti and George Pepper supervised the construction of a control room the day before the scheduled event was to occur. It never dawned on any of the Freex, amid the construction, flying sawdust, and nonexistent set, that this might not work. Nobody was worried because none of them had ever done a show like this. Revelling in blissful ignorance, they invited everyone in the underground New York art scene to come the following evening and sit in the bleachers to watch their historic pilot for network TV. When the electricity proved inadequate for the mountains of equipment they had brought in, Don West hired an outside generator and had it parked on Prince Street with cables coiling mysteriously into the building. The Freex's dream of themselves as a video version of a rock 'n' roll group was becoming a reality.

On December 16 West finally insisted on seeing the tape. After looking at it, he thought he would die. After all these months there was virtually nothing, with the exception of the Hoffman and Hampton tapes, the latter of which the Freex still refused to include. West was desperate. He called the farm in East Durham and chartered a plane to fly down with the tape masters. He spent the next 24 hours learning how to edit, trying to put together something he considered palatable for the fateful show. Haggard and gaunt, he arrived the following evening at five minutes to seven with his own 30-minute rough assemblage of the Hampton interview butt-edited with network coverage of the funeral. He was met with a wall of opposition. When Parry Teasdale flatly refused to put on his tape, West threatened to do it himself. Then Teasdale, backed by Cort and Ratcliff, told him that if he put the tape on, they would pull all the plugs in the loft, and there would be no show at all. It was a rash decision since none of the Freex had seen West's tape. But the fundamental issue was control; West had lost long ago whatever control he once had over the project. The Freex's defiance, pinned to political grounds, was the final mutiny. West stared into Teasdale's face and said somberly, "I won't put this on because I don't have any choice. But I'll never work with you again. If this is the greatest show in the history of American television, it's all yours. And if it's the worst show, it's all yours."

Three limousines were waiting at the door bringing the most important executives in American television to the oil-slicked cobblestone streets of lower Manhattan's Soho. Mike Dann, Irwin Siegelstein, and Fred Silverman climbed the narrow stairs and entered the loft. They had been out eating, and the smell of expensive liquor and imported cigars was breathed into the already charged air. West had insisted that the CBS executives sit in a room separated from the live performance; it was after all a TV pilot, and he wanted them to have a "viewing room" where they could view the pilot as people at home would, removed from the live hijinks. So the trio were led into a nearby loft and seated on an unmade bed. The Freex were offended by what they considered the arrogance of the network biggies in refusing to mingle with the masses. Misunderstandings and miscommunications touched off emotional bombshells all night. Next door in the control room, Eric Siegel, Chuck Kennedy, and Parry Teasdale were working feverishly to get the video signal to travel across the hall, squeezed through Siegel's primitive colorizer, and onto the glowing monitor around which Dann, Siegelstein, and Silverman were clustered. The contrast was deeply ironic between that dark, silent loft of network television's elite tastemakers and the throbbing excitement next door, where musicians like Buzzy Linhardt and Major Wiley were performing to a packed house of people, all of whom looked to West's jaded eyes like "Viva Zapata."

Recollections of what happened after that are fuzzy. Carol Vontobel recalled David Cort hurling the acetate credits into the bleachers instead of having them crawl up the screen. Cort recalled the show was a bomb. Parry Teasdale remembered the show going smoothly except for some technical problems with the CBS executives' monitor. Davidson Gigliotti recalls the big problem being the Siegel colorizer, which produced a garish array of magentas and greens and oranges, although he never saw the tape since he was running one of the three live cameras covering the performances. The bank of monitors arranged in a circle impressed the fans in the bleachers, who cheered enthusiastically like members of Howdy Doody's peanut gallery.

What everyone does remember is the evening's finale. At the end of the 90-minute extravaganza, Mike Dann allegedly staggered across the hall and into the Freex's loft, where he delivered a tactful speech. He said it might be several days before he knew what he thought of the show because it would take him that long to figure it out. That statement gave him enough time to get out of the loft alive, West recalled. Dann then added, prophetically, that it might turn out to be five years ahead of its time, five years before television was "ready" for this.[5]

3.

Guerrilla versus Grassroots

The Media must be liberated. Must be removed from private
ownership and commercial sponsorship, must be placed in the service
of all humanity. We must make the media believable. We must assume
conscious control over the videosphere. We must wrench the
intermedia network free from the archaic and corrupt intelligence that
now dominates it.

—Gene Youngblood, *Radical Software*[1]

The video underground's first encounter with broadcast television—
an adolescent confrontation with a patriarch—proved disastrous. Despite the underground's dictum that "VT is *not* TV,"[2] they had
jumped at the opportunity of having their work broadcast. They had
tasted the power of television: they had had money to burn, engineers
to command, state-of-the-art equipment to experiment with, and the
prospect of audiences in the millions. And they had blown it. Furious
over their expulsion from the Garden, the video underground vigorously rejected "beast television" and entered a period of disarray and
notoriety.

In 1970 the video underground began attracting press coverage
and funders' attention, and as new organizations began appearing,
the various identities of the different video groups began to coalesce.
With the infusion of CBS's money and engineering support, the Videofreex functioned as the movement's preeminent production group, acting as its technological and aesthetic innovator. Ken Marsh's new
organization, People's Video Theater, proved to be the most politically
and socially radical group then in New York, using live and taped
feedback of embattled community groups as a catalyst for social
change. With Rudi Stern, John Reilly founded Global Village, the first
closed-circuit video theater to show underground work (this was rap-

idly followed by the Philo T. Farnesworth Obelisk Theater, a project of Electric Eye in California). And Raindance, as publisher of the journal *Radical Software*, served as the movement's research and development arm.

Together the video underground shot hundreds of hours of documentaries, tapes on New Left polemics and the drama of political confrontation, as well as lifestyles and video erotica. Turning the limits of their technology into a virtue, videomakers were inventing a distinctive style unique to the medium. Tripods with their fixed viewpoints, were out; handheld fluidity was in. Gritty, black-and-white tapes were generally edited in the camera, since editing was still only a primitive matter of razor-blade cuts or else a maddeningly imprecise backspace method of manually cuing scenes for "crash" edits.[3] The technological limitations of early video equipment were merely incorporated into the style of "real time video," a conscious style praised for being honest in presenting an unreconstructed reality and opposed to conventional television "reality," with its quick, highly edited scenes and narration by a typically white male figure of authority.

Video's unique ability to capitalize on the moment with instant playback and real-time monitoring of events suited the era's emphasis on "process, not product."[4] The absence of electronic editing equipment—which discouraged shaping a tape into a finely finished "product"—further encouraged the development of a "process" video aesthetic.

Early video shooting styles were as much influenced by meditation techniques like t'ai chi and by drug-induced epiphanies as they were by existing technology. Aspiring to the minimal presence of an "absorber" of information, videomakers such as Paul Ryan believed in waiting for a scene to happen, trying not to shape it by directing events. The fact that videotape was relatively inexpensive and reusable made *laissez faire* work as feasible as it was desirable.

Observers outside the video scene found these early tapes guilty of inconsistent technical quality. Although some critics faulted video for being frequently infantile, they also praised it for carrying an immediacy rarely seen in establishment television.[5] The video underground's response to such criticism was to concede there was a loss in technical quality when compared to broadcast TV. But then they reminded critics that Hollywood had also been fixated on glossy productions until the French "New Wave" filmmakers in the early '60s created a demand for the grainy quality of *cinéma vérité*, jump cuts, and handheld camera shots. Like the *vérité* filmmakers 10 years before them, video pioneers were inventing a new style, and they expected to dazzle viewers with their radical approach and insider's ability to get stories unavailable to commercial television.

The competition for CBS dollars began undermining early camaraderie. With the availability of the first public funding for video from the New York State Council on the Arts, intense competition widened the growing rifts between individuals and production collectives and between video art and activism. Angling for a hefty grant of $263,000, Raindance proposed to NYSCA the creation of a "Center for De-Centralized Television," which would house a permanent video exhibition site where various video groups could show tapes and create new viewing environments. Equipment for video production and editing would be housed in a downtown Annex, available to individual artists and community groups. A portion of the grant would be allocated to support the production of tapes, and the balance would finance a newsletter and cultural databank of tapes indexed on computer. Global Village's competing proposal (which ironically was almost identical to the one from Raindance) called for a "Global Village Resource Center." The Videofreex wanted to own a cable channel and have a "media bus" to take video out of the city to universities and exurban communities. In their proposal, People's Video Theater wanted an outlet for "community video journalism," which would do roughly the same things everyone else had proposed.

"The debate among the groups sounded like an aphorism contest between Marshall McLuhan and Buckminster Fuller," Chloe Aaron wrote in *Art in America*. "In struggling for money they lost the sense of cooperation vital to the new, wider community to be achieved through video technology."[6]

The solution NYSCA chose was to fund none of the major proposals, opting instead for smaller grants for individual projects. Outside funding had become a necessity, but dissension and power politics threatened to undo everything. The debate played out in the back pages of *Radical Software* (1970–1974), Raindance's irregular journal. The large-format pages were filled with graphics and embraced the whole spectrum of tendencies within the movement. In it video chronicler Marco Vassi offered his impassioned analysis of the situation at the time:

> What was to have been the brightest jewel in the latest social disruption to call itself a "revolution," ie., the shock troops of media ecology, has become the latest stale turd to be tossed on the proliferating tombstone of western civilization. In NYC, communications central, the v.t. gang is a gaggle of white and jewish, middle class, twenty to thirty-five, long-

haired hippy businessman into dope. Who have not yet learned that all their complex equipment is just so much metal junk, toys and tools, which have no more worth than the hands and hearts of the people who work them.

Here there are frantic hustlings in lofts and storefronts, ripping factional gunfire, open warfare over the placatory chunks of breadmoney tossed into the pit by the State to keep the dissenters busy bickering. One sees no sexual honesty, one does not hear the questions of children, one does not sense that fierce inner passion for truth which alone purifies all activity. One feels one's tenderness drying up, one's silence invaded by the murmurs of people blinded by tissues of lies. They rarely touch one another, not with their hands or their eyes or their vibrations. The Invasion of the Sensitivity Snatchers.

Women are conspicuous by their absence or relegation to minor tasks. One sees no black faces; the gay have not been involved. Several Wall Street advisers are on the scene. No plants, four-footed animals, or parties. The rationalizations are all avant-garde, caressing each nuance of the current hip rhetoric. There is neither the focus of aim nor the relaxation of aimlessness. Ritualized confusion reigns.[7]

Amidst the chaos, inklings of what lay beyond could be gleaned by astute observers like Vassi. In another issue of *Radical Software*, he offered some rare insights into the video future:

> Tape will soon be everywhere. CATV will bloom, and electronic neighborhoods will be the rage. Home cassettes will rival the hi-fi markets in sound recording. There will be a computer in every pot. . . . Tape as an art form will develop its modes, its classicism, its surrealism, its abstractions. The boobs who have been staring hypnotically at the tube for thirty years will come to with a start, rub their eyes, and discover that they have a radically new medium on their hands. Finally it will become good business. And the race for exploitation rights will be on. . . . Every innovation in technology brought about by heads will be used by the power-trip neanderthals to furnish a more sophisticated 1984.

Vassi's advice to forestall this was to suggest

> that there be as little talking about this as possible, not to keep the enemy from overhearing or any of that nonsense, but to guard against coming to believe one's own rhetoric. The next thing you know, there will be a videotape movement. And theories of videotape. And videotape critics. And the whole superstructure of the very scene that tape is supposed to help get us out of.[8]

Vassi's advice, naturally, went unheeded. Video rhetoric, couched in a language dubed "cyberscat," kept pace with the rhetoric abounding in society at the time. Mixing technobabble and pie-in-the-sky theorizing with frontline reports of video activity and startlingly perceptive insights into the issues facing alternative video, *Radical Software* kept lines of communication open within the contentious video scene. In 1971, the journal gave birth to a book that became the movement's bible: *Guerrilla Television*, written by Raindance member Michael Shamberg and published by Holt, Rinehart and Winston.

The term "guerrilla television" was adapted from "cybernetic guerrilla warfare," an expression coined by Paul Ryan, who believed traditional guerrilla activity (such as bombings, snipings, and kidnappings) was ecologically risky compared with the "real" possibilities of "portable video, maverick data banks, acid metaprogramming, cable TV, satellites, cybernetic craft industries, and alternate lifestyles." For Ryan, portable video was "guerrilla warfare" insofar as it enabled you to fight the "perceptual imperialism of broadcast television" on a small scale in what was then an irregular war.[9]

Shamberg was quick to differentiate his notion of guerrilla television from Ryan's: while acknowledging it shared strategies and tactics with its counterpart in warfare, Shamberg insisted it was not a form of violence any more than evolution is. Avoiding any volatile political associations, guerrilla television was configured not as a weapon, but as a cultural tool bringing people together.

Shamberg's technoradicalism was conspicuously lacking in political analysis. Despite its militant name and rhetoric, guerrilla television was not aligned with the New Left. Members of the video collectives often considered student radicals to be hopeless Luddites. The Left's distrust of high technology, which had been associated with political and cultural repression and the military–industrial complex, may even have provoked some of Shamberg's exaggerated claims for new electronic media.[10]

In the late '60s, Leftist theories of media production had begun appearing that took seriously the possibility of using high technology to different ends.[11] Marxist critic Hans Magnus Enzensberger wrote that television immobilizes, depoliticizes, isolates, and pacifies individuals because centrally produced and controlled media can only stifle political participation and encourage passive consumer behavior. According to Enzensberger, television systematically prevents true perception of social reality. But by decentralizing the system structure, organizing collective production and transforming receivers into transmitters, the repressive use of mass media could be thwarted. Such ideas had been prefigured earlier in the century by Bertolt Brecht[12] who envisioned turning radio into a two-way interactive communication system. Enzensberger's writings were influential for

Marxists like Todd Gitlin, whose 1972 essay "Sixteen Notes on Television and The Movement"[13] may have influenced more politically conscious video activists, but rigorous Marxist analysis had little bearing on the video underground's post-political McLuhanesque thinking.

Shamberg's ideas[14] derived from McLuhan's view that political problems were caused primarily by communication breakdowns, not by the conscious clash of political interests. McLuhan viewed these breakdowns principally as a clash of generations; young people demanded involvement and harmony because they were retribalized by TV and radio, while their elders remained remote because they saw the world in fragmented patterns induced by print. Conflict was resolved, according to McLuhan, not by directly assaulting the system—as in a political revolution—but by extending the unifying properties of electronic media to everyone.[15] Shamberg wrote:

> It's nostalgia to think that . . . balance can be restored politically when politics are a function of Media-America, not vice versa. Only through a radical redesign of the information structure to incorporate two-way, decentralized inputs can Media-America optimize the feedback it needs to come back to its senses.[16]

Post-political video guerrillas believed that strikes, sit-ins, marches, and the like were chiefly significant as raw material for their cameras.[17] Political actions had little value in and of themselves; their greatest worth was as symbols, as electric drama.[18] Social problems, Shamberg reasoned, were solved not by "boorish" behavior in the streets but by redesigning the technological means by which people communicate. "Change the way a culture communicates, change the culture" was their daily litany.

Like McLuhan, Shamberg assumed that the economic prosperity enjoyed during the '60s would continue indefinitely, replacing the industrial age of scarcity with a leisure-time society "presided over by machines of loving grace."[19] Video visionaries saw distinct similarities between the electronic circuitry of the media and the functions of the human brain and nervous system. Believing themselves to be on the verge of becoming a cybernetic society in which the old paradigms no longer applied, they reasoned that by controlling the evolution of electronic media the cultural evolution of the human race could be directed.

Where they differed with McLuhan was in his acceptance of the commercial media more or less as he found them.[20] Shamberg believed the mass media numbed more than they enlightened, depending for success on accumulating mass audiences. "A standard of success that demands thirty to fifty million people can only trend toward homogenization," he wrote. "Information survival demands a diversity of options, and they're just not possible within the broadcast technology or context." McLuhan thought nothing could be done about the way a culture communicates, but alternative video theorists believed they could indeed do something. What they proposed was low-cost, decentralized TV made by the citizenry itself for its own purposes.

Guerrilla Television asserted that no alternative cultural vision could succeed without its own alternative information structure, not just alternative content pumped across the existing system. Underground video's experience with CBS had served as an important object lesson. By working outside the context of broadcast TV, guerrilla television had the potential to become a grassroots network of indigenous media activity. Rather than trying to reform broadcast television (which would be, in Frank Gillette's words, "like building a healthy dinosaur"), guerrilla television would coexist with broadcasting, restoring balance to the "media ecology" of America. By linking decentralized portable production with distribution technologies such as cable TV and videocassettes, guerrilla television would ensure that small-scale, non–mass-market information could be supported.

Not everyone making video at the time subscribed to guerrilla television's post-political thinking. Canadian media theorist McLuhan may have been its inspiration, but other Canadians were infusing video theory with political praxis,[21] inventing practical models for alternative video aimed at social rather than cultural change. The government-funded National Film Board of Canada launched the Challenge for Change/Société Nouvelle program in 1966 using film and later video to foster citizen–government dialogue.

The Challenge for Change was rooted outside the realm of broadcasting. Working collaboratively with a consortium of federal agencies and departments, the program's objective was to help eradicate the causes of poverty by provoking basic social change, using film and video as a catalyst. The idea had its roots in the social documentary movement of the '30s—in particular the classic film *Housing Problems* (1936), a documentary made "not *about* people but *with* them." John Grierson, father of the British social documentary, had also founded the NFBC. Shortly before his death in 1972, he acknowledged the influence of neorealist Cesare Zavattini who dreamed of arming Italian villages with cameras so they could send film letters to each other.[22] But the Challenge for Change went further: by training community people to make their own films and videotapes, they were freed from dependence upon liberal strangers who wandered into their lives and then out again once a documentary had been made.

"We feel the technology of communications should be understood and used by the people who are trying to find solutions to their problems, and who normally have no access to the media," wrote Dorothy Todd Hénaut in an article for the first issue of *Radical Software*. Hénaut and Bonnie Sherr Klein were the first staffers at the Challenge for Change to recognize the potential of portable video.[23] Hénaut's 1970 article, "In the Hands of Citizens: A Video Report," detailed the experience of the Comité des Citoyens de Saint-Jacques, a dynamic citizen's organization in a poor neighborhood in downtown Montréal.[24] The group decided health care was their most immediate problem, and they organized to start a clinic when the Challenge for Change approached them with the idea of using videotape as a community organizing tool.

Half-inch video allowed community people complete control of the media. They used the cameras to view themselves and their neighborhood with a new, more perceptive eye, conducted their own interviews, recorded their own discussions, and edited tapes to convey a particular message to a particular audience invited by them. Their aim was making changes in the community; making tapes was just a byproduct of this process.[25]

In this model the role for professional filmmakers was radically altered; instead of being producers, they became social animators. Creative control of one's work, refined aesthetic criteria, and professional standards of production were abandoned for a more democratic process in which the ultimate goal was social change not artistic excellence.

In issue two of *Radical Software*, Dorothy Hénaut took community video to its next step—"television as town meeting." Canada was ahead of the United States in its development of cable television (by 1968, 25 percent of all Canadian households had been connected to cable). It seemed natural to expect the concept of community film and video to be extended to cable television. After outlining a model community television service, Hénaut wisely cautioned

> The foregoing theory of communications has not yet been put into practice, and it will not be easy to do. It disturbs the status quo; it risks controversy; it could generate a lot of changes. The owners of the facilities are very jealous of the prerogatives of property-owners, and the impact could be so great on the established media that they too may feel very threatened. Local governments may also feel nervous about all this free debate of public issues. Advertisers may dislike the active, questioning mood of the public. There will be a lot of talk, mostly vague and self-righteous, about "responsibility." It will take some alert, determined, convinced and committed people to make it come true.[26]

Unlike the authors of guerrilla television, community video activists like Hénaut grasped the larger political and economic factors that would block the realization of a video democracy.

The Challenge for Change's model of community video activism crossed the border, carried by innovators like George Stoney and Bonnie Sherr Klein[27] and spread by tapes and by articles in publications like *Access* and *Radical Software*. It profoundly influenced the development of grassroots or community video in the United States, but since the United States was different from Canada (in political structure, attitudes toward government support of media production, cable television systems, etc.) the Challenge for Change model had to mesh with indigenous theories of community organizing and existing social structures for it to succeed. Some of the most dynamic examples of early community video arose in the southern United States, where cable television was widespread and a rich tradition of political organizing and community education had been revived by the civil rights movement. Equally important to its spread was the impact of two Johnson administration programs, the War on Poverty and Model Cities, which had created a social ideology and a bureaucratic infrastructure that helped support video access centers in the '70s.

A U.S. mecca for early community video was established in 1971 when George Stoney, who had left his post as guest executive producer of the Challenge for Change, joined with Red Burns in founding the Alternate Media Center at New York University. The Center became a training ground for community video activists and an important lobby for public access to cable TV. It was not, however, an American Challenge for Change: without the Canadian tradition of state-operated public communication systems, the community television movement in the United States was dependent on nongovernmental sources of support—private foundations and, ultimately, the cable television industry itself.

Shamberg equated guerrilla television with community or grassroots video, but they were actually different species of video activity. Guerrilla television producers professed an interest in community video, but they were generally far more interested in developing the video medium and getting tapes aired than in serving a localized constituency. Grassroots video, by stressing the participation of community members in making their own electronic information, was less concerned with polished "products" than with animating the "process" of social change.

But in 1971, *Guerrilla Television* appeared to rally the competing factions within the contentious alternative video scene under one banner. As guerrilla television, underground video emerged above ground, determined to challenge the hegemony of broadcast TV. Eager to experiment with a new video language and distinctive documentary video style, Shamberg began to hatch his own plan to turn guerrilla television theory into practice.

4.

The World's Largest TV Studio

Michael Shamberg was practicing yoga at the McBurney YMCA in New York City when a name came sailing at him out of the blue. Top Value Television. The 28-year-old author of *Guerrilla Television* was delighted, realizing that Top Value Television would also read TVTV. It was the perfect name for the video group he was getting together to cover the upcoming Presidential Nominating Conventions.[1]

It was February 1972, and Michael Shamberg wanted to put into practice some of the theories he had been formulating about alternative video. He had worked as a journalist for newspapers in Chicago and done brief stints at *Time* and *Life*. He had been to the '68 convention in Chicago, and in 1970 he took a half-inch portapak to the Conservative Party Convention, where he experimented with political interviews and event coverage, producing a "Media Primer" for Raindance, the theory-and-practice video collective that he helped form. He knew his way around the political scene; he also knew that if a group of video freaks went to Miami and did a good job, they could get major recognition because the networks and the national press corps would be there.

TVTV was not alone in seeing the conventions as an opportunity to sell itself. Anyone in America with something to sell came to Miami expecting to get a piece of the power and the money. As Timothy Crouse noted in *The Boys on the Bus*, "Hookers peddled ass, Mr. Peanut peddled goobers, pushers peddled dope, managers peddled dark horses, and the networks peddled themselves."[2] Why not peddle alternative media? Reporters had attended the first convention in 1831. In 1926 Lee DeForest, broadcast pioneer and inventor, speculated that what television needed was a live event to draw attention, such as a national convention. The networks later used the conventions to introduce their innovations—coast-to-coast network broadcasting in 1952, Huntley–Brinkley in 1956, the "creepie-peepie" camera[3] in 1960, then color. It was time for half-inch video to make its convention debut.

Shamberg and Megan Williams moved to San Francisco and joined Allen Rucker and members of Ant Farm,[4] an art-and-architecture group located in the Bay Area, to plot their coverage of the Miami conventions. Rucker and Shamberg had been college roommates at Washington University in St. Louis in 1965. Rucker went on to study communications at Stanford where he discovered video and ultimately cofounded the Portolla Media Access Center, a project of the Portolla Institute, the nonprofit umbrella of Stewart Brand's *Whole Earth Catalog*.[5] Rucker was working at the Center when Shamberg enlisted him in his new video venture.[6] Combining the talents of the East and West Coasts, Shamberg brought the think tank of Raindance and the technical wizardry of the Videofreex, while Allen Rucker contributed the graphic inventiveness and high spirits of the Ant Farm and the organizational know-how of Stewart Brand's *Whole Earth Catalog*, plus journalists like Maureen Orth. What started as a fantasy project became a reality in April when TVTV received full press accreditation. They set up a business and living commune in San Francisco six weeks before the July Democratic Convention and operated around the clock organizing and fund-raising.[7]

The people who worked on the convention tapes were chosen because of their various organizational or production skills, as well as whatever equipment they could provide. For the Democratic Convention there were twenty-eight people: four from Raindance, four from Ant Farm, four from Antioch College in Ohio, and three from the Videofreex; the rest were independent videomakers from New York, Chicago, San Francisco, and Los Angeles.

For the first tape, TVTV raised money from four cable systems: Teleprompter and Sterling Cable (now Manhattan Cable) contributed $1,000 each; Continental Cable in Ohio gave $500; and Cypress Communications pledged an unrecorded amount. Although the cable systems provided only 25 percent of the funding, the precedent of selling programming to cable stations was established. The agreement made with the cable systems was that the program would be completed within two weeks of the convention; the systems then would own a copy of the tape and could decide whether to air it. An additional $3,000 came from two private foundations, the Vanguard Foundation[8] and the DJB Foundation. Shamberg and his old friend Tom Weinberg from Chicago each kicked in $3,000. In the end, TVTV spent roughly $16,000 to make the first hour-long documentary; this included tape, equipment, a trip to New York for final editing, transportation, living expenses, and the princely salary of $50 a week for everyone.[9] TVTV finally put their expenses on credit cards and came away mired in debt but covered with glory.

A few weeks before the convention, Tom Weinberg traveled to Miami and rented a white stucco house in a posh suburb where TVTV's ad hoc production collective would live and work while covering both Conventions. His amazing luck in "scoring" the house as mission control for their operations won him the lasting nick name of "Score" Weinberg. Once the Democratic Convention began, activity sprawled from upstairs bedrooms where crews logged tapes, down into the living room—an informal screening room and mission control center cluttered with Sony portapaks, tapes, wires, cables, newspapers, and large handlettered signs and assignment sheets—and out around the azalea-bordered pool.[10]

TVTV's first big coup was in securing press credentials for all its members, one of a hundred officially accredited non-network TV groups from around the world given access to the conventions on a revolving basis.[11] Security guards on the convention floor were hesitant accepting press credentials from this unconventional group of blue-jeaned, long-haired alternate media guerrillas, and they gave hollow assurances it was "nothing personal, you understand." TVTV just kept their cameras on, recording it all. "By showing our equipment and ourselves," Megan Williams told *Rolling Stone*, "by putting our own lifestyle into the programs we make—we'll show the average guy who watches broadcast TV there's more than one kind of video."[12]

The TVTV crew believed their equipment would allow them to approach events more as participants than as threatening or dictating TV crews. Compared with the beefy network cameramen—laden down with scuba-style backpacks and cumbersome television cameras, tethered to a soundman, a floor reporter, and often a producer—a slim young woman holding a lightweight camera in her hands was considerably less threatening and much more flexible. This meant their finished tapes could emphasize informal, unstaged interactions between people, some of whom might not even be aware of their presence. To this end, Raindance adapted a vidicon tube (originally designed for military surveillance) for the portapak, thus giving TVTV the possibility of picking up images in poorly lit areas.

TVTV knew there was no way they could compete with the networks, so their tape would be about "us trying to tape the Convention and have it make sense as tape." Their emphasis would be on the "feel of the events" and on "the social space that has been neglected, rejected and missing from media coverage to date," in other words, on the reactions of real people involved, including themselves. The work would resemble a video collage—not of hard-edged, well-cropped images, but of "found art like snapshots, postcards, and sketches."[13]

In the briefing instructions to the crews, recorded in *Radical Software*, they listed the following "Things to Tape"

Delegates: Because we will not have unlimited access to the floor, we want to pick up on specific behind-the-lines Convention-related activity. If we can develop a rapport with delegates and hang out with them we can be there at the informal moments which the networks can't cover but which can give a better sense of the Convention than staged interviews.

Specifically, we should try to be with delegates at dinner, in caucus rooms, in their hotel rooms, at parties, etc. We already have pledges of access. . . . The continuing saga of a delegate may make a good continuity device in the final edit.

In terms of what types of delegates, they should be chosen as to color and articulation of viewpoint, and whether or not you'd want to hang out with them. Specifically we're thinking of people like a middle-aged Texas liberal friend of LBJ's, and Wallace people.

The Media: We need to document the media presence. This can be done partly through visuals which show equipment, crews, and interviews: and partly through sound: either newsmen talking to each other, or interviews with newsmen. In fact, newsmen are the only people we would consider doing a formal interview with.

You should also make friends with newsmen as they'll give you tips about events and processes. Chances are they won't feel threatened by us but will be amused and want to help.

Pseudo-Events: Anything which happens for the media will be over-covered by it. Yippies,[14] for example, will stage media events. Instead of taking them at face value we need to shoot behind-the-scenes and debunk them just as we would the straight media or straight culture. A lot of people are coming down here to get press attention. They will. By the time our edit appears people will be tired of hearing and seeing them. Moreover, demonstrations and press conferences tend to be didactic in that it's people telling you what to think. That makes slow, talky tape. Better to have spontaneous behavior which happens in process (as in hanging out with delegates).

Confrontations: People in Miami Beach are real edgy. . . . Some hippies may be into violence although their leaders have been cool. Some shots of trashing might be worth it. But chances are it won't turn into permanent confrontation like in Chicago in 1968. Our feeling is that confrontation tape is a cliché of Porta-Pak video and we're tired of it.

One reason for TVTV is to give viewers an idea of the range of alternate video, because too often they mistake the possibilities of the equipment with the fact that it's always used in the service of the same content.

We're not into declarative, explicit typed action or statements done wholly for the media. At best, we want to cover the media covering those actions and cover the people planning for or reflecting on them. The actions themselves are of negligible importance to us.[15]

TVTV deployed its motley staff into crews, using five to seven cameras at a time; each crew followed a story, and by rotating, everyone got some time on the convention floor. Instead of jobs, crew members had "roles." Organization was crucial: a central coordinator (a different person was assigned each day) remained in the house at all times to oversee the overall production. Two telephones at the house and at their booth at the convention hall insured communication between the coordinator and crews. Each morning, assignments were given on the basis of the day's convention schedule, the UPI wire, and what people wanted to do. Taping had priority over everything.[16] In an effort to get what the networks did not, TVTV taped everything from the construction of the convention floor to a guided boat tour of Miami.

TVTV's success was based on doing careful behind-the-scenes preparation. They were thorough about figuring in advance what they wanted to do and careful about how money was spent. Megan Williams recalls that it was not so much the editorial content that preoccupied them at the time, but rather getting people to Miami. When she arrived, the notion of actually going onto the convention floor seemed "terrifying," but once she got over her fear, the carnival atmosphere held sway.[17]

The convention floor was "the world's largest TV studio," lit for TV with rows and rows of hard white spotlights and wired with 150 miles of electric cable. The networks dominated the conventions: CBS had a staff of 500; NBC and ABC had 450 each. It was a cliché to say the National Conventions were conventions of media people and the stars were reporters not politicians. Although the conventions offered a chance to study a cross-section of the nation and examine the party system, it was mainly good business. The networks did a more expensive job than anyone; they spent about eight million dollars on the Democratic Convention (Cronkite's glass box above the hall alone cost nearly $100,000), while the Democratic candidates and the party spent a little less than three million.[18]

"The Democratic race would boil down to a quick civil war, a running death-battle between the Old Guard on the Right and a gang of Young Strangers on the Left," gonzo journalist Hunter Thompson reported in *Fear and Loathing: On the Campaign Trail '72*.[19] Less than a dozen of the 5,000 media sleuths accredited at the convention knew exactly what was happening at the time.[20] The strategy employed by George McGovern's forces to secure the first ballot was so "byzantine," according to Thompson, that not even Machiavelli could have handled it on TV.[21] The networks failed miserably; while Cronkite told the nation of McGovern's defeat, his "boiler room" at the Doral Hotel cheered knowing victory was theirs. But TVTV never lost sight of the story, following the complex plot of delegate challenges, capturing the thrill of victory and the agony of defeat, political style. In short, TVTV succeeded where their establishment "betters" failed. Machiavelli with a portapak.

TVTV's hour-long documentary, *The World's Largest TV Studio*, concentrated on two key events at the convention, the California and Illinois delegate challenges. In both cases TVTV provided exclusive material, including fine portraits of California's state representative Willie Brown and Billy Singer, the Chicago alderman who successfully challenged Mayor Daley.

The big question looming over the convention was whether George McGovern would be stripped of more than half of the 271 delegates he had won in the California primary. If the "ABM" (Anything but McGovern) movement could pull 151 delegates away, McGovern would lose the first ballot, and then the nomination would be up for grabs. The Old Guard, led by labor leader George Meany and Chicago Mayor Richard Daley, made a naked power grab pressing Hubert Humphrey into service as front man followed by Scoop Jackson, Terry Sanford, and Shirley Chisholm. The ABM people knew that nothing short of fraud, treachery, or violence could prevent McGovern from securing the nomination. Their plan was to hold McGovern under the 1,500 mark for two ballots, then confront the convention with an ABM candidate on the third ballot. If that failed, then another candidate would be tried on the fourth ballot, and so on until they could nominate someone acceptable to the Meany/Daley axis. What happened reads like "an extremely complicated murder trial," according to Thompson. On TV it was "like somebody who's never played chess trying to understand a live telecast of the Fisher/Spassky . . . duel in

Iceland.''[22] A surprise parliamentary maneuver from the Women's Caucus forced a premature showdown that effectively decided whether McGovern would get the nomination. McGovern's strategists deliberately lost the vote on the South Carolina challenge on whether the delegation included enough women. Humphrey's forces planned to settle two procedural issues on this challenge: who could vote and what constituted a majority. What had never been explained to the press or even to most of the delegates was that McGovern would win the nomination by either clearly winning or clearly losing South Carolina, thus postponing any procedural vote at that time. Since the numbers were much better for McGovern to win in California on the question of what constituted a majority, McGovern needed to hold that question off as long as possible.

The parliamentary question of the California challenge was explained by the networks as though it were Goedel's theorem, Renata Adler noted in *The New Yorker*. "Top Value Television," she continued, "did much better . . . in simply eavesdropping—if a reporter with videotape equipment can be said to eavesdrop—on an explanation by a McGovern aide to several delegations."[23] TVTV showed Willie Brown instructing his followers on the South Carolina challenge, saying to vote for it, when Shirley MacLaine (a California delegate) interrupted to say she thought the whole trick was either to win big or lose big. Brown, who apparently had not meant to explain that subtlety even to his floor whips, ran through the strategy, noting they should look solid behind the challenge so as not to tip their hand to Senator Humphrey's forces. But before explaining the ins and outs of all the challenges, Brown assured the delegates that the TVTV crew was "unaffiliated," a fact that "may have served the video group to more advantage than the portability of their equipment," as one critic later noted.[24]

Illinois had two delegations: one was led by Mayor Daley; the other was a "new politics" delegation led by Chicago alderman Billy Singer and Reverend Jesse Jackson. The convention had to decide which delegation was "official." Most expected a 50–50 compromise, but in an upset, the "rebel" delegation was voted in over Daley's "regulars." TVTV covered the contest right up to the moment when Billy Singer walked down a hallway, into the credentials office, and took possession of the documents, stuffing them into a brown paper bag while smiling at the cheers of colleagues who had crowded into the small room. As *Chicago Sun-Times* writer Anthony Monahan later wrote, "the scene has the disorganized ring of reality, a contrast to the often-manipulated dramatics of network convention coverage."[25]

In addition to focusing on the political players, TVTV followed the network media covering the convention. They interviewed NBC's Cassie Mackin, the first woman floor reporter for the networks,[26] who glowingly admitted, "It's a piece of cake. There's nothing a woman couldn't have done a long time ago." Dan Rather confided that conventions make him feel like a kid turned loose in a candy store. And CBS anchor Walter Cronkite proclaimed, "I enjoy an open-ended broadcast. It gives you a chance to say a few things." Veteran reporters Douglas Kiker and Roger Mudd also put in cameo appearances.

In a mirror-within-mirror moment, TVTV explored the media's response to the group itself by including a *Newsweek* reporter interviewing them, followed by a voice-over reading of the unflattering results of that interview. The seriousness of the group was apparently lost on the reporter, who stressed their reliance on laughing gas for achieving a new perspective on the convention.

TVTV's new perspective owed less to laughing gas than to a satirical grasp of political absurdities, a true-believer's faith in the possibilities of a new medium, and a remarkable ability for being in all the right places at all the right times. TVTV owed far more to the Marx Brothers than Karl Marx in their understanding of how to tell a political story. The nitty-gritty account of McGovern's brilliant if confusing strategy to win the nomination is sandwiched between TVTV's witty approach to what was happening outside as well as inside the convention hall. The tape opens with an off-key rendition of "Moon over Miami" sung by TVTV member Frank Cavestani, the first in a series of funky, TVTV-signature style elements. Group members pop up at odd moments throughout the tape: a hairy Allen Rucker complains, "I'm sick of being a media junkie"; Videofreex Nancy Cain—wrapped in a towel—poses beside a life-sized poster of Colonel Sanders propped against the TVTV media van; and Michael Shamberg zooms around like the Roadrunner cartoon character, muttering "Eagleton, Eagleton"[27] while interviewing delegates in the back corridors of the convention hall. The tape closes with sardonic snapshots of Miami including close-ups of a palm tree, a plug for the beef stew at Wolfie's restaurant, and several hilarious man-on-the-street interviews. In a short sequence called "superb" by one critic,[28] an elderly man in shorts and sunglasses, gingerly walking with a cane, passes the camera. TVTV calls after him, asking what he thinks of the convention. Turning ever so slowly, he explains in a flat, measured tone: "I am not interested in the convention," then slowly turns back and continues down the street. The last word is had by a souvenir hunter amid the debris of the convention floor, who asks, incredulous: "How could anyone really vote for Nixon?!"

In the end, TVTV had 80 hours of tape and two weeks to edit their sprawling coverage. Shamberg, Williams, and Rucker flew to New York, checked into the Chelsea Hotel, and began the final edit at C.T. Lui's new production and postproduction center, The Egg Store. They edited from half-inch tape onto one-inch using Sony equipment. Parry Teasdale, one of the Videofreex, handled most of the technical matters. The idea was to edit by committee, and it was, in Megan Williams' words, "pretty experimental and grueling." They worked in 24-hour shifts, then crashed in the studio for five hours until someone would come and wake them.[29] Their biggest problem, aside from the limits imposed by state-of-the-art video editing technology, was in finding a way to organize the material. The result, given the unprecedented effort, was amazingly good though rough. Not everyone was pleased.

Parry Teasdale disagreed with Shamberg over his approach to the Democratic Convention coverage. He told Shamberg he found nothing new in producing a tape about conventions to be broadcast on cable television "after the fact." Teasdale thought the event should have been covered live. Shamberg, he decided, was a "producer" employing "artists" to shoot what amounted to a conventional idea of television. The Videofreex were technical wizards still married to an idea of live, participatory video as "happening." Their live, low-power TV show in Lanesville was more what Teasdale had in mind.[30]

TVTV's formal innovations were less radical than Teasdale clamored for. The group knew they did not want voice-overs and cutaways. They edited what worked without stopping to think why, borrowing more from twenty years of watching television (especially commercials) than from any knowledge of film or documentaries. Editing proved an act of attrition. At the start, there would be many people in the room, wanting to see what would happen to the sequences they had shot, but as the hours grew longer and the process duller, people would stray, and it would finally come down to two or three who were just insane about the project and wanted to finish what they had started.[31]

That insanity was best expressed in one incident close to the end of the edit. As an organizing solution, they discovered they could use handlettered graphics to identify various storylines, as well as the names of famous and not-so-famous people on camera. Allen Rucker was awarded the magic marker because he had the best penmanship in the room. Early in the morning after working through the night with the tape three-quarters completed, Rucker walked across the street to a neighborhood bar to get a bullshot so he could wake up enough to continue his lettering. He strolled out of the bar and into a street sign, cracking his head open with a six-inch gash that bled like a war wound. He thought, with the clear logic of the exhausted, he was going to die making this tape. When he staggered back into the editing room, Megan Williams was ready to rush him to an emergency room, but Shamberg said, "Wait a minute! Before you go, you've got to finish these graphics." And Rucker sat there, holding his head and moaning he was bleeding to death, but he wrote all the graphics.[32]

Shamberg shrewdly calculated that the critical audience for the tape might be five or ten key people who wrote for influential publications. Low on money and worried about the prospects for raising any funds to make the next convention tape, they arranged a screening in filmmaker Shirley Clarke's[33] loft at the Chelsea Hotel.[34] Attending were several critics, including *New York Times'* TV critic John J. O'Connor, who devoted an entire column to *The World's Largest TV Studio* the day it was cablecast in New York. Although he was not entirely enthusiastic, criticizing it for "that peculiar brand of smugness that infects many underground visions of on-the-ground society," O'Connor nonetheless judged it "distinctive and valuable." The mere fact of a full-length *New York Times* review gave the tape and TVTV the kind of credibility the group desperately needed. The day before the review appeared, Sterling had reneged on its promise of $1,000 to produce the Republican Convention tape, but after the review, the cable company agreed to make good on its offer. TVTV considered O'Connor's review responsible in large measure for their ability to raise funding for the second show.[35]

O'Connor wasn't the only critic to find TVTV's coverage to his liking. Richard Reeves, writing for *New York* magazine, gushed

> [TVTV] does exactly what CBS and NBC with all their millions didn't do enough of: TVTV *reports* more than it interviews; it *shows* the confusion on the floor as delegates look for telephone and hand signals from George McGovern's manipulators; it *shows* what the networks only tried to talk about. The film [*sic*] . . . is an uneven and flawed little masterpiece . . . the best electronic coverage of the Democratic Convention that I've seen. And I've seen too much.[36]

Renata Adler, writing for *The New Yorker*, agreed with Reeves that TVTV had done a better job than the networks. And Anthony Monahan, writing for the *Chicago Sun-Times*, branded it "good lively television."[37]

TVTV's scrapbook program on the Democrats' often chaotic "open convention" was rough even by their own standards. Though praised by veteran analysts for their fresh reporting style and astute grasp of the real stories at the convention, TVTV knew they could do a better job the second time out.

TVTV's Scrapbook

TVTV kept a scrapbook in which shooting schedules, phone numbers, artwork (on the order of Crumb cartoons) and assorted memorabilia were jotted down and collected. Inscribed within was a Shooter's Guide, a mix of practical advice, hip philosophy, and TVTV humor drawn from their experience at the July convention.

Shooter's Guide
1. Track vidicon so the zoom is good
2. Clean vidicon, lens, & viewfinder
3. Check all connections
4. Clean heads (occasionally)
5. Check mic & headset
6. Do test record & playback
7. Check threading occasionally when out shooting
8. Make sure there is no recording on the part of the tape that you're about to shoot
9. Turn on the camera when something is about to happen
10. Make sure you've a good frame
11. Pan & zoom slow & steady
12. Keep aware of what's happening & try not to disturb the sane
13. Constantly check audio & video
14. Make sure the red light is on when you're recording
15. Don't jostle the pack
16. Keep both eyes open
17. Playback as soon as possible after recording
18. Get your timing together—sing, dance, do yoga, swim, run, pray, climb a mountain, smoke a little dope, watch your breath, witness yourself
19. *Consider the edit*
20. Don't take any of it seriously but have respect, peace, love, & Woodstock, remember the revolution, & do it for the Gipper
21. Put your equipment away & check it to make sure you haven't fucked anything up in the meantime

Appended in the margin was the following piece of mystical advice, inspired by the writings of Carlos Castaneda: "Find a spot for shooting (see Don Juan), then move the spot with you." Whoever wrote the quote was a little hazy on literary sources, since "Juan" is scrawled over a crossed out "Quixote," however, both allusions seem equally suited to TVTV's improbable and ultimately successful foray onto the turf of establishment media.

5.

Mountain Guerrilla

Ted Carpenter was a self-described " '60s run-around activist" who was interested in adult education. In 1968 the young Canadian came to the Upper Cumberland area of Appalachia to work as a VISTA volunteer.[1] Appalachia's problems were varied and complex, and government and private programs often neglected the people of the region, concentrating instead on industrial and natural resource development. Carpenter supervised VISTA's community development programs for several surrounding counties in eastern Tennessee.[2]

When his VISTA service ended, Carpenter and his family continued living on a small farm in the hills, doing odd jobs in order to remain in the region. In 1970, out of the blue, he was awarded a Ford Foundation fellowship for leadership development. The fellowship gave him the freedom to do whatever he wanted for a year, with a substantial stipend to travel, live, and study.

Carpenter was particularly interested in investigating techniques for adult community education that emphasized learning from experience rather than formal curricula—"learning with a culture around it," as he phrased it. It was a principle he found perfectly expressed by a storekeeper in Blackey, Kentucky, who said: "I've a feelin' that any kind of learnin' by adults will be incidental to their learnin' of something that they're vitally interested in. I'd just expect that more middle-aged coal miners have learned to read since they've been tryin' to find out about the black lung benefits, than in any time in history."[3] During the fellowship year Carpenter studied at the Highlander Center in New Market and at the Tennessee Technological University at Cookeville. At Highlander, he was introduced to a model for understanding Appalachia[4] and the new regionalism emerging from the traditional mountain culture. The University at Cookeville introduced him to video.[5]

The Highlander Center was founded in the '30s, an outgrowth of the folk-school movement. According to the theory, mountaineers were viewed as a legitimately distinct population, separated not only by geography and history but by ethnicity. All mountaineers were assumed to have the cultural and psychological capacity to participate in the usages of their culture, and the folk school was seen as the agency teaching the mountain folk their own culture so that they could become themselves.[6] Carpenter described this concept of "self-education" in a write-up for the Alternate Media Center's *Catalog*:

> People learn best in terms of their own situation and their own life; they learn best in a group that is familiar and natural to them; they learn through confronting a problem and sharing that struggle with other groups with similar problems; and, however inefficiently, they learn by being responsible themselves for the solution and by participating in that solution, however ill equipped they may be by professional standards.[7]

Highlander was opposed to organizing the Sol Alinsky way, where, according to Carpenter, "you ramrod an organization and point of view down people's throats and organize very effectively behind it." That model implied a top down way of doing things. Once the outside organizers left and whatever seed funding was gone, the model usually went as well. Highlander's approach was different, dedicated to giving people the instruments to empower themselves within their own community context.

At the university at Cookeville in 1970, Carpenter was chatting with a friend on campus when he suddenly noticed the picture on the TV set was frozen on the screen. He was stunned. He had no idea there was such a thing as video and immediately was taken with the potential of this new technology. Carpenter had always had an interest in the arts. As a VISTA volunteer he had known Earl Dodder, the still photographer who chronicled Appalachia. Dodder would attach himself to a volunteer who was highly active, a bull-in-a-china-shop whirlwind, and follow in his or her wake, quietly taking pictures. Dodder never seemed to agonize over how to act constructively for social change; he was a photographer. While others went to great pains to develop rapport with local people, Earl was careful to stay back. Carpenter thought that to do still photography you had to be like Earl, slightly removed in order to click that shutter. Distance—emotional or aesthetic—seemed essential. But Carpenter hated the separation still photography seemed to require. He had been looking for a tool that would allow him to stay involved and be a good chronicler—that tool was video.[8]

He decided to use some of his fellowship time to learn more about video and turned to the Ford Foundation for leads. The Foundation steered him to a conference on video being held at New York University. Carpenter travelled to New York where he met many industry people trying to figure out how to create a business out of video. He wandered around saying he was from Appalachia and wanted to do something different with video, until finally someone suggested he find George Stoney. Stoney was well acquainted with Highlander and what it stood for; more important, he understood what Carpenter was trying to accomplish. That evening they stayed up half the night looking at tapes of Canadian coal miners produced by Challenge for Change. Stoney was trying to transport the Challenge for Change experience to the states. Carpenter, smart enough to grasp the potential of video to help solve social problems, had found someone to help him figure out how to do it.[9]

Carpenter stayed in New York studying about portable video at the Alternate Media Center, where he also became acquainted with the beginnings of the public access cable movement and the politics of narrowcasting. The term "narrowcasting" was coined in opposition to the pervasive concept of broadcasting, with programming designed to reach the largest possible viewing audience and thus featuring material of interest to the broadest spectrum of the public. Narrowcasters contended that this insured a built-in bias against—and subsequent exclusion of—programs of interest to local or narrow audiences. Although by definition narrowcast programs do not compete with broadcast programs, they can compete well within highly targeted audiences. But for this to happen, an alternative distribution needed to be found for their delivery to targeted audiences. Cable, with its 40 or more channels, offered just such a vehicle. The alternate media movement seized upon public access to cable, then known more popularly as "the electronic soap box." As a result, most of the legal and philosophical questions generated by alternate media centered around issues of freedom of speech, censorship, government control, and licensing. The mandate for local-origination programming was virtually ignored by the movement.[10]

While visiting his brother one weekend in Connecticut, Carpenter asked if anyone knew where he might buy a video portapak. Someone reported that a local hospital had bought some Sony equipment, but the union would not let them use it because they were afraid it would replace people. Carpenter purchased the portapak at a distress sale price, but had to race back to Tennessee to borrow money against his farm to cover his check.[11]

Back in Tennessee, Carpenter met Mike Clarke, a local fellow determined to stay and build a social change base for the region. Together they began to explore how video could become one of those empowering tools.[12] Miles Horton, Highlander's director, was hostile to video at first. Although he trusted Carpenter and tolerated his efforts, Horton was adamant about not building video into Highlander at that time.[13] At first Mike Clarke was also skeptical about carrying technology around into places where they had been having trouble dealing with people. It was not easy to go into a conservative Appalachian community and convince people to speak out and challenge existing ways of doing things. But Carpenter believed video offered an ideal way of carrying other peoples' experiences along—the "each one, teach one" Highlander way.

In 1971, when Carpenter became regional coordinator of a Stanford University-run project on urban and rural adult community education,[14] he began combing the hills and hollows of Eastern Tennessee with his portable video, talking with farmers and shopkeepers, midwives and miners. The standard technique he developed was to find someone who, for whatever reason, was finally angry enough to stand up against the strip miner or the local school system and do something. Carpenter always began by playing a tape. People would see someone just like themselves talking about familiar issues, things that they had been struggling with alone. Being able to watch someone speak from the heart about your problem proved a very powerful communications tool. Meanwhile, Carpenter would have set up his equipment unobtrusively, and when the tape had ended, he would switch into the record mode and simply say, "Now, why don't you talk about this too." With this method, he and Clarke found it remarkably easy to unbolt inhibitions in what was ordinarily difficult, painstaking, and often volatile work.[15]

Also critical to Carpenter's approach was his use of an RF modulator in the video recording deck, which allowed him to plug in a small (9-inch) TV set and monitor his camera work.[16] Instead of looking through the camera eyepiece while recording someone, he held the camera in his lap, occasionally glancing at the TV to check on the picture. As a result, people felt they were talking to a person, not a camera, and felt at ease instead of intimidated by a detached cameraperson. Carpenter was convinced that the camera operator had to be a participant, not just an observer.

Another cardinal rule was playing back the interviews immediately, which gave people an opportunity for self-criticism and self-evaluation. "When people can see themselves . . . they get a greater sense of their own and other people's involvement," he later told a reporter.[17] Because the tapes would circulate to other mountain people, creating problem-centered dialogues within the region, it was important that speakers feel what they had said was something they wanted others to hear.

At first there was no editing of the tapes, partly because editing was anathema. "Militants don't interfere with the people speaking" was the Alternate Media Center tradition, according to Carpenter.[18] The other reason was more practical: there was little or no editing equipment available in the early days of portable video. Carpenter was able to create his first editing system by turning disaster into good fortune. He had his portapak for about nine months when he came to New York to show some work at the Alternate Media Center. During the screening, his uninsured portapak was stolen out of his car. George Stoney and AMC director Red Burns were so upset, they loaned him one of their own to take back with him. When the Ford Foundation heard what had happened, another portapak was produced out of a closet and given to Carpenter. With two portapaks, Carpenter could run a cable between them and attempt rough, backspace editing. Carpenter quickly discovered the power of editing, which allowed him to respect the needs of the end viewer as well as the integrity of the individual speakers. When the Ford Fellowship ran out, he was given an extension grant to decelerate; the money was designed to help a fellow get back into real life or set up something he had already started. Carpenter used his money to buy editing equipment.

In time Carpenter and Clarke created VideoMaker, a video distribution service, to get their tapes out to schools, colleges, libraries, and regional groups. They followed the mountain barter system: purchase-or-swap. People could either buy a tape or else send in blank or used tapes in exchange for a copy.[19]

Carpenter used video to explore the relationship between citizens and a public institution, the Model Cities Project in Cookeville, Tennessee. He got the City Council, County Court, Model Cities staff, and city officials to talk on camera as well as ordinary folks who spoke about their kids being in Headstart or about their jobs. One speaker was the man who ran the tractor for the sanitary landfill. In Appalachia, that usually meant dumping garbage in a ravine. Having the tractor operator, who got his job because of the Model Cities Project, explain land-use planning made an otherwise abstract concept real and meaningful. With video, Carpenter found he could explain institutions to people.

Joe Farris, a writer for Cookeville's *Herald-Citizen,* wrote an article on Ted Carpenter and his camera titled "He Starts People Thinking."[20] Farris stressed that Carpenter "doesn't tell anyone how to solve his problems or even talk about them very much. But he provides a new medium for the discussion of problems, both old and new." Farris cited a tape Carpenter was making on strip mining, one of the first edited projects. "The films [*sic*] aren't what one sees on the evening news. And they're not quite the sort of thing one finds in the network TV documentaries," he concluded.

Strip miners bulldoze the topsoil and trees off Appalachian mountainsides to get the coal from under the dirt, and they were ruining the land around Arden Franklin's farm in Fentress County (Tennessee). Carpenter visited Franklin in his home, showed him tapes of other mountain people concerned about strip mining, and Franklin listened intently, nodding in agreement, absorbed by the words and experiences of people like himself. Afterward, he spoke eloquently and at length about his problems. Then Carpenter put his portapak in a back harness and, using batteries, climbed a mountain, scrambled over rock ledges and fences, and made his way across a quagmire by way of a fallen log, following Franklin to get a closer look at a strip-mined hillside. Franklin pointed out the damage already done and the beautiful valleys threatened by the stripper's bulldozer. Franklin appeared confident and at ease; having seen other people on tape, he knew his would reach people like him in much the same way. With minimal editing and the addition of a song written by a member of an anti–strip-mining group, the Franklin tape was turned into a half-hour work of quiet eloquence, *A Mountain Has No Seed*.

The next week, Carpenter traveled with mountain farmers and residents of the coal camps to Knoxville, Tennessee, to talk with the Tennessee Valley Authority, whose policy of buying cheap coal encouraged strip mining. Carpenter recorded their discussion and a tour of the TVA's Bull Run Steam Plant, as well as an experimental site where the TVA was trying to reclaim stripped land. The tape was replayed that evening at a workshop meeting of mountain people along with Arden Franklin's tape. Both tapes were later edited into an hour-long program, *To Raise the Dead and Bury the Living—Strip Mining*, and sent to Congressman Ken Hechler and Senator Fred Harris in Washington, who were sponsoring strip-mining legislation. These tapes also were shown in closed-circuit screenings at local public schools and colleges interested in providing an Appalachian curriculum as well as on Appalachian cable TV systems.[21]

Cable began to play an increasingly important role in Carpenter's strategy. Isolated by hills and hollers, mountain people had a rich history of oral learning and culture, yet they had little access to the mass media. Locally-produced programming over cable offered a significant alternative to mainstream media. It promised that people could generate true-to-life images of themselves and respond to the demeaning stereotypes broadcast on national television in series like "The Beverly Hillbillies" or films like *Deliverance*, which portrayed the mountaineer as lazy, shiftless, backward or degenerate. The possibility of being able to put programming on cable became more and more appealing to Carpenter, especially when it promised a way of economically supporting the production of such work. Without fully realizing it at the time, Carpenter began to move away from the ideal of intimate, "holler-to-holler" videotapes aimed at sharing self-enlightenment between like-minded mountain people and into something bigger and broader.

6.

Four More Years

Thrilled with their sudden prestige among the press corps, TVTV returned to Miami in August to cover the Republican Convention. The group quickly discovered the Republicans were as controlled as the Democrats were disorganized. This made the job much easier, especially since the media inadvertently had been handed the Republicans' minute-by-minute script of the Convention, including all the "spontaneous demonstrations" held by the Young Republicans. The story at the Republican Convention was not about a fight for the nomination (since Nixon's anointing was a foregone conclusion), but about the clash of styles and values espoused by the people inside the convention hall and those outside.

TVTV covered Young Republican rallies, cocktail parties, antiwar demonstrations, and the "scheduled" frenzy of the convention floor. Posted in the living room of their Pine Tree Drive headquarters was the following reminder

The Big Stories
1. The Underbelly of Broadcast TV
2. The Vietnam vets
3. Those zany Republicans, young and old
4. The White House family/celebrities

Are *you* on a big story? Does your big story *connect* with the others? Is your Little story part of the big picture?

The Management[1]

Once again aiming their cameras away from the podium and into the crowd, TVTV produced *Four More Years*, an amazingly coherent and exhaustive chronicle of the convention. From the Nixonettes to the Vietnam Vets, from the ego-driven media stars to the power-hungry political czars, the characters included in *Four More Years* provided a complex portrait of America poised at a moment when a contentious war was about to end and a political debacle about to unfold. Perhaps without intending to, TVTV was recording the untidy demise of the '60s and the complacent rise of the '70s.

Four More Years intertwined the abovementioned four "big stories," leading off with a devastatingly funny portrait of Nixon's Young Republican supporters. Operating on the premise that if you give someone enough rope he will hang himself, TVTV hung out, equipped with rope—and tape—to spare. One Nixonette holding an Illinois sign blithely revealed she was a local sorority sister recruited for the convention. A busload of Young Republicans, when asked whether there was any truth to the "rumors" they were tightly organized, answered in unison, "No!" And an enthusiastic organizer commented to her staff, "The balloons alone will give us the fun we need!" prompting one TVTV member to observe later, with mingled awe and delight: "No one can write lines like that! They'd never believe you."[2]

By contrast, the extended interviews conducted by Maureen Orth with the Nixon daughters, Julie Eisenhower and Tricia Cox, revealed them to be surprisingly articulate. Whether their campaign arguments were persuasive or not, their ability to handle themselves under a barrage of tough questioning was admirable; that they appear as such in the tape counteracted any charge of bias in TVTV's handling of the Republicans. Edward Cox, however, fared less well, providing another candidly funny moment as he awkwardly tried to save himself from foot-in-mouth disease. Well-known political figures including Henry Kissinger and then-governor Ronald Reagan are seen entering and leaving private parties as well as in more public appearances. Ominously, a bashful Ronald Reagan delivers a sentimental speech about saluting the flag, which is met by raucous cheers of "Yeehaw!" from Young Republicans seated adoringly at his feet.

Maureen Orth's brief interview with Henry Kissinger emerging from a party was particularly startling. Orth asked the chief U.S. peace negotiator whether there was any sign of peace. Nixon, whose campaign slogan was "Peace is at hand," might have been surprised at Kissinger's declaration that "we" didn't care what effect the peace process was having on domestic politics. Orth's third follow-up question, asked just as Kissinger was about to escape into his limo, was "How are the girls?" Surprised, the suddenly smirking Kissinger stopped and replied, "Very nice. Very nice." Clearly Kissinger, who had a reputation as a ladies' man, was caught off guard by the attractive Orth's fast thinking.

The media stars play a much greater role in this tape than in *The World's Largest TV Studio*. Adopted by avuncular reporters who enjoyed the sudden attention paid to them by these young and talented upstarts, TVTV was able to explore the range and variety of personalities and opinions displayed by the network biggies. Several provided helpful tips, such as NBC's Douglas Kiker, who explained the merits of washing with vinegar rather than soap and water after being teargassed. By the second convention NBC's Cassie Macken had lost some of her enthusiasm, confiding she was bored by the lack of spontaneity and exhausted from all the "busy work." Another reporter, when asked "What's news?" replied inscrutably, "Things that happen." Gradually a family portrait of an ego-driven press corps emerged. Caught are some of the internecine jealousies between competing journalists: CBS's Mike Wallace grumbles that Dan Rather is over with the VIPs while he is stuck on the floor where nothing much is happening, concluding: "I'd rather be watching this at home." And in a lengthy and thoughtful interview, Walter Cronkite comments on the dangers of too much introspection for journalists and voices his worries about people who rely exclusively on television for the news. Only Roger Mudd refused to talk to TVTV's camera. Baffled by Mudd's muteness, interviewer Skip Blumberg asks Nancy Cain, who was taping, if she believes he was just tired. Then, in a typical TVTV moment, Blumberg whips out a harmonica and plays "The Republican Convention Drag" as the TVTV logo appears in the screen's lower right-hand corner. Using graphics, wit, and charm, TVTV playfully turned broadcasting conventions—and personalities—inside out and upside down.

From the "spontaneous" chant, "Hey, hey, waddaya say? Nixon, Agnew, all the way!" TVTV cut to the edgy retort, "Hey, hey, ho, ho! Trickie Dick has got to go." The chants, with their identical rhythms and similar phrasings, recalled for those old enough to remember, the earlier refrain: "Hey, Hey, LBJ! How many kids did you kill today?!" The lingering issue of the Vietnam War and its protest, an issue that lay beneath the carnival surface of the convention (and at times erupting) was woven throughout TVTV's tour de force work.

The Democratic convention had attracted its assortment of dissenters, including Yippies, Zippies, SDSers,[3] Jesus Freaks, and an unaffiliated assemblage of drug-tripping, party-going convention groupies, but there was never any serious threat of confrontation like the kind that marked the 1968 convention in Chicago. In fact, differences between the Democratic delegates inside the convention and the hippies outside seemed marginal. The Republicans, on the other hand, represented a class and a worldview distinctly at odds with the often contentious protesters who flocked that August to Flamingo

Park, the free-speech area. Some of the different groups there got on very badly, while heat and fatigue heightened hostilities. Gay men and feminists were needled and sometimes attacked by visiting local thugs; Jesus Freaks antagonized everyone. Serious drugs were on hand, including heroin. Following the directives of the benign Miami police chief, the demonstrators tried to police themselves, but that failed to preclude daily battles. Movement people from the '60s were conspicuously absent, and veteran observers noted that almost no political education took place in Flamingo Park during the convention.[4]

In one brief sequence, TVTV managed to capture the silly side of the protesters. Lined up in opposing camps, militants fiercely shouting "Jesus loves you!" engaged in a verbal sparring match with the irate hippies. In mid-sentence, one of the more vocal debaters did a double take as he noticed the TVTV camera taping his tirade. As their images faded out, the plaintive protest heard is: "No one wants to freak on Jesus 24 hours a day!" and superimposed on the screen is one of many campaign buttons TVTV used to punctuate the tape: "Acid Amnesty Appeasement—Vote for McGovern."

TVTV was also on hand for more sober moments. The demonstrators' "Street Without Joy" (named for Highway One in Vietnam) was a guerrilla theater event few delegates ever saw, because the demonstrators were given the street and the delegates entering the convention hall were rerouted. With hands and faces dripping with red paint, a hundred acted out the death of Vietnamese peasants, screaming and falling down while papier-mâché bombers were rushed over their heads and smoke bombs exploded. Locals laughed since, as journalist Nora Sayre observed, "guerrilla theater probably moves only those who already agree with what it states—unless it's very, very good—or funny."[5] TVTV gave the event the drama some felt it lacked in reality, using their wide-angle lens to render the young people's frozen postures as a moving frieze of lost innocence and eloquent outrage.

But the real threat of violence—with its potential to unseat Nixon—came from the only antiwar group with any "psychic leverage,"[6] the Vietnam Veterans Against the War. Just as TVTV had scored at the Democratic Convention with its insider's grasp of the California challenge, so TVTV triumphed at the Republican Convention with its eyewitness coverage of the "Last Patrol."

The scrapbook page for Tuesday's activity at the Republican Convention centered on the following crew assignments:

1. McCloskey—Political Fight: Steve & Anda
2. Young GOP—Wendy & Jody

3. Media: Megan, Skip, Nancy
4. VVAW: Bart & Chuck
5. GOP Style: MAS T.L.
6. Hippys: Chip & Fire

Surrounding the plan of action were phone numbers of airlines, restaurants, and the networks, the calling card of *TV Guide*'s Neil Hickey, shipping data for cameras and tapes in transit, an inventory of missing equipment, assorted caricatures of TVTV members, and, in bold letters, the salient reminder: 4^{00} Vets at Ftableu!!⁷

TVTV was there early and taped an informal conversation among three women standing around the veterans' compound, discussing the VVAW and whether there would be violence. Casual and conversational, Maureen Orth offered her own belief that none of these guys would ever hurt a woman. But one woman in pointy Gary Larson sunglasses insisted, "They're aimless creatures!" convinced the men were all just pretending they had been in Vietnam. A grey-haired man who fought in World War II echoed the peculiar denial that operates when unpleasant realities confront the unwilling or the unprepared. He insisted these guys were "all *hopped up* on dope," and that is why they came back. "Their buddies died, but they came back." He tells then about his own war wounds: "I zigged, when I should have zagged!" he says, laughing, but TVTV interrupts to ask how come he came back. Was he "all hopped up?" Wasn't that the same thing? "No," he said, and he shook his head uncertainly, "No."

At 4 o'clock, as the Vietnam Veterans Against the War marched up Collins Avenue, most of the press was either at the Convention Hall covering the liberal versus conservative floor fight over rules for seating delegates in 1976, or standing around in the mid-afternoon heat at the Miami International Airport waiting for Nixon to arrive. The Last Patrol was led by three men in wheelchairs, and it moved up Collins Avenue in dead silence; 1,200 men dressed in battle fatigues, helmets, and combat boots followed orders given by "platoon leaders" using hand signals. In total silence, the eerie procession confronted 500 heavily armed police stationed at the Fontainebleau Hotel, the vets forming a tight semicircle that blocked the three northbound lanes. For the first time during the convention, the police were clearly intimidated. After five minutes of "harsh silence,"⁸ a platoon leader spoke into a bullhorn: "We want to come inside."

Suddenly and unexpectedly, Congressman Pete McCloskey shoved his way through the police line. He talked with a few vets long enough to convince them a frontal assault on the hotel would be futile. Few cameras were there to catch the drama, but TVTV's portable video rigs were trained on the scene as outright conflict was narrowly averted. The VVAW settled for a series of bullhorn speeches that were drowned out by the whirring of two Army helicopters that appeared overhead. The only one who made himself understood above the chopper drone was a paraplegic ex-Marine Sergeant named Ron Kovic.[9] As Hunter Thompson later noted, "his words lashed the crowd like a wire whip . . . If Kovic had been allowed to speak from the convention hall podium, in front of network TV cameras, Nixon wouldn't have had the balls to show up and accept the nomination."[10] Unfortunately, as far as the general public was concerned, the vets' silent march and sober speeches were obscured by the media's focus on the street hijinks of prankster protesters. The Young Voters for the President saw no distinctions between the Vietnam vets, the Jesus People, the SDS, the visiting American Nazis, YIP, the feminists, the gay activists, or the Zippies.[11]

No scenario could have worked to ensure that the protesters' "militant nonviolence" would not erupt into something deadly the last night of the convention. Despite Rennie Davis's pledge, "We won't be violent with individual delegates," the SDS and Zippies had refused all along to cooperate with the Miami Convention Coalition, and unaffiliated outsiders were on hand, so a clash seemed inevitable. As the delegates began arriving for the final evening session, gas billowed down the avenue, cries arose from blocks away, formerly peaceful police grew rougher, and there were bouts of tire-slashing and trashing as cars and buses were randomly damaged. The protest, which was intended to delay the session of the convention and knock Nixon out of prime time coverage, postponed the program by only seven minutes. The delegates, after inhaling tear gas and Mace, came hawking and retching into the convention hall, frightened and angry.[12]

One delegate interviewed by TVTV recommended firing on the demonstrators, adding enthusiastically: "We might end up with something larger than Kent State—but it would be worth it!"

During the final session, what was happening in the streets was hardly acknowledged by the convention celebrants. Inside the Hall were the realities of the '70s—Richard Nixon exulting in a warmth binge—while outside was the last gasp of the '60s.[13] As Girl Scouts and Boy Scouts dashed through the police barricades and into the hall, marching around the floor and singing "The Star Spangled Banner," protestors behind the fence sounded a different note with their dissonant rendering of the national anthem.

Ron Kovic addressed the convention that night, but not from the podium as Hunter Thompson had fantasized. TVTV had followed

Kovic throughout the convention, profiling him and his cause. On the last night, Hudson Marquez gave Kovic his TVTV press pass so that Kovic could get onto the convention floor. What happened then became part of the moving climax of *Four More Years* as Kovic mournfully stared into TVTV's camera, surrounded by security guards and a few network reporters. Yelling into the tumultuous crowd of cheering Nixon supporters, his voice nearly drowned by the throng, Kovic shouted: "Stop the bombing . . . Stop the war. Stop killing human beings!"

TVTV boldly crosscut Kovic's gravely heroic image with the manic frenzy of screaming conventioneers, focusing on Henry Kissinger, politely applauding the renomination of Richard Nixon in the company of a pint-sized child clone, as a shower of balloons rained down on the assembled zealots and a skinny kid, hysterically laughing, shrieked until he became hoarse, "Four more years! Four more years!"

Despite their negative experience with *Newsweek*, TVTV enthusiastically continued to give interviews to visiting journalists throughout the convention. Timothy Crouse dropped in one afternoon in August and interviewed Shamberg, who, as self-appointed group spokesperson, explained TVTV's belief in a different style of television:

> The networks have never understood that the expensive equipment they have dictates a style, which is what's pissing people off. They have to force behavior. When they're on live, or even when they're filming, they have to have something happening when the camera's on. Everything they do costs so much that they can't afford to be patient. That's why they have correspondents who are always talking to give you the illusion that something's happening. They can't wait and really pick up on what's happening.
>
> We never do that. We just like to hang out. It's more of a print notion. Like, when you do a story, you probably don't do formal interviews as much as you hang out. We're trying to do the same thing.
>
> The network people are essentially giving people a radio with a screen. If you turn the picture off, you don't miss a thing. They never let you hear environmental sounds. They always make people express themselves in a format determined by the announcer. They never say, "How do you want to explain the problem? Do you want to take me around and show me or what?"
>
> Another thing is, they shoot film and take it back to the studio and process and edit it, and the subject of the film never gets any say in it. But we can play a tape back for people immediately. If they don't like it we'll erase it. People rarely ask you to do that. But you can establish a rapport with people that way if you're working in an alien situation.

That's how we got our stuff on the Nixon Youth. They were very uptight about us shooting, so we let them see themselves and get a feeling for how they came across, and it relaxed them.[14]

In *The World's Largest TV Studio*, TVTV had included several such "feedback" moments: Wallace delegate Alberta Johnson says, "I think all the media's slanted," then she is shown watching herself on tape as her cynicism melts in the glow of her own image on the TV screen. Anda Korsts interviews Billy Singer after the success of his challenge. He watches himself on tape as the result of the vote is announced while Korsts asks if TVTV's presence was in any way intrusive. He reassures her that he was too absorbed in what was going on even to notice they were there and taping. In *Four More Years*, this same "feedback" technique was used to deflect hostility and win acceptance, but such sequences were not included in the final tape.

TVTV's notion of just hanging out and letting things happen—rather than structuring interviews to conform to the packaged reports favored by broadcast news—yielded a style that was, for journalists like Crouse, strikingly different. The mere fact that narration was absent was cause for comment: "Except for a few handwritten titles," Crouse remarked, "the pictures and sounds of the conventions spoke entirely for themselves; watching a narratorless news broadcast was a strangely exhausting and disturbing experience. There was no easy gloss to take the sting out of what was happening on the screen."[15] Although proponents of American-style cinema vérité[16] had introduced narratorless documentaries to television in the early '60s, the style had never become acceptable to broadcasters accustomed to the voice-over narrators or on-camera journalists who conferred credibility along with neat conclusions to their stories. TVTV's approach was actually more open, more "objective" than the networks' coverage. "Surprisingly, they reflected no particular ideology," Crouse added;[17] for *Time*-dropout Michael Shamberg, there was perhaps no greater praise for TVTV's journalistic integrity than such bewildered admissions.

After *Four More Years* was cablecast, TVTV was approached by someone from Westinghouse Broadcasting, who said if they would cut the two tapes together into a 90-minute version, he would broadcast it. He paid TVTV $4,000, which helped pay their debt, and transferred the program to two-inch quad tape, which was then standard gauge for broadcast transmissions. As far as TVTV knew, it was the first time half-inch portable video tape was bumped up to broadcast standard.[18] The convention tapes were broadcast at the end of October on Westinghouse's five VHF stations: in Boston, Baltimore, Pittsburgh, Philadelphia, and San Francisco. It was also shown on San Francisco's public broadcasting station, KQED. The listing in *TV Guide* for Sunday evening, October 29 read as follows:

> 11:45 (5) UNDERGROUND TELEVISION LOOKS AT CONVENTIONS '72
>
> *Special:* An unorthodox view of last summer's Presidential nominating conventions, filmed [*sic*] by a group of young, free-lance cable television reporters. Informal—without an anchorman, this documentary has been acclaimed as a "video verite" masterpiece. (90 min.)
>
> (Pre-empts regular programming.)[19]

Charles E. Downie of the *San Francisco Sunday Chronicle and Examiner* waxed enthusiastic about the show in his television column:

> Did you ever suspect that the almost antiseptic view of the Republican and Democratic conventions presented by the Big Three networks did not convey the full flavor of either? . . .
>
> You're tired of politics? Can't imagine any coverage of the two conventions that would be worth lighting the tube for? You're wrong. You may not like what you see on "Conventions '72" but you should find it fascinating—all one and a half hours of it.[20]

Westinghouse received nearly one hundred letters from enthusiastic viewers who agreed with Downie. They wrote raves like these:

> It's not very often an average citizen has an opportunity to be exposed to the behind the scenes goings on of a national convention. I still can't believe what I saw. Keep up the work & try to get to Cleveland.

> It was like a breath of fresh air to have someone give the feeling of the event instead of the canned—programmed prepackaged version we were spoon fed at the time of the conventions[21]

TVTV had set out to prove alternate media could be more than disjointed, herky-jerky images of confrontations or out-of-focus eroticism—and they had succeeded. As one columnist for the *San Francisco Chronicle* reported: "These kids, crawling around with their hand cameras, did such a fantastic job that in New York, a top CBS exec called a meeting of his convention staff to grump 'Our network spent more on coffee than these kids did to cover both conventions, and they did a better job.' "[22] TVTV's achievement spurred the networks to accelerate their development of small, lightweight electronic news gathering (ENG) equipment, which would give them the mobility and unobtrusiveness TVTV had displayed so well.[23] But the unguardedness of people as yet unfamiliar with this new "Mickey Mouse" technology would only last a brief time, long enough for TVTV to make a few more memorable tapes.

7.

Communitube

What can non-professional production and small audiences offer that nation-wide television can't?

Social change.[1]

Minneapolis was a hub for Midwestern interest in video, proving that video activism was not solely a bicoastal phenomenon.[2] The people who flocked to video in the late '60s in Minneapolis were more likely to be drawn by its utility as a social change agent than by its potential as a medium for artistic expression. This was due as much to a legacy of Midwestern populism and progressive values as it was to the zeitgeist. Thus the three young men who joined forces to create University Community Video were '60s students already using video as a tool for community activism. In 1971, Stephen Kulczycki—a University of Minnesota journalism and television student influenced by the Challenge for Change ideal—went to work for the American Friends Service Committee using video as a vehicle for community organizing. Ron McCoy, a Minneapolis College of Art and Design graduate, joined the staff of the Model Cities' Communications Center, where he used video in citizen participation projects. And Miles Mogulescu was hired by the University of Minnesota in 1972 as the video access coordinator for the West Bank Student Union's storefront community center.[3]

The University of Minnesota was largely a commuter school with 40,000 students and three student unions dating back to the '30s. In 1972 the student government set up three nonprofit corporations, an attempt by the relatively weak body to generate income and interest. Ron McCoy was hired as Coordinator of the University Student Telecommunications Corporation (USTC), responsible for developing a radio station, investigating cable television, and programming the university's own closed-circuit cable system. The funding for the corporations, just like the funding for the student unions, came from student fees.

The university had constructed a new television and theater complex, the Rarig Center, which included five studios located on Minneapolis' West Bank, a feisty community then embroiled in housing battles. Both the Telecommunications Corporation and the West Bank Access Center had their headquarters in Studio A's control room, roughly 15 by 30 feet in size. Although McCoy had been involved in campus politics and citizen participation video, he was more interested in the arts, whereas Mogulescu, who grew up attending socialist summer camps, was a born-and-bred activist. While Mogulescu was taping campus demonstrations against the mining of Haiphong Harbor in the Spring of 1972,[4] McCoy was more likely to be found taping a music performance. The chemistry between the two men never quite worked, and they had trouble communicating in their close quarters.[5] This clash between artists and activists would be resolved differently at various junctures of University Community Video's history.

Stephen Kulczycki, who had been hired by McCoy in 1973, saw value in what both McCoy and Mogulescu stood for and persuaded them to pool their interests and resources to create the University Community Video Access Center (UCV). In October 1973, UCV absorbed the West Bank Video Access Center and the Minnesota Student Association Video Project. Kulczycki became UCV's Programming Coordinator and Mogulescu became its Administrative Coordinator, while McCoy retained his title as Coordinator of the Telecommunications Corporation.

The Video Access Center began its programming in October 1973 over the university's closed-circuit cable system, which went to dormitories, auditoriums, and classrooms. Using the fifteen minutes of empty time between closed-circuit TV classes, UCV cablecast short tapes "ranging from public service announcements to rock concerts," shown at the top of each hour between 10 A.M. and 2 P.M. Wednesdays through Fridays. A staff of six produced an average of one tape a week for cablecast. In addition to producing and programming the CCTV channels, UCV also taught a credit course, "Advanced TV Lab," where six students each produced a 10-minute tape during the quarter session. Monthly workshops were offered free of charge to 15 students and community members, with alumni from the "Advanced TV Lab" helping to run them.[6]

Although UCV's closed-circuit audience was captive, it was also silent, and staff received little feedback for their programs. Anxious to have a more visible outlet for their work, the staff was persuaded that cable television for the Twin Cities was on the horizon and began dreaming of the future community cabling would bring. In an article on the access center for a community newspaper, one writer speculated on whether cable would democratize the airwaves. "What can non-professional production and small audiences offer that nationwide television can't?" he asked. "Social change," Kulczycki replied, brashly adding that cable was "an excellent vehicle for people telling their own stories, without the distorting filter of outside reporters and editors."[7] McCoy told a student reporter for the university paper that with the advent of the time-base corrector (see Chapter 8) it would soon be possible to broadcast half-inch video, but his hopes were still tied to cable television. Only Mogulescu looked soberly into the crystal ball, announcing that the prospect of cable appeared to be at least five to eight years away.[8]

Charged up by the national fervor surrounding public access to cable, UCV staff attended several conferences on public access in 1973, where they met many of the better known figures in the video field, including members of Top Value Television, the Ant Farm, and the Videofreex.[9] But 1974 was the year of the oil crisis and the big bust of the cable industry,[10] and much as Mogulescu predicted, it would be nearly ten years before the city negotiated its franchise and was wired for cable. So when all the momentum preparing the community and university for cable had nowhere to go, UCV decided to turn to what was available—public television. Public television fought them so hard and with such dedication that it served as a red flag spurring their determination to get their programs on the air.[11]

To begin with, public television station KTCA refused to deal with UCV directly. Then the station objected that it already had a "public access" program, "People & Causes," which aired on its UHF channel and was received by few people. When the university, which was a major client of the educational television station (spending possibly a quarter-million dollars a year for airtime[12]), stood firmly behind UCV's proposal, KTCA had to capitulate. The University sold UCV part of its airtime to put on a show that aired through the "back door" of the university's contract, effectively eliminating any further debate between UCV and KTCA.[13]

Communitube was scheduled to air on January 30, 1974, but it was preempted by another historic event, President Richard M. Nixon's last State of the Union message. As staffers waggishly wrote later, "Both programs were tedious, amateurish and visually dull. The difference is that UCV's show got better."[14] Rescheduled two weeks later for February 13 in the 9 P.M. time slot, *Communitube* received favorable reviews in local newspapers. The program was edited from 12 different tapes produced during 1973 by community groups, university students, and UCV staff. One can see the split between art/entertainment and activism from the mix of excerpts selected: a peace rally, a dance group, a documentary on rape, another on the United Farm Workers, the San Francisco Mime Troupe, singer Bonnie Raitt performing at the Marigold Ballroom, Angela Davis appearing on campus, a black history conference, and a documentary on the Vermillion Lake Indian Reservation.

The sampler clearly emphasized how video could be used to stimulate citizen participation in local governance. In one segment, a man stood looking at a St. Paul swimming pool, explaining why his neighborhood wanted its own pool; the camera also showed traffic flashing through the busy intersection, demonstrating why parents were so fearful. The tape led the St. Paul City Council to consider the neighborhood request for a swimming pool. Although the request was not approved, it set in motion a new citywide policy and organized a community around an issue. As May Pesina, chairwoman of the citizen's group, explained: "We learned a great deal about local government and, though some people said it couldn't be done, we worked with people from all over town, learning to appreciate each other's needs and interests and how to work together."[15]

The *TV Guide* listing for *Communitube* read

Wednesday
Evening
9:00 (2) *COMMUNITUBE*
Special: Using a video magazine format, this experimental pilot examines how citizens can use TV to express their attitudes and values.

The magazine format was virtually unknown for television when UCV invented its own version.[16] UCV's program opened with Miles Mogulescu as host wearing a plaid lumberjack shirt to differentiate him from the men in suits—the obligatory authority figure/TV host—making it clear from the start this was *not* your typical public television program.

Mogulescu was interviewed by one reporter about the show's rationale. "Most people probably get most of their information from television,[17] so why not open it to ordinary people to express their views to the world? Anyone can learn with a few hours' training. And just like everyone knows how to read and write, everyone ought to know how to use television."[18]

Communitube offered UCV staffers a chance to create a bridge between their earlier video activism and UCV's current mission. The tape on the Vermillion Lake Indian Reservation was part of a continuing story for Stephen Kulczycki, who had collaborated with the reservation in northern Minnesota while he was working with the Quakers. The reservation had been trying to raise enough money to build their own health clinic. Their healthmobile was scheduled to stop rolling because of federal funding cuts, and the residents did not want to have to drive 70 miles for medical care from a hospital that would often to turn them away, even when they presented their Blue Cross or Bureau of Indian Affairs medical cards. Kulczycki shot a tape that was edited by the tribal members, who then traveled around screening it to local groups. Viewers watched a baby cry as he received an injection at the healthmobile and an old man tell the camera, "If it wasn't for the people and the doc, I'd be deaf and dumb." With the tape, they were able to raise enough money to keep the healthmobile open.

At one screening for a church group, the wife of the hospital administrator saw the tape, told her husband about it, and he contacted the reservation and demanded they edit out their complaints against the hospital. The reservation refused to do anything until they settled their differences. Because of pressure brought by the tape, the hospital administrators negotiated with the reservation and resolved the problem. The reservation continued its organizing; in three years, they had secured a 1.5 million dollar grant to build a health clinic of their own, one that would serve other area reservations as well.

Before joining UCV as a staffer, Barry Morrow had been working with writer Paul Gronseth, using video to document the ethnic history of Beltrami, a small deteriorating neighborhood once called "Little Italy." The tape showed old-timers telling how the people used to brace their floorboards for the dancing that always followed a big wedding or baptism. One storekeeper described the 52 years she had watched her neighbors pass her store, mothers taking their babies to the clinic at the Settlement House, immigrants going to their English lessons. Although the videotape did not persuade the city planners to stop a roadway from cutting the area in two, it did create a living record of a historic neighborhood. As *St. Paul Pioneer Press* writer Ann Baker noted, "Youngsters saw that their own streets and homes had a history as fascinating as that of any ethnic neighborhood pictured in their schoolbook."[19]

Kulczycki told Pat Aufderheide, film critic for the university paper *Minnesota Daily*, that UCV's people-oriented video was rough "in the sense of not being sophisticated. It's not that it's a first attempt, because the people at UCV do know what they're doing and they've made a good watchable half hour out of it. It's that it demonstrates other people's first attempts." Aufderheide responded:

> Yes, the half hour is rough. It's also exciting as you watch the possibil-
> ities, the implications of people's video beginning to grow: The arts—
> Pilobolus, or Bonnie Raitt, as you like. Or activism—Chile Solidarity,
> UFW, AIM. Or people's education, like "Rape and the Law," or an
> interview with Minneapolis–St.Paul, Minnesota, high schoolers on wom-
> en's liberation. It's a grab bag of human concern, and if one's first
> impression is of disparate diversity, links between these different groups
> soon appear. All these projects are projects by and for people who don't
> usually get air time or programs aimed at their interests.[20]

Staff writers for the *Minneapolis Tribune* wrote a story on "Do-it-yourself TV" prompted, in part, by the broadcast. Unlike Aufderheide, they downplayed the more radical aspirations of "people's video" and played up its acceptability, opening with a faintly mocking tone:

> Once upon a time there was television. Mostly it was Ozzie running down
> the stairs looking for Ricky.
> But lately there is a broader concept of television that goes by the
> grander name of video. And the new species of video freak or (more
> politely) videophile is using the once-forbidden electronics of television
> in all sorts of unusual ways.

The writers situated University Community Video in a bustling land-scape of unthreatening video production, which included elementary school children making tapes on the energy crisis, college music students watching themselves learning to conduct, and Minnesota Twins coaches studying pitching styles using slo-mo gear. Distinguished from the "video freaks" was "the straight community" and its use of video: the Ford Motor Company used it to train salesmen and mechanics, and the U.S. Navy used it to show football games to sailors on ships. "Devoted to the ideology of public access and social change," UCV's "homemade TV" was presented as just one more aspect of "do-it-yourself" television.[21]

The University was happy with the broadcast of *Communitube* but KTCA's president John Schwartzwalder wrote letters to the president of the university, the regents, and the state arts board raising questions about UCV's irresponsibility.[22] Part of the reason for his outrage had to do with the fact that KTCA had not expected to be broadcasting a half-inch videotape. Perhaps expecting the kind of homely programs produced with 35mm slides for their public access program, they did not find out what the format would be until the day before broadcast. The only way for the station to transmit half-inch video—without transferring it to quad tape or putting it through a time-base corrector—was to scan it optically from a TV monitor using a broadcast studio camera. Although this meant viewers at home would see a fuzzier picture than usual with a horizontal scan line regularly coursing down the screen, this video version of a kinescope had already been used by the networks to air half-inch tapes of news events.[23] There was really no technical reason for KTCA to flinch.

In 1974 UCV had a staff of seven, assorted studio equipment, seven portapaks, and a budget that had grown from $30,000 in 1973 to nearly $80,000.[24] Approximately 1,200 community users walked through the door that year to learn how to use video. At first confined to studio A's control room, UCV gradually spread out, taking over both the 40- by 60-foot studio and additional storage space.[25] By the spring UCV was the only video access center in town: the Model Cities' Communications Center had been phased out and a video storefront run through the College of Art and Design had folded because of lack of a funding base. Groups like St. Paul's Public Service Video relied on UCV's equipment to be able to run its community program.[26] Ron McCoy referred to the Video Center in an interview as "the last bastion of public access in Minneapolis," noting, with a characteristic threat of the era, that funding hassles might force UCV to "fold up and go underground." Because of their reliance on student fees, UCV had to compete each year for their money, vying with the student newspaper and the band for a few more cents. Without a visible outlet, apart from the CCTV programming on campus, UCV had little funding clout. Finding a more public outlet seemed essential if UCV was to continue to support their unique blend of student– and community–made work. A regular series on public television was their best bet.[27]

8.

Gaga Over Guru

TVTV effectively abandoned all claims of being an alternate video group when they decided to re-edit the convention tapes for broadcast on Westinghouse television stations. As Allen Rucker later recalled, "We broke the sacred rule: our friend Paul Ryan's dictum that VT (videotape) is not TV, that alternative TV does not truck with broadcast."[1] TVTV knew that many in the alternative video movement believed the group had sold out, but TVTV had learned the hard way that cable television was not interested in funding original programming. Cable operators were not the showmen and entrepreneurs who had started television—instead they were used car salesmen and TV repair shop owners, businessmen with no clear vision of what cable programming could be. TVTV believed there was no future (and no money) for them in cable, so when Westinghouse showed an interest in their work, they began to think of themselves as television makers.[2] The next projects reflected this shift in identity.

After the convention tapes, TVTV members Michael Shamberg, Megan Williams, Allen Rucker, Hudson Marquez, and Tom Weinberg returned to San Francisco and began to organize for the future, developing new fund-raising strategies and better technical skills. In March 1973, they received $2,200 from public television station WNET in New York to produce a tape on *Rolling Stone* magazine for its "Behind the Lines" series. What TVTV produced was a 17-minute puff-piece for the magazine and its brash young entrepreneurial founder, Jann Wenner. A far cry from the rough but complex storytelling of the convention tapes, *TVTV Meets Rolling Stone* has the look and feel of bad boys[3] getting off on being young, hip, smart, and successful. After a promising opening with "dueling cameras" held by Shamberg and Rucker, the tape goes rapidly downhill with a series of fairly conventional ego-stroking interviews with Wenner and staff. Unlike the "event" tapes, this was a nonevent made by TVTV's core group from Ant Farm and Raindance. Clearly lacking is the energy, talent, and sharp focus of the earlier collaborative tapes.

The subject should have fit TVTV like a glove. Wenner's goal was not unlike that of TVTV: packaging countercultural ideology into a mainstream commodity.[4] Wenner succeeded by hiring some of the best "New Journalists" around, and TVTV was the video version.

About a dozen styles were loosely grouped under the umbrella term "New Journalism." Everyone had their own way of defining it: participation in the event by the writer, the transcendence of objectivity, the use of fictional techniques or of composite characters—all elements that TVTV would eventually explore in their work. While there was really nothing very new about this—Paine, Voltaire, Hazlitt and Twain had all written work that could pass as "New Journalism"—a flock of talented young writers and farsighted editors in the mid-'60s had stirred up the world of nonfiction writing with their subjective journalism. Shamberg claimed to be the only one in his college who had read Clay Felker's *New York Herald Tribune*, but everyone read *Rolling Stone*.

Many of the New Journalists were informed by populist politics, working-class backgrounds, and respect for writers like Norman Mailer, Murray Kempton, Jimmy Cannon, and I.F. Stone. From these writers one learned irony; a sense of history; reverence for facts, truth and justice; a sense of drama; the legitimacy of rage and the folly of politeness; and a sense of the concreteness about the lives of ordinary people.[5] From writers like Tom Wolfe, considered a "French Impressionist among the New Journalists"[6] with "the social conscience of an ant,"[7] one learned how to parlay social fads into fame and fortune. Wolfe was Shamberg's hero; other TVTV crew members admired Hunter Thompson's "fear and loathing" concept of journalism.

What TVTV got on tape at *Rolling Stone* was Tom Wolfe demurely discussing his new series on astronauts and Hunter Thompson recounting a story about a girl being arrested in his room during the 1972 conventions, providing the locker-room tone that is further reinforced by a shot of him wrapped in a towel strolling about the office. Ant Farm's Hudson Marquez and Chip Lord provide the obligatory TVTV interaction on camera, doing a stand-up satire at a newsstand that plays off Wenner's business savvy. But Ant Farm's imitation of the Merry Pranksters on video is not only the surface of the tape, it is the substance as well. Allen Rucker's disgusted reaction at the tape's end—"This is boring. This is not television!"—registers his frustration with their clowning around and with the fact that they had not recorded anything good on tape. What is also registered was a new measure of success: producing "television," not "alternative television."

About that time, TVTV came up with a new strategy for funding. The group produced a magazinelike prospectus entitled *Prime Time*, which was designed to acquaint potential investors, funders, and television sponsors with TVTV's own history and ideas for the future of television: "We grew up with TV. We remember its early days as a time of high energy, looseness, and creativity. Since the late 1950's, though, TV seems to have burned itself out . . . . Recently we decided that simply starting TV all over again might be the best answer."[8] This was their modest proposal.

TVTV's master plan to revise television had three stages: first, a survey of new developments in video hardware and software; second, a prototype program; and third, a total programming package—an entire evening of alternative television. Westinghouse helped fund the survey, which was published a year later as *The Prime Time Survey*. In the original version of the prospectus, TVTV outlined seven program ideas that contained the seeds for subsequent works like *Gerald Ford's America* and *Super Vision*. As for the big program package, TVTV never got around to producing it.

Prime Time was optimistic, persuasive, and remarkably free of the jargon and countercultural rhetoric that characterized early guerrilla television manifestos. Businesslike in its appeal and McLuhanesque in its graphic design, the stylish prospectus revealed a global approach to funding, open to both profit and nonprofit sources—foundations, cable television, independent broadcasters, investors, patrons, and institutional and commercial advertisers. The only two sources excluded were public and network television because, according to TVTV, programming policies of the new Corporation for Public Broadcasting precluded any innovations, and the networks would never "give up the time and control necessary to make *Prime Time* a success." Ironically, it was public television and, much later, network television that aired TVTV's subsequent work.

In June 1973 TVTV incorporated with Allen Rucker as president. Together they raised $100,000 by selling shares in the company mainly to family, friends, and the Point Foundation.[9] Incorporating proved more effective than trying to raise money through grants. The group paid off $55,000 in debts, bought equipment, gave themselves salaries of $100 a week, and moved into a new office in a storefront at Sacramento and Fillmore, whimsically keeping the sign over the door: "Joe Cruz Tennis Shop."[10] Their new San Francisco headquarters afforded several large rooms furnished with comfortable furniture and one wall covered with 8 × 10 glossies of network newscasters.[11]

While TVTV was working on their *Rolling Stone* tape, a breakthrough occurred that had a major impact on TVTV and on the future of alternative television. In March, the National Association of Broadcasters met in Washington. Attending the meeting were David Loxton, director of the Television Lab at WNET in New York, and John Godfrey, a supervising engineer at the Lab. They wandered around the floor and heard a lot of whispers about suite 311, but nobody could tell them what was there. Curious, they went to the suite and discovered an extraordinary piece of equipment engineered by a California-based company called Consolidated Video Systems. It was the first stand-alone time-base corrector. CVS had just finished a working model a week before the show and had neither the time nor the money to book themselves a booth on the main floor. A time-base corrector measures the lines in the video picture and the spaces between them. Through electronic processing, the lines are made even, producing a stable signal. Recognizing that with the new device it would now be possible to broadcast half-inch portable video, Godfrey insisted they get the first unit off the production line, and in June they put it into the studio and began experimenting with it.[12]

Loxton was in charge of one of public television's three experimental laboratories created by a grant from the Rockefeller Foundation. Until 1973, the Television Lab at WNET was exclusively devoted to experimental video productions by artists like Nam June Paik and Ed Emshwiller. But Loxton, who was interested in documentaries, wanted to expand the productions at the Lab to include nonfiction programs. This was no easy task. In the wake of the vicious attacks on the media (especially television journalists) by President Nixon and Vice President Agnew, public television's interest in documentary was at an all-time low. This coincided with the introduction of the video portapak, which made a new era of lively documentary programming possible. TVTV's convention tapes for cable were precisely what Loxton thought public television should be doing. He knew he could be going out on a limb, because the station and the video art community would look dubiously on his diverting any money for documentaries, but he was convinced it was a necessary broadening of the mandate of the TV Lab. He thought: "If we could break the technological back of how to get half-inch videotape onto broadcast, then I could sort of slide in the back door of getting documentary programming back onto public television. Not necessarily under the

guise of programming, but maybe under the guise of experimentation."[13] The stand-alone time-base corrector was just what he was
looking for.

Meanwhile, Doug Michels of Ant Farm suggested to TVTV the
idea of doing a tape about the Guru Maharaj Ji.[14] The guru was a
15-year-old who claimed to be god. His followers were the faded flower
children and drugged-out hippies of the '60s who were having a hard
time making the awkward transition to life in the '70s. Without the
antiwar movement or the counterculture to guide them, many young
people were lost. In their yearning for a leader, they were easy prey
for a religious demagogue like the guru and his even more frightening
Divine Light missionaries. In November, his followers were holding
"Millennium '73," a celebration at the Houston Astrodome, and billing it as "the central event in human history." It was perfect for
TVTV—a national story that commercial television would either
ignore or cover inadequately. TVTV had to be there, so they set out
to find financial backing and broadcast sponsorship.

TVTV approached foundations six months before the event, tried
to get seed money from the Corporation for Public Broadcasting, and
talked to KUHT, the PBS affiliate in Houston. Although KUHT
expressed public support for the project, they privately offered no help
in fund-raising. All foundations turned them down. In a last-ditch
effort, the group approached the Stern Fund. Partly because Stern
was interested in video as a new territory for its funding and partly
through a personal contact, TVTV secured $20,000 contingent on
being able to raise another $5,000. In the nick of time CPB decided
to contribute the $5,000. Because TVTV was a for-profit organiza-
tion, it needed a funding conduit and a coproducer for the show.[15]

Exactly what brought Shamberg to Studio 46 at the TV Lab
remains lost in memory. An edit of the convention tapes had been
included in the May broadcast of a WNET program called "The Television Show" (the 90-minute pilot for a live series) that also featured
a discussion of TVTV's *Prime Time* TV proposal, and this may have
been how Shamberg and Loxton first became acquainted. But when
Shamberg walked into the TV Lab studio with the guru project on
his mind, Loxton was ready to talk business.[16] TVTV would produce
the first half-inch video documentary commissioned for national
broadcast.

Following the convention model, TVTV rented a house in Houston
ahead of the event and collected 24 crew members to work on the
tape. Elon Soltes, who joined TVTV for the first time to work on this
tape, had a brother-in-law named Michael who was one of the guru's

followers. Soltes and crew joined his brother-in-law in Boston and followed the Soul Rush '73 bus caravan of the guru's followers from Boston to Houston. This trip was TVTV's first experience with the "gurunoids." The journey provided some of the wittiest moments of the tape, including a hilarious four-way conversation involving an elderly Jewish couple who ask whether Maharaj Ji is another Jesus or Father Divine. One of his followers, a suburban matron, explains she did not know she was searching, but now she has found the light, heard the music, and tasted the nectar—and so have five members of her country club. Their quartet of voices overlap in the familiar fashion of real people too busy to listen to one another.

Not all encounters with the devotees en route proved as delightful, such as the time a mahatma in Washington threatened Soltes that he would return in his next life as a frog if he revealed any of their secrets. As outlandish as the threat sounded, it was also unnerving. When the location crew arrived in Houston, they debriefed the production collective and an unspoken understanding arose that they would all watch out for each other: there were only 24 of them and thousands of "gurunoids" who thought they had found God. It had been easy for TVTV to maintain perspective on the Youth for Nixon, but the guru's followers were people their own age and shaped by the same experiences. The guru had persuaded his followers that he had all the answers, and some TVTV members were seduced even as others were repelled by his promise of "peace now."[17]

This preview helped TVTV prepare for three intensive sixteen-hour days covering the event. The group came up with categories—disciples, the Guru and his family, "the knowledge," outsiders—and they divided into five crews of two or three people each, charged with developing a facet of the overall story. As with the convention tapes, each crew was responsible for managing their own equipment as well as screening and logging the tape they shot. Each evening they assembled for editorial meetings to share information, watch tapes, and chart the overall direction of the production. Because TVTV had so many people in the field, they generally knew more about what was going on than anyone else there, including the media and the guru's followers.[18]

Since TVTV was the largest and most persistent element of the press, they were welcomed at first. But the Divine Light Mission quickly realized TVTV was not satisfied with canned information, so they switched tactics and tried to contain them by constantly changing the rules and spontaneously invalidating their press passes. The most menacing confrontations were with the "World Peace Corps," a misnomer since the neatly dressed, English-accented members actually comprised the guru's goon squad. Their ministrations ensured lots of shots of hands over lenses and arguing voice tracks. TVTV was too caught up in the fracas to be able to record how the paramilitary wing of the guru's organization functioned.[19] But TVTV did engage one bodyguard in a confrontational conversation that yielded some eye-opening statements. The fanaticism and casual violence of the guru's security force proved just as disturbing as the passivity and desperation of his followers.

Paul Goldsmith, an accomplished film cameraman, was brought in to operate the new "portable" color camera TVTV was experimenting with. Goldsmith had been hired to shoot a film about the Democratic Convention when Wendy Appel first introduced him to TVTV. Because Goldsmith was a filmmaker, TVTV initially viewed him with outright suspicion. As alternative videomakers, they were determined not to fall into patterns of an older, dominant technology like film. But later when the TVTV people realized they were going to need a skilled cameraperson to handle the one-inch color camera, they turned to Goldsmith. An important key to TVTV's success was this reliance on talented outsiders—journalists like Maureen Orth, filmmakers like Paul Goldsmith and Stanton Kaye, video innovators like Skip Blumberg and Nancy Cain—people with a keen sense of how and what to shoot and then how to assemble it all. Goldsmith's expertise was tested in Houston under the most physically demanding circumstances. It was, he later recalled, like being an astronaut.[20]

TVTV thought the new Asaca color camera would give good color quality with a portapak feel. At that time only CBS had a more portable color rig (the Ikegami), and it would be another year before JVC introduced the first half-inch color portapaks. Unfortunately, the Asaca was tethered to a one-inch recording deck loaned by the TV Lab, and it required an hour for setup and a five-person crew—hardly portable video. Although the color on the camera was good, it was badly designed with a fixed, built-in lens and slow power zoom that added noise to the signal, a factor that seriously handicapped Goldsmith's shooting style. Even more crippling was the weight of the scuba-style back frame which he had to wear; in one position, he was briefly paralyzed. Goldsmith shot only 12 hours of color tape over three days, and only ten minutes were used in the final work. TVTV would have had better luck using a color camera on a tripod, but they were determined to test the portability of color equipment.[21]

By the early '70s, color had become an important technical consideration in television production, because networks were now billing themselves as "all-color" and looking down on black-and-white pro-gramming.[22]

Goldsmith found TVTV's approach to its crews as active partici-pants in their tapes—something he attributed to the conceptual art background of some of TVTV's founders—refreshing. He liked that this meant he did not have to present "balanced truth" but rather a facet of the story that might be interesting or stir things up. What surprised him was finding that when TVTV took objective, nonin-volved positions they got noninvolved interviews, but when they were outspoken, they got "real content and real feelings."[23]

Goldsmith quickly found TVTV's approach was slanted toward verbal information, which carried the danger of too many talking heads. He could contribute strong imagery to balance this, so on the first day out shooting, he recorded a fine sequence of hands grasping flowers and fingers waving desperately for the "god-touched" blos-soms, which captured the unnerving devotion of the guru's followers.[24] It took TVTV's crews time to absorb the message, but soon they became highly self-critical of careless shooting, crew members' in-ability to build narrative sequences, and problems following nonverbal action. New standards of professionalism began to influence the ear-lier, looser guerrilla TV style.[25]

Lord of the Universe was an extraordinary achievement, arguably TVTV's best journalistic tape. The 58-minute work is complex in its structure and devastating in its indictment of a fakir and his unsus-pecting victims. If the convention tapes chronicled the demise of the '60s, then *Lord of the Universe* witnessed what became of that lost generation in the '70s. Well before the Jonestown massacre and the rise of the reverend Sun Myung Moon, TVTV captured a religious impostor exploiting the vulnerable, in this instance, survivors of the Vietnam War years who now were searching for inner peace or a new leader or simply a shared sense of community—people too burnt out or too drugged to tell a phony from a god. *Lord of the Universe* also revealed how the guru's message of world peace, which gathered the fragile faithful into the fold, barely concealed the greed, deception, and hunger for power at the core of the movement he fronted.

The tape dexterously weaves together opposing stories: desperate devotees with sinister security squads; true believers with disillusioned ex-followers; antiwar-activist-turned-PR-man-for-the-guru Rennie Da-vis with Abbie Hoffman, a fellow Yippie and cynical guru observer. At the core of the tape is the guru himself, a rotund teenage prankster who likes to ride his minibike around the Celestial Suite and push photographers into swimming pools. Compared with his frenzied followers, the guru appears colorless and bland. TVTV contrasts his teachings about spiritual values, plus his followers' rejection of their middle-class parents' materialism, with his fabulous wealth. The guru business is a family business. His mother, Mata Ji, is an unabashed materialist who openly solicits donations of cars, appliances, and other goods at a press conference. Bole Ji, the guru's chubby older brother and an unlikely Elvis Presley imitator, leads the rock band Blue Aquarius, providing "celestial music" for Millennium celebrants. And Bal Baghwan Ji, the guru's other brother and a Hindu version of a Madison Avenue ad man, is coordinator of the three-day event, although he modestly asserts he does nothing as minions bow to kiss the ground when he passes by.

Whether viewed at press conferences, rehearsing the band, having their feet kissed, directing construction workers, or gloriously displayed on stage, the "holy family" seems a carnival facade for the more sinister behind-the-scenes workings of the Divine Light Mission. TVTV tracked down freelance reporter Pat Halley who played a practical joke on the trickster guru—a pie in the face—and was rewarded with a severe beating that crushed his skull and required a plastic plate to mend the damage. When asked about the incident at a press conference, the guru nervously sidestepped the question as his handlers attempted to catch the flack, but a bodyguard interviewed later was not so reticent on the subject: he admits he would have slit the guy's throat had he been there.

TVTV got hold of Abbie Hoffman to serve as foil for Rennie Davis. Given TVTV's avoidance of narration, Hoffman functions as TVTV's surrogate spokesperson. Both men were well-known radicals who had taken different paths once the antiwar movement began to dissipate. Davis opens the tape proclaiming the Millennium to be the central event in human history. Next he is seen in video flashback at the May 1971 March on Washington tensely declaring, "If the government doesn't stop the war, we will stop the government." Asked by TVTV how he reconciles his past political activism with his new role as advance man for god, he laughs while holding a child in his arms and says the past was all a warm-up for this moment.

As SDS founder Todd Gitlin noted, Rennie Davis's conversion to the world-saving enterprise of the Guru Maharaj Ji was a logical continuation of years spent in New Left politics "organizing with mirrors," Rennie's own expression for making a project real by creating a reputation for it when it was less than real. (On the tape, Abbie Hoffman describes this talent in his own words when he claims Rennie was a good propagandist because he was able to establish vision as reality.) Davis' transformation was an odd "transcendentalized" conclusion to years of leaping after an effective agency for social transformation.

> Rennie's conversion . . . was both an extension of the New Left's utopian vision and an abdication . . . misconceived as a higher calling. . . . [It] was his spiritualized attempt to overcome an untenable position in a disintegrating movement: from a movement that had overstated its real political possibilities to the mysterious power of a teenage god incarnate was not so great a leap.[26]

Abbie Hoffman, who makes his first appearance in a TVTV tape here, has the last word on Davis's conversion: "Rennie was always arrogant about the future. . . . There's a difference in saying you've found God and in saying you know his address and his credit card number!"

As before, TVTV captured people candidly saying amazing things. One "gurunoid" remarks inside the Astrodome, "I don't know whether it's the air conditioning, but you can really feel something!" Another skipping devotee attempts to convert a bystander, asserting: "People are not only working for peace, they're experiencing it now!" Goldsmith was convinced it had to do with the fact the video cameras were soundless (unlike 16mm film cameras), so people were caught off guard. It was like the early days of handheld cameras when people had no reference for this novelty.[27] Religious fanatics of different persuasions also made cameo appearances in the tape, including a tambourine-shaking Hare Krishna follower eager to debate the superiority of his theology and an irate born-again Christian berating devotees for following the devil. Moved by the passion of their beliefs, unselfconscious and unguarded in their remarks, these people lent emotional intensity and even greater irony to the unfolding drama.

Threading through the tape is the story of Michael, who has come to Houston to get "knowledge" which is given only to the chosen. He is successful in his quest, unlike the many humorless followers stuck on lines and passed from one organizer to another, fruitlessly complaining they were promised knowledge if they came to Houston and asserting they are not going home without it. "I'm ready to crawl the walls," one woman says through clenched teeth, "I've got to get Knowledge now!" Their suppressed rage and helplessness is both funny and pathetic. Michael, once he has become a member of the elect, defends the ritual's secrecy, as TVTV juxtaposes him with several ex-premies (followers) who describe their initiation and subsequent disillusionment. One man wittily comments upon the peculiar jump the mahatma made right after he received "knowledge." Without skipping a beat, he explained, the mahatma told him his "free" gift now required a lifetime devotion to the guru and a generous donation of worldly goods.

TVTV members agonized among themselves whether they should reveal the secret knowledge; one TVTV crew member even volunteered to be initiated but this idea was promptly vetoed. They finally decided it was essential that they disclose the occult practice, both in terms of debunking the guru and resolving the narrative of the tape, but they opted to have an ex-premie do the telling. Tom Weinberg found a man who described in precise detail the various meditation techniques. When the dreaded "knowledge" was finally exposed on tape, most of TVTV's fears—from physical violence to being turned into a frog—dissolved.

The lasting image of the tape occurs during an Astrodome session of satsang (discourse about knowledge) after the guru relates a simple-minded parable about a boy who comes to Houston in search of a Superman comic. As he speaks from the huge platform throne, the banality of his remarks is further set off by his appearance: Garbed in gold-spangled clothes, Guru Maharaj Ji wears a glittering crown perched precariously above his smugly grinning face. TVTV captured the Lord of the Universe in living color, surrounded by flashing neon signs and an extraordinary frieze of garlanded girls hailing the guru ecstatically to the insipid strains of Blue Aquarius playing his theme song. The nodding heads of blissed-out followers in the audience completed the zany if devastating picture. Abbie Hoffman's final comment seemed to sum it all up for TVTV: "If this guy is god, then he's the god America deserves."

One might expect *Lord of the Universe* to be sympathetic in its presentation of deluded hippies, yet TVTV's cameras reveal the hysterically giggling devotees in much the same way as they had shown the argumentative hippies in Flamingo Park in *Four More Years*. Although some might claim it as adherence to that illusory journalistic standard of "objectivity" that prompted such detachment, other explanations vie for consideration. TVTV's core members were neither hippies nor antiwar activists themselves, despite their long hair, beards, and youth. For the most part they were witnesses, not participants, of the marches and bloody confrontations of the antiwar years. Some crew members felt kinship with the young people gathered for Millennium '73. Megan Williams recalled that the guru show was probably the closest TVTV ever came to people who had shared an experience with them. It had been easy to view the Young Republicans as "horrible, creepy people," but the guru followers were people their own age and, like them, had been through a lot of communal experiences only to emerge and find there was no support for them anymore. "One day you're a flower child, and the next you're just wandering around as a lost soul. . . . All the promises held forth in the Sixties and early Seventies never materialized." The guru answered a need. Observers like Williams found it sobering to contemplate why some people burned out and others survived.

Despite this sympathy, TVTV generally remained separate from the gurunoids—and a few members may have even felt themselves superior to these lost souls. In *Lord of the Universe*, as in all TVTV tapes, everyone comes across as more or less foolish. TVTV's sarcasm was the ultimate leveler: they scrutinized both the mighty and the lowly with equal irony.

After Millennium '73 ended, TVTV spent weeks editing 82 hours of tape into a 58-minute show. It was a total nightmare, according to Megan Williams. It began with throwing out everything that was technically unstable, which represented a good portion in those days. A team of six did a rough half-inch edit using the backspace crash method. For 1973, the system was "amazingly fast."[28] TVTV consistently pushed their equipment. Having projected it would take four weeks to edit, TVTV had to revise estimates when faced with the mass of tapes and post-event fatigue. People laughed at them when they talked about broadcasting. They finally arrived at the TV Lab in New York having roughed out the edit on one-inch equipment. Accustomed to editing for themselves, they felt strange having John Godfrey pushing all the buttons during the on-line quad edit. But John Godfrey proved crucial to their creative process. More than an engineer, he offered TVTV valuable editing suggestions and helped solve some lingering continuity problems.[29] At a time when other engineers turned up their noses at small format video, Godfrey rolled up his sleeves and went to work to put it on the air. Without Godfrey's willingness to find answers to numerous broadcasting problems presented by portable video, TVTV would have been stymied at the eleventh hour.

Because *Lord of the Universe* was edited on quad, special effects like dissolves, still frames, and slow-motion—at the time not possible with helical formats—made the visual texture of *Lord of the Universe* strikingly fluid and brisk. The editing team had constructed story sequences using TVTV's signature graphics, so essential for providing basic expositional information and thus sidestepping the need for narration This time the graphics were in color and electronically generated for a slicker, more professional look. They also served another purpose, allowing a clever way of getting around a potential broadcast problem. TVTV had to add color burst to the black and white portions of the program so that home television receivers could read the color portions. But FCC broadcast standards did not allow the addition of burst on more than five minutes of uninterrupted monochromatic video, and jumping from burst (color) to non-burst (black-and-white) caused a glitch each time in the tape. They solved the problem by adding genuine color information every five minutes in the form of color (yellow) titles and credits.[30]

Loxton worked out a $4,000 post-production budget which TVTV raised on its own. Loxton then convinced the station's accounting office to attach the 44 percent overhead charged for its projects to the editing budget only, because the tape was not being shot in-house. He then covered the overhead with TV Lab funds. His creative, sleight-of-hand maneuvering made it possible for TVTV to complete the tape for $36,000, or roughly 45 percent of the costs for a conventional PBS film production.[31]

Lord of the Universe was broadcast nationally by PBS on February 24, 1974. Although the program was completed the first week in January, TVTV shrewdly decided against an early airdate for the sake of publicity. Shamber's print background taught him about the lead time newspapers and publications like *TV Guide* need for reviews. While WNET handled New York publicity, TVTV tackled the nation, working with local affiliates' PR departments. This meant personal visits, preview videocassettes, publicity, photos and, occasionally, personal letters to TV columnists explaining the project and their production methods, excellent substitutes for personal interviews. TVTV's bread-and-butter approach to publicity—an infinitely more sophisticated PR campaign than anything guerrilla television was used to doing—paid off.[32]

Ron Powers of the *Chicago Sun-Times* had this to say about *Lord of the Universe*: "It is highly recommended viewing, both as an example of skeptical, unimpressed (but never vicious) journalism, and as a peek into—well, into the future of television."[33] John J. O'Connor of *The New York Times* agreed, noting that "Videotape's advantages of portability and flexibility can now promise a thoroughly professional picture quality." O'Connor continued to be favorably impressed with TVTV's work, adding: "TVTV came away with a terrific documentary. . . . The visual results created a devilishly appropriate Wizard-of-Oz context. . . . After TVTV superbly dissected the guru, his 'holy family' and his followers, more objective viewers might have chosen to laugh, cry, or throw up."[34] Even the respected TV critic of the *Christian Science Monitor*, Arthur Unger, found TVTV's guerrilla TV production a fascinating study and a shockingly accurate account of the guru and his followers.[35] But it was Katy Butler writing in the *San Francisco Bay Guardian* who offered the most incisive criticism:

> The TVTV style . . . has smoothed out considerably since the group first won national recognition for programs on the 1972 conventions: This show has fewer interjections from TVTV personnel, fewer moments that drag, more technological razzle-dazzle (color footage, slow motion, stop motion, tight and rapid cutting). . . . But the guru's entourage is an easy target, anybody can look like a fool when a smartass wide angle lens distorts their face, and teenage ex-dopers who think a fat boy is God don't stand a chance. Time now for TVTV to move on to subjects with more ambiguity, more challenge.[36]

Butler's astute view that TVTV was too reliant on "easy targets" and cheap effects was possibly the first published criticism. As for "cheap effects," TVTV had used the wide-angle or fish-eye lens in *The World's Largest TV Studio* out of practical necessity: the cheapest wide-angle lens was a 9mm that was fairly fast; it allowed one to shoot in relatively low light and include a crowd in one shot.[37] It also covered a multitude of camera errors, since one could shoot close without showing any shaky camera movements.[38] Megan Williams recalled:

> When we first started we didn't have the money to be able to afford good lenses. So we borrowed this $30 attachment that you just put on a zoom lens, and that creates a fish-eye distortion. We wanted it for the flexibility of being able to shoot both close and distant. . . . In terms of the fish eye distortion, our effect wasn't intentional. But in terms of shooting close and showing people as they really are . . . that was intended.[39]

But once TVTV mastered the portapak camera, no longer needing it to cover up their mistakes, the wide-angle lens stayed because they also liked the effect it had—making weird people look even weirder. Despite persistent and mounting criticism of its uses in subsequent tapes, the wide-angle lens became another TVTV signature.

Leendert Drukker, a columnist on audio and video for *Popular Photography*, took issue with TVTV's active presence in the tape and with video tape in general:

> To this viewer, the outstanding characteristic of video tape has always been the verbosity, the endless interviews, and "The Lord of the Uni-

verse" doesn't convince me otherwise. . . . In film, the documentarian has striven to keep himself and his camera as inconspicuous as possible, to avoid upsetting whatever he was trying to shoot, for as realistic, as honest a recording as possible, as the term goes, "cinema verite."[40]

Drukker's notion of cinema vérité adhered to the distinctly American concept of direct cinema; had he been familiar with its French version, he would have understood TVTV's interactions with and provocations of subjects placed them in another grand documentary tradition. Admittedly, much early video did tend to excess, but this was partly because editing equipment was poor or nonexistent and a concomitant "real time" aesthetic was in force. *Lord of the Universe*, however, was markedly different from "the-run–of-the-mouth" video Drukker conjures in his review. It is more likely that Drukker's bias may have reflected the growing fears of film loyalists as the upstart, low-cost, flexible medium of video began to challenge film's preeminence along with cherished notions about what film and television and a documentary could be.

One further possibility for Drukker's antipathy to TVTV's work is that Drukker had sided with Global Village in the early funding battle waged against Raindance, given the fulsome way Drukker goes on to praise Global Village's John Reilly. If such partisanship were the case, then nothing TVTV did could hold against the bitter feelings stirred by early funding competition in the underground video community.

Perhaps the most outspoken in his criticism of the guru tape was Bob Williams, writing in the *New York Post*. Calling it a "deplorable film [*sic*]," and "flat, pointless, television," he then went on to insult all Indians and their religions. Essential to his review was the fact that *Lord of the Universe* had been aired during a PBS fund-raising week, and he concluded his review thus:

> The hour-long program was remiss in not providing some small examination of the available box-office take of the goofy kid guru, much less telling prospective contributors how it got involved in spending how much of its foundation grants and viewer subscription money in such a questionable venture without more inquisitive journalistic endeavor, or ignoring gurus.[41]

William's off-the-wall response to TVTV's fresh approach to the documentary pointed up a pervasive problem that all independent producers have had to face whenever public money is spent to produce experimental work. Williams, however, appears to have been the only writer at the time to question TVTV's seriousness as New Journalists.

The question of funding lurking behind Drukker's review and boldly stated by Williams had always been a sensitive issue for TVTV; even before TVTV's inception, there was the debacle over the New York State Council on the Arts' funding of a Raindance proposal for "The Center for De-Centralized Television," which Shamberg help architect. Persistent difficulty in raising grant money led to TVTV's businesslike incorporation, yet another factor that propelled them on a different course from most other alternative video groups at the time. TVTV's views about grants and the people who receive them was rather petulantly displayed in an interview with Richard Casey for a feature story on *Lord of the Universe* in the *Berkeley Barb*:

> Allen [Rucker] said that the first four years of independent video work, in which millions were spent, produced some good experimental educational development, but a lot was spent on "people hanging out in the woods with porta-paks being hippies." Those who got regular grant money tended to become secure and comfortable, and Hudson [Marquez] characterized them as, "Well, let's go tape this old guy down by the fire house, and if somebody comes by we'll show it to them."[42]

Such disparaging remarks about early alternative video hint at the intense competition for funding that by 1974 had rent the once chummy underground video scene as people vied with one another to get federal, state, and private grants to keep making portable video work. TVTV had depended upon the skills and generosity of members of early video groups like Videofreex, Raindance, and Ant Farm, among others. Without their willingness to temporarily subsume their identities within this new entity and contribute technical know-how and aesthetic innovations, TVTV never would have been able to create ground-breaking programming, first for cable and then for public television. *Lord of the Universe* benefited from the camaraderie and the all-for-one spirit that initially defined the group and the movement that spawned it. But as the once fluid roles of TVTV's production collective began to solidify into assigned jobs, fewer video freaks would flock to participate in TVTV's coverage of subsequent events.

Parry Teasdale, whose contribution to editing *The World's Largest TV Studio* was essential to its success, argued with Michael Shamberg during the edit about the direction the tape was taking. Teasdale could not see what was new about producing a tape about the conventions "after the fact" when it could have been done live. Frustrated with the outcome, he declined to work on *Four More Years*, sensing that Shamberg had already locked down a format wedded to a "conventional" idea of television.[43] Teasdale was a founding member of the Videofreex, which moved from New York City in 1971 to a rural village in upstate New York where they began weekly live "narrowcasts" to their neighbors. "Lanesville TV" was just the kind of homely hippie video Rucker and Marquez were knocking in their comments to the *Berkeley Barb*, sad testimony to how wide the split between VT and TV had already grown.

There is also a curious postscript to the Ji show. After *Lord of the Universe* was broadcast, a major audience for the tape was the guru's followers. Although the Divine Light Mission had been wary of TVTV and there was some talk of a lawsuit,[44] once the tape had been aired, they eagerly bought copies of the tape for their far-flung communities around the world. Some followers saw the tape as an exposé, but many others were glad to be able to view the Millennium event and witness the guru on tape. Whether Divine Light Mission edited the tapes they bought is unknown, but it would seem TVTV managed to suit both themselves and the guru's followers.

9.

Prime Time TVTV

What pecksniffery lurks in the hearts of men? TVTV knows, bwooo-hooo-hooo-hahahahahaha. Does a poltroon, a mountebank threaten the lives of decent citizens? Looks like a job for . . . TVTV! "Extry, extry! TVTV Rips Veneer Off Fake Guru!" "Here, son, I'll take one of those . . . keep the change." "Gee, thanks, Mister. Say, aren't you . . . ?"

TVTV has struck again. TVTV is part League of Justice, part television's answer to the New Journalism, part guerrilla style Front Page and part Samuel Beckett. Television of the Absurd. Through a lens, starkly. Witty, irreverent, deadpan—but never quite able to conceal the cold eye of the reformer.

—Ron Powers[1]

Soon after the Presidential Nominating Conventions, Allen Rucker of TVTV and Alvin Duskin, a millionaire clothing manufacturer turned political and media activist,[2] began work on a tape about the people behind television commercials. The idea was in keeping with TVTV's interest in exposing the inner workings of the television industry. Duskin's San Francisco group, Public Interest Communications, was involved in counteradvertising and was to have produced the program with TVTV. But when Public Interest Communications proved unwilling to provide full funding for the tape, TVTV severed their ties and decided to produce it themselves.[3]

Raising funding from foundations for *Adland* continued to be difficult. TVTV suspected this was because they planned a vérité approach to the subject rather than a didactic documentary. Money was raised by setting up a limited partnership, in which shares in the production were sold to individual investors who, in turn, received a portion of the profits or write-off against income taxes. By selling twenty-four shares at $500 a share, TVTV raised the $12,000 budgeted for the tape.[4]

Because *Adland* was not event oriented, the production was spread out over six months with shooting in New York, San Francisco, and Los Angeles. Without the compact time and place of the event coverage, *Adland* cost more to produce than anticipated, a little over $18,000. But when TVTV members compared this with the cost of a recent CBS special on advertising—$120,000—they were satisfied. Through Tom Weinberg's efforts the PBS affiliate in Chicago, WTTW, agreed to underwrite the $3,400 cost of the quad edit in exchange for the right to broadcast it first.

Thirteen people worked on *Adland*, but TVTV principals formed the core with friends joining in at various points when the production called for a second unit in New York or Los Angeles. Because the production was so different from TVTV's sharply focused, event-oriented blitz, *Adland* suffered from a lack of direction. In *The Prime Time Survey*, they soberly analyzed some of their problems

> Good television is about people interacting with something, usually other people. Generally this happens through transactions between subject(s) and camera, subject(s) and environment, or between subjects themselves. On all our productions we were part of "the media" and had a much more distinct role in our subjects' minds. In "ADLAND," however, our presence became special. Thus, we weren't able to get total access to the advertising process, particularly to those moments of transaction between admen and clients. Indeed, "ADLAND" was initially stymied by the refusal of most large agencies to cooperate. Finally, we found that the people at the top who had made it on the strength of their personal and not corporate images were the most open, and also the most interesting . . . In retrospect it would have been best to have focused on a personality like [George] Lois and used his process to get into other facets of advertising. Nonetheless we did get good, strong material from a variety of sources.[5]

TVTV's postmortem reports consistently emphasized the flaws and mistakes made in their work. *Adland* was no exception, but the tape was nowhere near as disappointing as the commentary would suggest. What is interesting is the way in which TVTV articulated their understanding of what makes television work and how critical they saw being part of "the media" had been to their past success.

George Lois (of Lois, Holland & Callway in New York) is *Adland*'s most prominent character in every sense of the word. "If my wife don't know a product, it ain't famous. I ask her, I ask cab drivers, I ask somebody else. If those people don't know it, it ain't famous," he exclaims. Also featured is famed ad man Jerry Della Femina, who made the first feminine hygiene commercials for Feminique. He speaks about his sincerity in selling, swearing that his wife "loves the stuff, she uses it all the time."

Many of the people interviewed are pleasant, intelligent people, like Marshall Efron (who had done anti-commercials for public television, but by then was making ads for the residuals) and Dagne Crane, the actress for Adorn hairspray, who speaks about the model's role. She attributes her success to having a rubbery face and looking like she comes from Ohio, which she does. Perhaps the most chilling interview is with child-star Mason Reese, who obsesses about food as he rehearses for a frozen dessert commercial. More like a little old man than a child, Reese is accompanied by his normal-looking parents who fuss about preserving his "gentle, loving quality." Normal is as normal does, or so TVTV seems to say. TVTV takes you behind the scenes with Jay Brown, all-night TV car dealer, and on location for commercials at Marine World and McDonaldland, where we are led through hamburger patches to Fillet O'Fish Lake. With their video cameras, TVTV captured the surreal landscape of Adland.

One problem TVTV had not anticipated was a run-in with the unions. The screen actors' union did not recognize journalistic license or distinguish between an ad being made and a program about one being made. TVTV feared it would have to pay actors' fees equal to the entire production budget merely to use their McDonaldland footage. In the end, the actors and directors agreed to sign waivers. The technical unions were a different matter; TVTV found that if they were nice to the shop steward on the day of shooting, he would waive requirements. "In any case, it's best to get your tape first and waivers second," was TVTV's parting advice on the subject.[6]

Although *Adland* was shot with black-and-white portapaks, the tape included film clips from a number of color commercials, so they resorted to the same ruse that had worked for *Lord of the Universe*: they put color burst throughout the tape using color graphics whenever needed to adhere to FCC broadcast standards. During the edit someone commented that what they had learned from making the tape was that "TV ads tell you more about the fantasies of ad men than those of consumers."[7]

Adland was first broadcast in Chicago on April 8, 1974. Both Gary Deeb of the *Chicago Tribune* and Ron Powers of the *Chicago Sun-Times* loved the tape. Ron Powers so reveled in TVTV's exposé that his witty description of *Adland* is worth quoting at some length:

There is the ad exec who gushes, "The important t'ing's gotta be, is, dat you . . . Implant an Idea out There"; an idea, he says, that hopefully will expand "like poison gas."

There are the balding, bearded, 50-ish executives in their open, flowered shirts who reach for another Scotch and swear sanctimoniously that they'd "do this work for nothing," although they are already making $100,000 a year and want more. There are the close-ups of admen's faces, showing the tics, the twitches, the compulsive tumbling of sentences.

There are the segments taped during the filming of commercials—such as Fabergé's $100,000 Christmas commercial production—that show how quickly child actors pick up the breezy, tough cynicism of their adult colleagues.

Finally, there are clips from the commercials themselves, to show the mentality hammered into the American consciousness each night by this narrowly informed, acquisitive, cunning, superficial subculture of men and women: commercials that tell nothing about the product's merits, but only ingratiate. Commercials that play on this country's sentimental notions of holidays. Commercials that suggest sexuality, power, youth, and happiness are inherent in the purchase of the product.

An ad executive discusses the notion of "mind-bending" commercials, which are commercials that "make people t'ink somet'ing dey shun't t'ink."

"Doesn't that go on a lot in the advertising world?" asks the interviewer.

"Naw," says the exec. "I don't t'ink anybody's dat good."

Hopefully, TVTV will hurry up and complete a lot more documentaries like this one before everybody realizes how good THEY are.[8]

Powers was not alone in his enthusiasm for TVTV's way of "putting the screws" to admen. Terrence O'Flaherty of the *San Francisco Chronicle* echoed Powers' tone in a review he wrote when *Adland* was broadcast there in August:

Anyone who wondered about the graceless vulgarity of television commercials owes it to himself, his family, his country, and his sense of humor to watch "Ad-Land" tonight. . . . This suicidal behind-the-scenes look at the making of commercials is mandatory viewing. . . . You will never again wonder how those ignorant slobs who haggle over deodorants got on television.[9]

O'Flaherty thought "the oafs in the crowd don't understand what caricatures they really are." Powers postulated that TVTV's relative obscurity explained their success in getting people to hang themselves on camera: "People let their guards down during TVTV's interviews, assuming that their smartalecky asides, their false starts, their moments of obscene or 'off-the-record' candor will be dutifully edited out—as they always are in 'straight' documentaries. Uh-uh. Not here."

TVTV was working on a number of projects in late 1973 and early 1974 in addition to *Adland* and *Lord of the Universe*. They discussed a series for San Francisco PBS affiliate KQED called "Free-Lunch," interviews with interesting San Franciscans at the local restaurant of their choice. There was also a paperback book planned. Neither project materialized.[10] But TVTV did publish *The Prime Time Survey* with the support of Westinghouse and the TV Lab at WNET/13.

The Prime Time Survey appeared during the summer and was reviewed by TV critic Powers, who stated: "TVTV, with its use of Porta-Pak videotapes and its anticonventional blend of art, journalism, politics and satire, is easily one of the most creative forces in American TV's mostly stagnant universe." Calling TVTV "television's future," Powers found the survey to be a blend of self-serving propaganda and outrageous ideas that should not be taken lightly.[11]

The *Survey* opens brashly with a biblical-sounding note: "In the beginning, there was the porta-pak." TVTV goes on to soberly outline the future of video, noting that the growing interest of the networks in developing broadcast-quality portable video equipment for the news, coupled with the rise of videotape for entertainment shows like "All in the Family," meant that technological differences between alternative television and mainstream television would soon be a thing of the past.

Prophetically noting that commercial interests would pervert portapak techniques, using real human emotions, humor, and exuberance as candid camera filler for the news, TVTV advocated expanding alternative television beyond the notion of merely putting portapaks in people's hands. The *Survey* called for plans to use portable color equipment, microwave links, satellites, live studios, and sophisticated editing, so that all new technology could become countertechnology. It was time for a new form: nonfiction television. TVTV was aware they would have to keep a critical distance from mainstream TV, and that this would not be easy.

TVTV's taxonomy of the video movement reveals their growing drift away from their roots following their broadcasting successes:

> What began as a general movement towards "alternate television" has evolved into three distinct forms, more as a response to channels of distribution and funding than to anything inherent in the video medium.

The three forms are: Video Service, Video Art, and Video Programming (aka non-fiction TV).[12]

Video Service encompassed all uses of video where television was not an end in itself: this included cable access programs, closed-circuit showings, and other small group uses. Video Art was defined as experimentation with the video image itself or with the video experience. And Video Programming was what TVTV did, producing nonfiction television for broadcast.

The *Survey* explains:

> We believe now that building an enclave within the existing system is a viable strategy for change. By using whatever channels will get programming shown in as many places as possible, it may be possible to build audience recognition for a particular style and approach to information which transcends the quirks of any particular outlet.[13]

TVTV need not be alone in this; their experience could serve as a model for others, since technical precedents had opened the doors to anyone with "quality programming" for television. TVTV identified with a production group, not a video service organization. "Our choice of program topics has to be political—not political in the sense of favoring a particular ideology, but in seeing each production as both an important program and a demonstration of different approaches to producing TV."

In 1970 Shamberg had written, "Reforming broadcast television would be like building a healthy dinosaur. . . . Anyone who thinks that broadcast-TV is capable of reform just doesn't understand media."[14] He had clearly changed his mind. Having met personalities who were enthusiastic about experimenting with video—broadcasters like David Loxton and John Godfrey, critics like Powers and O'Connor—the possibility of reforming broadcast television by example became TVTV's new, improved goal.

Shamberg's use of the word "political" is an index of how dramatically TVTV diverged from "video service" groups, many of whom still adhered to the New Left politics of the '60s and who saw video as a way to work for civil rights, social equality, and needed reforms. Reaching large audiences and getting their work broadcast was not their aim; their goal was to change society, and video was only a means to that end. TVTV had ridden the crest of the '60s' political wave without ever being a part of it; now it was the '70s and the "politics" of broadcasting was their new inspiration.

There is a photo in the *Survey* which makes TVTV's attitudes toward "video service" more concrete: it is of a grey-haired nerd wearing a suit, carrying a portapak, and bearing the label "Video Servant." Coming from comfortable homes in metropolitan cities, some TVTV members had a class bias that may have contributed to their thinly veiled contempt for homegrown community video with its local interests and nonprofit status. Despite their countercultural appearance and attire, TVTV members had not rejected the materialism of their parents, and that may be why they viewed hippies, political radicals, and religious fanatics with such detached, satiric glee.

TVTV's "truly awesome satiric capability"[15] closes the *Survey*, which outlines four ideas for future TVTV programming. First was "The Washington Bureau," a video analog to New Journalism, which would experiment with alternative ways to run a news gathering organization in the nation's capital. Next was an examination of the Nielsen rating system. Third, TV2000 offered a witty and imaginative history of the future of television. Finally, "Alive One" proposed the first alternate television satellite to be launched (or leased) as part of the Bicentennial Celebration.

By midsummer TVTV signed a year-long contract with the TV Lab to put some of these ideas into production. Like Rennie Davis's "organizing with mirrors," Michael Shamberg's shrewd promotional ability, coupled with TVTV's four big production successes, had convinced public television that TVTV, with its special brand of "nonfiction programming," was the future of television.

10.

Broadside TV

JOHNSON CITY. A television viewer flips through the channels, searching for an after-dinner program besides "Gomer Pyle" and "Truth or Consequences."

Suddenly he finds a spontaneous mountain music session straight from someone's modest living room or a "very experienced" midwife telling her story.

And Bob Barker has lost his appeal.[1]

A two-year seed grant from the Appalachian Regional Commission allowed the 26-year-old Ted Carpenter to move to Johnson City, Tennessee, in 1972 and found Broadside TV, an extraordinary communications experiment based on a regional planning and development model. Building on his "living newsletter" experience, Carpenter determined to construct an economically viable, self-sustaining community media utility, an entity virtually unique in the nation.

Broadside TV's uniqueness lay in several areas. It would "narrowcast" small-format video programming over cable television, a strategy then in use mainly in urban areas; it would take advantage of the preexisting communications environment of Appalachia and its status as a primary cable market; it would take advantage of the Federal Communication Commission's mandate for cable systems to provide local-origination programming; and it would be based not on the concept of a TV station but on a community newspaper.

The cable television industry was born in the community antenna television (CATV) companies that sprang up in the early '50s in rural areas with poor television reception. Their sole purpose was to erect a tall tower wherever reception was best (usually a mountaintop) and equip it with a sophisticated antenna that would attract a broadcast signal, boost it, and then pipe it down to subscribers via coaxial cable. Areas that required cable as an essential service were referred to as primary cable markets, and Appalachia was preeminent among them. It was not until the '70s, when the FCC lifted its ban on cable services to the top 100 television markets in the country, that secondary cable markets in urban areas were developed.

Carpenter reasoned that he could ground the economic viability of Broadside TV in the healthy cable industry in the region by capitalizing on the FCC mandate for cable operators to produce locally originated programming. Acknowledging that cable TV could contribute to community development by telecasting public service programs, the FCC had ruled in 1969 that CATV systems with 3,500 or more subscribers had to provide a certain amount of locally originated programming, including some programming during the prime viewing hours. By providing all the local programming for the region's four multicable systems,[2] Broadside TV would offer an economical solution to the cable owners' production problem.[3]

Carpenter rejected public access to cable as a viable model, distinguishing himself from urban TV guerrillas who focused on the FCC's public access ruling to get their programming out to cable viewers. Carpenter was adamant in his belief that public access was ineffective, asserting that access to electronic media meant nothing: filling the media void with programming was what mattered, and that required people, institutions, and money.[4] Carpenter was prepared for Broadside to serve as a public access facility for community members, but his first concern was developing Broadside as a self-supporting video production center. Funding from foundation grants and commercial support from local businesses, school systems, etc., would grease the wheels of production, but these sources could not be depended upon for basic, ongoing support. By exploiting the local programming requirement, Carpenter theorized that income from the cable companies could provide the stable economic base necessary for Broadside's long-range viability.

Carpenter's plan was quite simple. He approached the cable companies and said: "Look, you've got to do this. You don't like it. If you do it yourself, your budget is limited. You're not going to want to do any more than you have to, and you can't afford to do any more than you have to. Why don't you let us pool all the resources on a regional basis and then let us use your studio and share some of your equipment. Rather than hiring somebody locally, why don't you help support an additional person on our staff?" And it worked.[5]

The region's cable companies paid Broadside TV annual fees (an average of about one dollar per subscriber per year) for the right to run the programs Broadside produced. In addition, the companies had to furnish some money and equipment and make their personnel available to help put the shows on the cable. Although the cable companies were designated as "active members of the production team," in fact all the local programming was produced by Broadside. Carpenter was so successful in setting up his contractual services as a nonprofit business that he had trouble getting a tax-exempt status from the IRS because Broadside operated in such a businesslike manner. Because there was no way for Broadside to be profitable at that stage of video technology, Carpenter finally won the case, whereupon he thanked the IRS for the compliment.[6]

Instead of thinking of his service as a little TV station, Carpenter took for his model the community newspaper, hence the name, Broadside TV. Carpenter was inspired by *The Mountain Eagle*, one of the few homegrown, successful Appalachian newspapers. He admired its strong intellectual focus, crusading image, and self-awareness. There were columns on Appalachian culture, articles written by local people, and articles by people in the Highlander network. *The Mountain Eagle* provided a model of both flexibility and built-in traditions for dealing with conflict. When the cable operator wanted to show bingo and the Broadside staff wanted to run into the hills and videotape a midwife, "shocked by the ugly greedy capitalists,"[7] Carpenter looked to the newspaper, which had to deal with such conflicts. What are people willing to read about, what are reporters willing to write, what are advertisers willing to pay for? The editorial concept of the newspaper offered a model that could satisfy all demands.

The concept of an electronic community newspaper also freed Carpenter from having to tie each of his programs to a funding dollar, because each article in a newspaper does not have an individual sponsor, unlike each program on a TV station. Using this model, he was able to convince the local CATV operators not only to turn over their production budgets to him, but also to allow him discretionary powers in the use of these funds. This revenue amounted to a sizable block of unrestricted production funding, the rarest and most valuable kind. In return, Carpenter promised to produce a certain number of hours of wrestling and bluegrass music, which had been the CATV operators' standard local fare. The result of this strategy was a considerably expanded and diversified spectrum of local programming.[8]

Carpenter considered three areas critical to nurture—first were the universities and schools, second were the public agencies that had built-in budgets and a need to communicate, and third was the cable industry. Carpenter made the same argument to the schools as he did to the cable companies. The local schools had video equipment, sometimes fully equipped studios, but they rarely had fulltime video staff or teachers trained to know what to do with the equipment besides turn a camera on and talk. Carpenter persuaded them to turn over their equipment and some money so that Broadside staffers could develop interactive programs with their students. He carried the same argument to local agencies. By 1974 these efforts added up to close to a $300,000 operating budget and a staff of 15.[9]

Broadside TV began operations in April 1973. Their promotional flyer explained they would use TV "more like a telephone providing citizens of Central Appalachia the opportunity to hear and respond to their own neighbors and their own institutions. We do not seek professional quality, but rather stress community and problem oriented communication."[10] Although cable television would be a major outlet for Broadside's videotapes, Carpenter still believed cable was secondary to the intimate, one-on-one exchange of tapes between involved people. The communications process involved in making these documentaries was at least as important as the final product.[11] Bringing the portapak to the problem—and only to those people involved in it—had been at the core of Carpenter's "living newsletter" work. "Under no circumstances are we trying to be 'teachers,' 'missionaries' or 'film-makers' taking a curriculum, message or other form of 'enlightenment' to people in the mountains," Carpenter had written. "We assume that people in the region have a ready access to experience, language and ideas when it comes to their own vital interests. . . . We create a disciplined exchange that allows people to generate the material for their own learning."[12] Broadside's challenge would be to maintain those goals under the pressure of producing quantities of programs for cable schedules, local agencies, schools, and outside contractors.

At first, production was limited by lack of equipment, and Carpenter had the problem of finding a standard format that would allow for both production and cable distribution of programs. Half-inch portable video was the only format that was both flexible and affordable, but it was unstable for cable transmissions. With the help of Gary Keylon,[13] Broadside's technical specialist, the group discovered that three-quarter-inch Umatic video cassettes had greater stability and hit on the solution of transferring half-inch tapes to three-quarter-inch cassettes for cable transmission. Tapes were then made available on either format to anyone interested in buying or borrowing a copy.

By the summer, Broadside was providing up to six hours of cable programming a week, from Appalachian studies, mountain music, bluegrass music and mountain history to regional news, entertainment, and sports. A typical programming schedule for the week of August 27–31, 1973, included the following:

All-Star Wrestling—1 hour
Bristol Music Festival—1 hour
Crossroad Boys—30 min.
Music in these Hills—30 min.
Governor Dunn at Davy Crockett Park—30 min.
TV Foxfire: Carter Co. residents demonstrate traditional mountain folkways—30 min.
Appalachian Schools: Benjamin Carmichael, TN Commissioner of Education, speaking at Eastern TN State University and a tape on the Blackey (KY) School situation where a group of parents are trying to save their community school.—1 hour[14]

In the fall of 1973, Broadside began work with the Elizabethton school system and helped produce "In These Hills," an oral history project in which students and teachers videotaped the history and traditions of the area. Junior high school students went to a local nursing home to interview 96-year-old Aunt Rosa, who had seen the town change into a bustling city. Others interviewed Aunt Minnie Conley, a midwife who had served Carter County women for more than 60 years. Their half-hour tapes had titles like *Granny Woman*, *Butter and Applebutter Making*, *Quilt Making*, *Tobacco Cutting*, and *Hog Dressing*. Other students went to local industries and workshops to interview laborers and employers about local job opportunities, which resulted in career education of the liveliest kind. Twenty-four tapes for secondary school students, produced in conjunction with the District's Manpower Task Force, helped identify job categories and skills appropriate to the Central Appalachian labor market.

Broadside cooperated with the Bays Mountain Park Environmental Education Center on a series of environmental education tapes for elementary and secondary school students. The programs for younger children featured a seven-foot chipmunk named "Bampy," who talked about waste control, fire prevention, and, in one grocery-store sequence for *Nature's City* (reportedly the most difficult to tape, since Bampy's huge tail kept knocking cracker boxes and olive bottles off the shelves), human and animal food-gathering behavior.[15] Broadside also covered local area school board meetings, city commission meetings, and other local meetings and hearings. The group made tapes on health careers as well as in-service training and local health problems for area hospitals.

The Tennessee Commission on Aging funded Broadside to do a series of 25 programs on the needs of senior citizens, including nutrition, transportation, health screening, housing, and recreation, all featuring the activities of community centers in Memphis, Chattanooga, and Nashville. With the support of the Tennessee Committee for the Humanities, Broadside examined three public policy issues—strip-mining in Southwest Virginia, the New River Dam Project in North Carolina, and the disappearance of small farms in East Tennessee. At its peak, Broadside provided up to 20 hours of programming per week to 12,000 homes.[16]

The people who came to work at Broadside came for a variety of reasons. Broadside TV had an open door and worked with whomever came in.[17] Although most staffers came from within the region, some, like Jo Carson, were intellectually sophisticated and quickly grasped how video could be used to further social change and nurture the cultural wealth of the region. But others, like Tom Christy, were mainly fascinated by the new technology. Few were able to combine, as Carpenter had, production skills (as camera operator, interviewer, and editor) with a larger vision of why tapes were being made.

Blaine Dunlap was one of the most talented producers to work at Broadside. He was a born filmmaker and had been making Super-8 films since grade school. He entered his "save the world" stage at 19 when he was hired as a camera operator on a documentary film shot at Wounded Knee. Determined to make "the great Indian movie," he received an NEA filmmaker-in-residence award and was assigned to the Sioux Indian reservation in Rosebud, South Dakota. Dunlap discovered what the Sioux wanted to do was learn how to shoot video for themselves. Quickly realizing the limits of his position as a "white liberal outsider," Dunlap put them in touch with the nearby public TV station and, in the process, got "turned on" to video. When he won the Sinking Creek prize for his film *Sometimes I Run*, he left South Dakota for Tennessee, where he discovered Broadside. Although he had grown up in Dallas, his grandparents had come from Tennessee, so settling there was really a return to his own roots.

To recruit him, Carpenter promised Dunlap whatever he wanted: video editing, color equipment, even broadcast of his work. But when Blaine arrived, all Broadside had to offer at the time was half-inch, black-and-white portable video. Curiously, that never mattered because Broadside gave him an unparalleled opportunity to produce numerous tapes. "That was the height of my youth," he fondly recalled. At 21 he ran around the hills of East Tennessee making mountain guerrilla tapes then plugging them onto cable, shows like "The

Amazing Live Monday Night Video Chautauqua," a crazy-quilt public access show. When the show was live, Dunlap often handheld the studio camera, sometimes so the audience could see him. He would shoot tapes in the afternoon, then play them on cable that evening. There was no way to electronically lock-up the machines, so he would just roll the decks and then hit the play buttons. "Boom! Chung-kashdunk. It'd roll, and you'd roll tape." He remembered going to a bar one night, and Broadside's signal was coming in poorly. He telephoned the station, and, while looking up at the monitor in the bar, gave the engineer instructions on how much to raise the video level, fixing the television set by fixing the station. "That," he recalled, laughing, "was the height of something!"[18]

In 1974, when Broadside was full of optimism about the future, a new project initiated by a local professor to record various aspects of Appalachian folk culture[19] received a sizable grant from the National Endowment for the Arts. The Southern Appalachian Video Ethnography Series (SAVES) was the project of Richard Blaustein, a professor of sociology and anthropology at Eastern Tennessee State University (ETSU). With additional funds from the Tennessee Arts Commission, SAVES began to explore, document and preserve traditional mountain music, crafts, and lifestyles.

Blaustein became aware of video's potential at a conference on Appalachian education held in the spring of 1973 at Highlander, where Ted Carpenter showed excerpts of his tapes. Once Broadside TV started in earnest, Blaustein borrowed a portapak and started videotaping some of the traditional musicians in his rural neighborhood. Then he got his students interested in using video. One produced a video essay on the growth of commercial country music in nearby Bristol, another recorded interviews and performances with Blue Ridge musicians and began a study of step dancing, and still another worked with a traditional storyteller living in her home town.[20]

The most spectacular project to emerge from ETSU's initial involvement with Broadside was undertaken by an undergraduate student. During the spring of 1973 several members of the Church of God in Jesus' Name in Cocke County, Tennessee, were bitten and killed by rattlesnakes during services. The church was drawn into a bitter confrontation with the courts, and network newsteams descended on the town, presenting biased and shallow reports on the Pentecostal church and its practices. Wayne Barrett, an anthropology student at ETSU, approached the church with the idea of studying their belief system from their own perspective using video. At first suspicious of Barrett's motives, the church elders finally agreed, and Barrett taped interviews and services for several weeks. Two videotapes were edited. *They Shall Take Up Serpents* included an interview with the assistant preacher who provided a detailed insider's view of the faith, segments of actual services, and a brief interview with the judge involved in the case. *Fire and Serpent Handlers* opened with additional excerpts from services, including fire handling, and concluded with a panel discussion by ministers in Bluff City, Tennessee.[21]

Blaustein realized video's value in anthropology: it could interest students in doing fieldwork, helping them develop a professional orientation to folklore and anthropology, as well as generating tapes that could be used in classroom discussions involving more students. According to Blaustein, students took an active role in determining the content and direction of their course work, using each other's projects as a basis for continuing research. He viewed this as another example of the "each one, teach one" method Carpenter had learned at Highlander.[22]

Blaustein showed his own tapes at professional meetings like the Conference on Visual Anthropology at Temple University. Alan Jabbour, the new head of the National Endowment for the Arts' Special Projects Division, saw Blaustein's tapes at one such meeting and came to Johnson City to talk with Carpenter and Blaustein about expanding the work. In September 1974 SAVES was launched. Nearly a year later the SAVES catalog featured 34 tapes made by various producers[23] on a broad array of subjects, including weavers, fiddle makers, broom-makers, farriers, and musicians performing in their homes and at festivals. The catalog described the project's purpose thus:

> The principal function of the SAVES project is to produce high-quality videotape documentaries dealing with various aspects of Southern mountain culture, and make these available to interested parties. SAVES videotapes are geared to two major audiences: academic institutions and the general public. . . .

This was a rather different approach than the "self-education" concept Broadside originally espoused, resembling more the agenda of the much-despised missionary and teacher than the folk school proponent intent on sharing information with like-minded mountaineers. Nowhere does the SAVES brochure mention any payments to the musicians and craftspersons whose performances provided credibility for the project and its director.[24] Certain inconsistencies between the folk school model and Broadside's pragmatic application of the concept began to reveal a fundamental rift between philosophy and practice.

At Broadside's beginning in 1973, Carpenter told Charles Childs, a staffer at the Ford Foundation, that it would follow the Highlander model of self-education. Avoiding impersonal studio productions, Broadside TV's programs would be made where people were most comfortable and continue the instant playback that was central to Carpenter's "Living Newsletter" experiments in person-to-person community empowerment. Eschewing "fancy programming," Carpenter would continue to produce videotapes of "self-criticism, self-evaluation, and self-education."[25] But the bigger Broadside grew, the more impossible it became for that model to flourish.

In almost no time Carpenter became a full-time administrator concerned with the operational issues of running a successful non-profit business—juggling the numerous contractual responsibilities Broadside had undertaken, writing grants, managing accounts—doing work that took him away from actual productions and the training of staff. He had become so busy keeping the organization running that he failed to realize that once the initial enthusiasm for Broadside had worn off, the contractors, who had put in a lot of money, expected to see something for their investment. In the midst of everything Carpenter had neglected to develop a staff that could fulfill those increased expectations on a regular basis. By the time he realized the problem and began to recruit staff like Blaine Dunlap, he was on the verge of an even larger problem, a blow so monumental it would knock the economic base out from under Broadside and leave the organization scrambling for its very survival.

11.

Impeaching Evidence

Following the success of *Lord of the Universe*, David Loxton offered TVTV an unprecedented year-long contract for almost a quarter of a million dollars to create five hours of programming for public television. The initial money came from the Rockefeller Foundation's grant[1] to the TV Lab; later, the Lab's discretionary money from the Ford Foundation figured into the total sum. TVTV's overall budget was $230,000; of that amount $138,000 went directly to TVTV for their production costs and the balance went to the TV Lab to cover postproduction expenses. Loxton had taken a huge risk with *Lord of the Universe*, and now he was going even further out on a limb by committing such an enormous sum of money (for public television) to produce TVTV's nonfiction television.

Joining TVTV's original gang of four were three new partners, Wendy Appel, Paul Goldsmith, and Elon Soltes.[2] TVTV stated the five experimental projects it planned to explore included new approaches to broadcast journalism, the videotape magazine, late night information-as-entertainment shows, fast-breaking news events, and short journalistic features.[3] Their first project evolved out of "The Washington Bureau" proposal detailed in *The Prime Time Survey*.

Determined that their New Video Journalism must pioneer a new structure for news gathering, TVTV asserted that The Washington Bureau would combine the stylistic and economic advantages of portable video with decentralized management. Four 30-minute programs were planned, plus an additional 60-minute documentary about the making of the bureau's tapes. Acknowledging that it would be impossible to gather comprehensive information on all of Washington, TVTV decided to concentrate on interpretive rather than expositional stories on the environment, personalities, and opinions of Washington. The entire proposal rested on the belief that Richard Nixon would be impeached and the hearings would form the heart of their coverage.

But history turned another page, and TVTV arrived in Washington the day Nixon resigned.[4] TVTV's flexibility was put to the test from day one, and their strategy for covering Washington necessarily was revised to accommodate a portrait of the first hundred days of the new administration.

TVTV's ideas for the Washington Bureau were ambitious, often innovative, and logical extensions of their brand of impressionistic reporting. Not everything TVTV planned to do was new, but some innovations included unconventional on-camera talent; reflexive sessions analyzing not only the biases of the subjects but TVTV's own prejudices; follow-up coverage of stories; and a mix of graphics, music, and video synthesis. All this promised a livelier, more democratic style and content to Washington reporting than television viewers were accustomed.[5]

The crew was drawn from past TVTV crews and other portapak professionals—15 people plus TVTV's four principals and two technicians. Engineer Steve Conant maintained equipment on a daily basis, while Winston Chao from WGBH flew from Boston for two days each week to check out the machines and match them, doing any major repairs. Mary DeOreo, a former Watergate reporter, joined TVTV as researcher as did Betsy Ross, a still photographer.[6] Although there were no "entrenched roles," people were assigned primary tasks. Administration was largely the responsibility of TVTV principals, while the production crews had relative autonomy over their stories. Having learned from the mistakes and mishaps of past productions, TVTV decided they needed skilled editors to review daily tapes and make recommendations from an editor's perspective on what worked and what was needed to make a story.[7]

Since there was no single event like an impeachment hearing to anchor the series, four separate stories emerged as topics for each half-hour program in the series. The President, The Press, Congress, and the Washington social scene emerged as themes for *WIN*, *Second Hand News*, *The Hill*, and *Chic to Sheik*. Decentralization of management looked great on paper but in reality strong direction for the programs proved lacking as individual crews drifted off in their respective directions, working with their own editorial teams. The final order of programming was changed[8] to lead off with the two strongest tapes, which offered behind-the-scenes glimpses of Washington society and the presidency; the other two were more rambling exposés that revealed the weaknesses of TVTV's heterarchy far more than the flaws in the inner workings of the press or the Congress.

TVTV had wanted to produce "The Nixon Tapes" and instead had to settle for "Gerald Ford's America."[9] What they proceeded to capture was the "style" of Washington. Over the course of three months, they shot over 150 hours of tape, approximately 80 percent in black and white and the rest in color. TVTV had hoped to be able to produce the first color documentary using the newly available portable camera and deck, but Jon Alpert and Keiko Tsuno of the Downtown Community Television Center in New York City got there first with their hour-long exclusive view of *Cuba: The People*, which was aired by the TV Lab in late December 1974.

Two portable color cameras were tried out on "Gerald Ford's America." At first TVTV used a JVC camera and portapak, but the camera had a slow tube, making shooting difficult in scenes with mixed lighting. In addition, the camera really was not portable; when the camera operator was in motion, the tape recorded an incomplete signal, making it virtually impossible to achieve broadcast, even with a time-base corrector. TVTV next tried the new Sony color camera and a cassette deck. There were no problems shooting with the portapak, and the camera, which had a faster tube, allowed work at light levels comparable to a standard black-and-white camera. The only complaint was the weight of the cassette (30 pounds); though mobile, it was not portable.[10]

While TVTV was in Washington working on the series, the TV Lab sent a crew to make a half-hour documentary about them and the making of "Gerald Ford's America." Aired in February 1975 as the premier show of the TV Lab's new "VTR" series, the group portrait was shot by Andy Mann, who had worked with TVTV on the convention tapes and had signed on for the Washington Bureau. Mann's eccentric, energetic camera captured the frenzy and playfulness of TVTV at work as well as a telling picture of TVTV's "hierarchy." Host for the "VTR" series Russell Connor commented in his introduction: "It is truly a Washington show—a tape of the tapers taping."

On camera Allen Rucker and Paul Goldsmith perform a comical roll-call check of their equipment before leaving San Francisco for the nation's capital; their inventory includes "the infamous curvitar lens" and the instruction book for the new color portapak, which they planned to read on the plane. "We're not going to look at the President. There'll be a million dollars' worth of gear all pointed in one direction and we're going to be pointed in another. We don't know exactly where yet . . . but we're going to try to find something interesting," Paul Goldsmith said.

Getting down to basics, Skip Blumberg explained their shooting style: staying away from interviews, TVTV would try to be more conversational, catching people on the run. The shooting ratio would be nearly 100 to 1 compared to the network reporter who shoots 10 or 5 to 1. Video, TVTV felt, allowed crew to function more like print reporters eavesdropping on a story than a network news unit. TVTV's flexible distribution of labor set them apart from network news units in yet another sense, because in television only the correspondent talks, and the cameraman (rarely woman) is neither seen nor heard. TVTV's different production style and emphasis caused a slight upheaval in the tradition-bound corps. When TVTV's camera pointed at the press instead of the President, one member of the press corps called it "unethical." And since TVTV did not require the lighting that film cameras demand, they decided not to contribute to the network lighting pool. In retaliation, TVTV was threatened with loss of lights if they did not kick in their share.[11]

Shamberg insisted TVTV represented a different but complimentary group of professionals to the networks' news teams, stressing they were not into competition. "What we're trying to do is make good, watchable programs." Admitting he might consider listing job roles in the credits, he bristled at any hint there was a hierarchy within the group: that "doesn't seem fair." The interview ends, perhaps characteristically, with Shamberg, who has been discoursing alone while reclining on a hotel bed, turning to the other members of the group clustered in a corner of the room. They start giggling and one jokes, "We're the sycophants around you."

In mid-November, after three months of production, TVTV moved to New York to edit the tapes at the TV Lab. After the rough half-inch edit, tapes were transferred to quad for the on-line edit with John Godfrey and Phil Falcone supervising.

"Gerald Ford's America" was distributed nationally by the Public Broadcasting System. It aired weekly in New York during January 1975. TVTV's sardonic humor and unflattering reportage came in for heavy criticism from the Washington press corps who charged them with superficiality and fun-house photography. "What that camera does to Gerald Ford's jaw shouldn't happen to a Watergate conspirator," wrote Anne Crutcher in the *Washington Star-News*."[12] But elsewhere critics were enthusiastic.

The establishing frame for many of the print reviews was the arrival of video to network television news. Not long before "Gerald Ford's America" was completed, St. Louis station KMOX announced its news department had gone "all electronic." It was only a matter of time and money before every TV station in the nation switched from film to ENG (electronic news gathering) production, and this provoked underlying alarm—and, in a few instances, delight—over video's imminent impact on television news and documentaries.

The development of truly portable equipment coupled with the advent of mobile microwave transmission and electronic editing ushered in a new approach to broadcast news reportage known variously as ENG (electronic newsgathering) or EJ (electronic journalism). Prior to ENG, live television newscasts depended mainly on prearranged events such as an inauguration or a convention. With ENG, spontaneous events could be covered live and broadcast within hours or minutes. When KMOX became the first to use ENG exclusively, only 10 percent of U.S. television stations were using any ENG equipment; seven years later only 8 percent would still use news film. Some critics accused "live" or "eyewitness" news programs of trivializing or sensationalizing the news, although others praised the new technology for increasing television's ability to cover unplanned newsworthy events. The first spontaneous event to be covered live on American national TV was in May 1974, when the Los Angeles Police Department fired on the Symbionese Liberation Army's hide-out. Although the availability of the technology made live news possible, the quality of that news continued to depend on the journalists behind the camera.

TVTV's challenge to entrenched ideas about television journalism sent some critics scrambling for a secure position from which to judge these video "interlopers," but there was also praise for that rarest of TV commodities, "the willingness to take a risk."[13]

The first tape aired in "Gerald Ford's America" was *WIN*, named after the button devised as a public relations effort to Whip Inflation Now. The tape pokes fun at the presidency by exploring the contrasting realities of life on the campaign trail with the belt-tightening existence of ordinary folks. Attacked by some critics for presenting the citizenry as "boobus Americanus" and faulted for not fully exploring Ford, it was also called exhilarating, irreverent, and fast paced.

The tape opens with a scene at an airport where citizens worshipfully await the president's arrival. Whether intentionally or not, TVTV manages to evoke the opening of Leni Riefenstahl's epic film, *Triumph of the Will*. But unlike Riefenstahl, TVTV is not interested in mythmaking. Rather, they succeed in deflating the elevated image of the presidency; after *WIN*, the public's "depressing infatuation"[14] with the president would never be the same. The most devastating aspect of the tape is the way TVTV undermined Ford's larger-than-life image by juxtaposing segments from his silly "clean plate" speech on inflation with a fund-raising auction where his autographed football sold for $2,700. Interlaced with these narrative strands are interviews with the Stevens family, middle Americans whose inflation-beating ideas are quoted in the presidential speech.

The frivolity of the black-tie fund-raiser and the casual way high rollers squander money on mementos takes an acid turn when contrasted with the frugality and decency of economically hard-hit people like the Stevenses. "I want the kids to know they can have a good life without money. I like the idea of hope. They need to know that they can survive beautifully without a lot," Mrs. Stevens says. The glamour of the presidency is considerably tarnished by tape's end. TVTV's technique of playing parallel stories off one another made *WIN* strong and disturbing.

In his review of *WIN* in *The New York Times*, John J. O'Connor detected a "note of cajoling in the questions, a touch of calculated put-on" that never shakes the suspicion that the "unsuspecting are being cynically trapped"—a notion of entrapment that was reiterated by other critics. But O'Connor concluded by saying the program "turns out to be less 'alternate news' than a clever, frequently imaginative exercise in counter-Establishment journalism. The TV Establishment can certainly use the competition."[15]

TVTV used their signature graphics again, notably displaying the title of the series in the shape of a football, an image that ties together the four half-hour segments, both recalling Ford's athletic image as well as the auction scene in *WIN*. The series' opening features a rendition of "Hail to the Chief!" heard over scenes of Richard Nixon boarding a helicopter leaving Washington and the presidency.

The next program in the series, *Chic to Sheik*, received the most critical attention of them all, stirring strong negative response to TVTV's alleged "cheap shots" at unsuspecting Washington society. Shamberg believed it was the best program in the series.[16] The tape opens with the following crawl:

> Parties are work in Washington. People go to trade information, see people in power and be seen with them. Parties attended by the President, or his inner circle, are the social center of Washington. In order to show you what exclusive Washington society is like, we had to attend parties, more as participants than as spectators.

Using their low-light tivicon camera, TVTV attended an array of parties, from a birthday celebration for Nancy Howe, assistant to Mrs. Ford, to a lavish birthday bash for the Shah at the Iranian Embassy.

Ant Farm's cover art for *Guerrilla Television*, the alternative video manifesto for reorganizing the structure of information in America, written by Michael Shamberg and Raindance Corporation (Holt, Rinehart, and Winston, 1971).

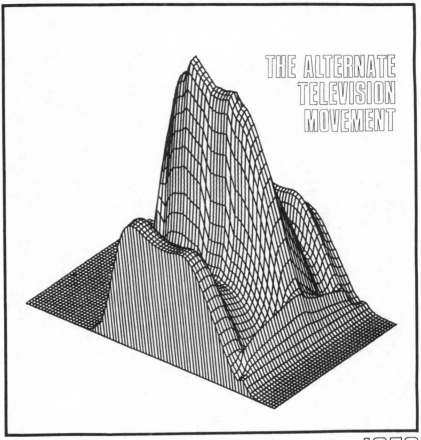

Cover of the first issue, Summer 1970, of *Radical Software*, an irregular journal edited by Beryl Korot and Phyllis Gershuny, which served as the chief networking tool of the video underground. *(Source: Beryl Korot)*

Cover of the third issue, Spring 1971, of *Radical Software*, published by Rain-dance Corporation. *(Source: Beryl Korot)*

Chicago 8 co-conspirator Abbie Hoffman, taped by the Videofreex for *"Subject to Change." (Photo by Michael Curran)*

Black Panther Fred Hampton in the disputed Videofreex tapes for *"Subject to Change." (Photo by Michael Curran)*

TVTV in Miami during the 1972 presidential conventions. *From left*: Allen Rucker, Anda Korsts, Tom Weinberg, Skip Blumberg, Michael Couzins (behind Blumberg), Judy Newman, Steve Christiansen, Chuck Kennedy, Ira Schneider (kneeling), Martha Miller, Michael Shamberg, Chip Lord (kneeling), Andy Mann, Nancy Cain, Hudson Marquez, Jody Sibert (sitting), Curtis Schreier, Joan Logue, and Jim Newman.

Nancy Cain of TVTV videotaping in Miami.

Skip Blumberg interviews Douglas Kiker as Nancy Cain records in "Four More Years."

Antiwar demonstrator in TVTV's "Four More Years." *(Photo by Kira Perov)*

Young Republican in "Four More Years."

Hunter Thomspon in "TVTV Meets Rolling Stone." *(Photo by Michael Curran)*

Abbie Hoffman in TVTV's "Lord of the Universe."

Megan Williams and Anda Korsts with the Iranian ambassador in "Chic to Sheik," part of TVTV's "Gerald Ford's America" series for WNET's TV Lab. *(Photo by Carlo A. Maggi)*

Skip Blumberg on camera and Hudson Marquez on mike with Speaker of the House Carl Albert in "Gerald Ford's America."

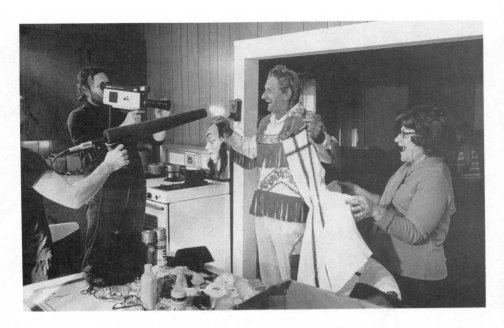

Allen Rucker videotapes country Cajuns dressing for Mardi Gras in TVTV's "The Good Times Are Killing Me."

Paul Goldsmith videotapes Nathan Abshire, Mr. Accordion, and his group in "The Good Times Are Killing Me."

SHOOTER'S GUIDE

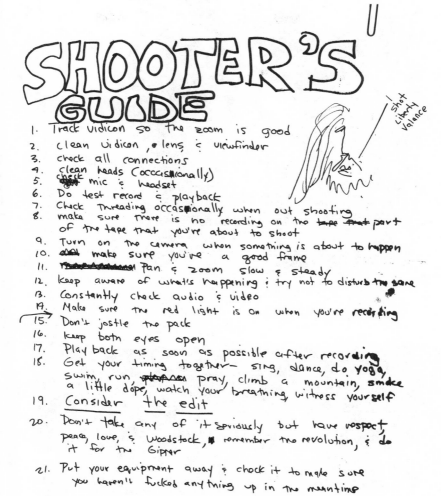

Shot Liberty Valance

1. Track vidicon so the zoom is good
2. Clean vidicon, lens & viewfinder
3. Check all connections
4. Clean heads (occasionally)
5. check mic & headset
6. Do test record & playback
7. Check Threading occasionally when out shooting
8. make sure there is no recording on the ~~tape first~~ part of the tape that you're about to shoot
9. Turn on the camera when something is about to happen
10. make sure you're a good frame
11. Pan & zoom slow & steady
12. keep aware of what's happening; try not to disturb ~~the scene~~
13. Constantly check audio & video
14. Make sure the red light is on when you're recording
15. Don't jostle the pack
16. keep both eyes open
17. Play back as soon as possible after recording
18. Get your timing together — sing, dance, do yoga, swim, run, pray, climb a mountain, smoke a little dope, watch your breathing, witness yourself
19. Consider the edit
20. Don't take any of it seriously but have respect, peace, love, & Woodstock, remember the revolution, & do it for the Gipper
21. Put your equipment away & check it to make sure you haven't fucked anything up in the meantime

"Shooter's Guide," a page out of TVTV's scrapbook of the 1972 Presidential Nominating Conventions.

Bart Friedman, Nancy Cain, Tom Weinberg, and Elon Soltes of TVTV tape Super Bowl X.

Steve Conant (with camera) and Bill Murray (with flash) in the stands for "TVTV Looks at the Oscars."

TVTV at the Oscars, *left to right:* Paul Goldsmith, Michael Shamberg, Megan Williams, Bill Murray, Hudson Marquez, and unidentified woman.

The Videofreex clowning around for a group shot, circa 1972–73: *left to right,* back row: Sarah and Parry Teasdale, Skip Blumberg, Bart Friedman, Chuck Kennedy; front row: Ann Woodward, David Cort, Murphy Gigliotti, Carol Vontobel, Nancy Cain, Davidson Gigliotti.

Broadside TV's Tom Christy taping banjo player Ralph Stanley. *(Photo by Dianne Snyder)*

Serpent handler in "They Shall Take Up Serpents" by Wayne Barrett, Broadside TV. *(Photo by Michael Curran)*

Program logo for University Community Video's weekly magazine show, "Changing Channels."

University Community Video, circa 1976: *left to right*, back row: Jim Mulligan, Greg Pratt, Mark Frost, Brian Lee, Stephen Kulcyzcki; second row: Arby Shuman, Jim Malec, Paul Burtness, Dan Melcher, John Velie; front row: Anne Ericson, Ellen Hyker, Elle Segal.

"Dairy Queens" (Ann Kanton, Patty Kakec, and Alice Trip), an award-winning documentary by Elle Anthony for University Community Video.

Jon Alpert tapes in the Philippines in the mid-80s for NBC's "Today Show." *(Photo by Maryann DeLeo)*

They were chaperoned by Betty Beale, a longtime chronicler of posh capital parties for the *Washington Star-News*. Because they were a novelty, these "cute couples" with portapaks were viewed as entertainment, hardly a threat, which allowed them a chance to capture some extraordinary unguarded moments along with the boredom, small talk, and frequent inanities of soused party-goers gossiping about the Fords.

The tape opens at a White House tea for Republican women. "I never leave the house without an elephant on," one woman says. Another, asked about Watergate, blames it on "the press and the Communistic elements and the young people working for him." Yet another praises Mrs. Ford as a "down-to-earth" person, but none of the party-goers seem equally earthbound. Betty Beale is first seen wearing a WIN button at Nancy Howe's party, but she is not wearing it at the Iranian embassy. "Doesn't it go with this party?" TVTV's Megan Williams asks. "Oh yes," Beale explains. "It can go with this party. Because if every American could eat at the Iranian Embassy, they wouldn't have to spend anything on food."

Tom Shales and Donnie Radcliffe, writing in *The Washington Post*, thought the soirées were not at all representative of working Washington parties. Moreover, TVTV's "shrewd or malicious" editing made basic pleasantries sound like "frozen deceits." Noting that it was futile to criticize the tape by the standards and etiquette of TV news since TVTV rejected those standards, Shales and Radcliffe raised questions of fairness, suggesting that few party-goers were aware of how ridiculous they would appear on camera because they were seduced by the glamour of TV.[17]

TVTV disagreed. Megan Williams, who shot much of *Chic to Sheik*, found the women taped at the tea parties to be staunch Republicans who were participating in a Washington ritual where favors were paid back and status displayed.[18] Betty Beale was upset with the tape and wrote TVTV a letter saying she felt she had been had. She had thought the program was going to be about her. She also complained about how things looked: the low-light tivicon tube wiped out details and was notorious for making men look like they had a five o'clock shadow. Mostly Beale was unhappy with the way she looked.[19]

One writer commented that the party-goers "look so foolish and decadent you half expect to see the French Revolution breaking out around them. That, or a grand entrance by the Marx brothers."[20] Yet another compared *Chic to Sheik* with *The Great Gatsby*, finding Fitzgerald's "brilliant and sympathetic handling of wealth"[21] superior to

TVTV's portrait of Washington society. Comparing a TVTV documentary about Washington in the '70s to a novel set in the '20s or
to a Marx Brothers comedy may seem odd, yet the allusions to fiction
about decadence was flatteringly apt given TVTV's aspirations as
New Journalists.

Despite the video team's "inflated smugness" and questionable
ethics, Shales and Radcliffe nevertheless concluded by saying the program had "certain refreshing qualities: the close-up immediacy its
technology affords, an absence of loquacious on-camera reporters telling viewers how to react, and a sense that the world is mad."

Marvin Kitman, writing in *Newsday*, was unabashedly enthusiastic
about *Chic to Sheik*, giving it four "antennas," his highest rating.
Praising TVTV's subjective, radical reporting style, he found a virtual
"cult of anti-personality" in TVTV's work because of the lack of
stand-up reports or sit-down analysis: the cameras were the superstars, the people interviewed the real attractions. Aware that TVTV's
ability to capture unguarded moments could not continue for long, he
concluded, "Some day man will adapt to TVTV, too. But for a while
at least we get to see a true picture of what people are really like."[22]

Second Hand News was the series' third installment. Its focus was,
according to the opening crawl

> on the men and women of the White House press corps, that elite group
> whose lives are geared to Gerald Ford's every move, and whose stories,
> columns and TV commentaries provide the basis for the public's under-
> standing of the president. The program examines the rituals and quirks
> of life in the White House press room, including the daily briefing and
> the photo session.

The much-abused White House Press Corps—"the widest, easiest
target in town"—was the perfect foil for the "new and intrepid young
purveyors of journalistic truth."[23] But *Second Hand News* was less
about the Corps than it was a three-actor showcase. Featured was
the Washington Bureau chief for the *Chicago Daily News*, Peter Lisagor, as unwitting "straight man to Sarah McClendon's bluster and
giggle." (McClendon operated her own Washington news service.)
And, in the unlikely role of the only real critic of the press, John
Ehrlichman, late of Watergate infamy, bemoans the lack of time given
for investigative reporting. The tape moves from scenes of a press
reporter's "pool" report to colleagues, to a press conference, an empty
newsroom, a hearing on the Hill, and foolish encounters with Senators
Hubert Humphrey and Robert C. Byrd.

"It is shot in herky-jerky style, alternating between black-and-white for press segments and color when the President appears and it often comes in a distorted image as if it were being filmed from inside a fish bowl. If this is the wave of the video future, God help the fishes," Haynes Johnson opined in *The Washington Post*. Citing reporters like Timothy Crouse and others who had successfully skewered the Washington press corps, Johnson concluded that television had yet to capture its own portrait of "our menagerie."

The last tape in the series, *The Hill*, was a jaundiced view of Congress. It received the least critical attention of any of the programs in the series. The UPI's critic Frank Swertlow simply found it superficial and incomplete, but Benjamin DeMott, writing in *The Atlantic*, championed it as loose-limbed and rambling.[24] The tape includes interviews with farmers, merchants, and kids on what was wrong with the United States and its government. Hubert Humphrey offers his lecture on "this country of ours," declaiming to Peter Lisagor, "It's a young country; it's a lively country; it's an undisciplined country; it's a—Somebody's got to get a *hold* of it!" says Humphrey, histrionically grabbing Lisagor's lapels. A Virginia congressman entertaining a flock of schoolchildren on the Capitol steps admits in stage whisper to the camera: "They'll go home, you know. They'll tell their mothers and fathers . . ." The viewer eavesdrops on backbench politics in Senate lobbies and caucus sessions and briefly hits the campaign trail with Senator Byrd.

Why was this "collection of snippets" so pleasing to DeMott? "The secret lies in style," he wrote. "TVTV's camera has a disheveled, wayward manner. It's never at attention, seldom knows what it's covering, roots about at random for 'telling particulars.' " One such is Representative John Brademas inquiring about senatorial responses to a presidential address. The subject, DeMott notes, changed on camera from taxes and energy to relationships among Senate stars and congressional workhorses. Brademas warily goes after Senator Jacob Javits, trying to appear among peers, but Javits's hand on his shoulder—"avuncular, condescending"—makes everything perfectly clear.

DeMott had watched the series with a former Washington correspondent. "And when it was over we told each other we'd just seen more essential Washington than in a year of nightly news and specials." DeMott's essay for *The Atlantic* stressed the importance of allowing such innovations by freelance video journalists to have a place within the tightly controlled structure of broadcast television. Calling for a demystification of the medium, he believed video could stimulate a freshly critical self-consciousness among network pros.

As matters now stand, the nightly news is some kind of holy church unto itself—impervious-portentous in manner, undeviatingly dim about significances lying in what happens between people, monstrously overconfident, not only about the discreetness of assignments and stories, but about the metaphors . . . by which importance is certified.

According to DeMott, the alternative video documentary, "infused with folk feeling . . . communal, small-scale, intimate, forgiving," just "might open up commerce between high culture and popular culture, disclosing Borgesian labyrinths in political life, decomposing 'official versions,' showing leaders operating in a darkness they only pretend is light."

DeMott closed his enthusiastic review by identifying with Maureen Dean. An elegant matron at the Iranian embassy in *Chic to Sheik* gushes at Ms. Dean, saying how wonderful she was on camera during "those hearings." "How did you do it? Did you take vitamins?" she asks. And Maureen Dean, smiling symmetrically, said, "I was fascinated. I didn't want to miss a minute." "I feel more or less that way about 'Gerald Ford's America,'" DeMott concluded, "and I think TV news moguls need a rocket."

Although many critics registered a generalized "dread"[25] over the coming revolution in all-video news gathering—especially if TVTV's work was any indication of what was to come—most grudgingly allowed that if the pioneers of tape refined their techniques, "they might soon constitute a bona fide alternative news media."[26]

Television reporter Les Brown wrote in *The New York Times* that "many in the industry believe that video groups, which heretofore had been technologically relegated to closed-circuit and cable television" would now begin to exert considerable influence over broadcasting. "Since the commercial networks do not normally buy independently produced documentaries,[27] the market for tapes made by video groups is expected to be confined, for a time, to the lower-paying entities in television," such as public television. "But a New York station manager expressed the belief that the young producers, who work outside the television system, will be the most significant new force in television programming within a year or two."[28]

Catherine Twohill, writing in a PBS subscriber magazine, raised a host of other questions occasioned by TVTV's success

As the reality and spontaneity of the portapak are discovered by the network news departments, will the search for alternative news fall flat? Can a group like TVTV—with everyone drawing a salary of $150 a week and celebrating their good fortune—possibly hope to compete with the well-funded network systems once the novelty of their effort becomes a commonplace of the six o'clock news? Can they maintain their political sting as they struggle for air time in an industry that—even in public TV—has a sensitive ear for political criticism?[29]

David Loxton at WNET's TV Lab was pleased with "Gerald Ford's America." Although he found the individual programs uneven, he thought that even the poorer ones had more energy and vitality than what was then found on television. Loxton felt they were pushing the system, doing exactly what they were supposed to do by exploring what could be done with the new technology.[30]

Early in January, as "Gerald Ford's America" began appearing over PBS stations around the country, Michael Shamberg received a letter from Elie Abel, Dean of Journalism at Columbia University, informing him that TVTV had received an Alfred I. duPont Columbia Journalism Award for *Lord of the Universe*. With the most prestigious broadcast journalism award acknowledging the group's work, TVTV jauntily embarked on the production of their next three programs for WNET. TVTV told a reporter that they planned to work on a smaller scale in the future and possibly do some scripted pieces.[31] Plans for a documentary about Cajun music were already under way even before "Gerald Ford's America" was edited. Riding high on the unprecedented critical and collegial response to their brand of "alternative television," TVTV was totally unprepared for the fire storm of controversy and condemnation that would surround their next productions.

12.

Changing Channels

Although some felt "Communitube" would have been a better title for University Community Video's biweekly series, it was "Changing Channels" that premiered Wednesday, October 9, 1974. Getting Minneapolis' PBS affiliate KTCA to accept the idea of a regular series took long hours of negotiations, partly because of technical obstacles and partly because the programs would not have the sophisticated look of broadcast television. A compromise was struck when UCV agreed to comply with the FCC requirements for color burst, borrowing the strategy TVTV had used with *Lord of the Universe* by inserting color graphics throughout their black-and-white program. The series' opening title was accordingly produced using color film animation. During the first season, the new series was optically scanned, producing what critic Will Jones observed to be a "less-than-perfect image . . . resembling news film, and with a bright line flashing through the picture every 15 seconds." But the argument of content over technique finally prevailed over KTCA's other objections.[1] The university arranged to buy the half-hour of airtime for $200 per show, and KTCA reserved the right to review each episode 48 hours before airtime for "appropriateness."

The series proved to be the best advertisement for UCV's community training workshops, attracting viewers who had seen the show and now wanted to learn how to produce a tape about an issue of concern to them. UCV staff told a reporter for the *St. Paul Dispatch* that they would train anyone to use video. The Video Access Center would then edit shows, selecting segments for their general interest although favoring "subjects not usually treated by commercial stations." They were careful to note that not all shows produced through the Center would be aired, due to time limitations and broadcasting requirements, but anyone could show their segments over closed-circuit TV. Although they aspired to "true public access," UCV acknowledged it was not possible at that time. As far as UCV knew, this was the first such regular programming in the nation.[2]

UCV matched a skilled student producer with a community member, combining technical expertise with a burning issue. After community people had taken the basic introductory portapak course, staffers would then organize production groups to help student and community members develop their projects so they could be edited and broadcast. During the first season of "Changing Channels," the majority of productions (roughly 60 to 70 percent) were made by community members working in tandem with staff and student producers.[3]

Minneapolis Tribune critic Will Jones devoted a column to the new show in which he approved of the program's "unfettered, unchallenged advocacy." "Changing Channels" was not meant to run in a familiar TV groove of balanced reporting, according to Jones, but to "use TV to bring the power of information to people who haven't had it before." He quoted Stephen Kulczycki at length on the philosophy behind the series.

> What we're working with here is an evolutionary process in democratizing television. . . . The development of the portapak camera can be compared with the invention of the printing press. Television has developed as an elite technical medium. But now, with these cheap cameras that are easy to operate, anybody can learn to express himself in the medium. . . . Before the printing press, all information and knowledge came to the people from the pharisees and the scribes. After the printing press, there was an incentive for other people to write, to express themselves. That's the kind of process we're encouraging here through television.[4]

Jones picked up on the potential for controversy in upcoming shows, a topic Miles Mogulescu discussed at some length in a feature written about the new series in the *Minnesota Daily*:

> The advertisers control the existing television medium . . . [so] few controversial views are aired. Occasionally a controversy such as a riot will get on the television. But what is covered is the riot, not the issue that produced it in the first place.
>
> Television is so powerful, yet its uses have been so limited and ineffective. The center is allowing people to break the stranglehold of major networks and their subconscious control.
>
> We're not expecting a 37 on the Nielsen television rating, but we do think there are lots of people who want to see something different on television.
>
> For any particular piece on "Changing Channels," something else

like it has been done on broadcast television. However, a subject given 30 seconds on the news may go for 10 minutes on our program and be done in a nonconventional style.[5]

Kulczycki and Mogulescu were well versed in the philosophy and tactics of alternative video, and they both proved able spokesmen for UCV's brand of guerrilla television. Although their quotes may not have been as polished as Michael Shamberg's, they were firmly committed to the cause they espoused.

The first program in the series was much like *Communitube* in its composition, although there were fewer works and each was full length at ten to twelve minutes each. Gone was the obligatory series host; UCV was determined that their tapes would stand on their own and unwilling to have the show's success depend on whether people liked some personality. Bonnie Raitt again was featured, this time singing at the Cabooze Bar. A story on municipal ownership of public utilities took a strong position in support of such self-reliance. It was the sort of story that would have had a difficult time getting sponsorship on a commercial broadcast channel, *Tribune* writer Will Jones observed, where representation from the private-power interests would be required in the name of balance. But Mogulescu, who narrated the segment, and Kulczycki, who shot it, defended their right to air a point of view, asserting the purpose of "Changing Channels" was to explore alternatives and the Circle Pines municipally owned utility was an alternative to privately owned gas utilities. When the community got to see the segment, about 20 people called KTCA to express their approval of the show, although some laughingly accused the chairman of the utilities company of hogging the camera. His reply was, "Blame the producers."[6]

Also included was a delightful and witty portrait of a tent revival "in which the faith healer conducts himself much like a pop-music star, complete with organ riffs accenting his sermon," Jones reported. "Questioned about the opulent style in which he and his staff lived, healer Wayne Parks told the camera: 'We God's people have a right to have the very best . . . our Cadillacs are blessed.' " Capturing the Billy Sunday appeal of a latter-day show-biz preacher, this was the second tape UCV broadcast that was made by Jim Mulligan, a newcomer to the staff.

Communitube had featured *Rape and Law*, an investigative study Mulligan had made while still a broadcast journalism student. Mulligan's ambition had been to become a TV reporter but he believed there was little hope of that happening. In the fall of 1973, he borrowed a portapak from UCV to make a ten-minute tape on the campus cable system that was shown closed-circuit over the system. Hooked on video, Mulligan spent half his senior-year credits on independent projects produced through the Center, one of which was a tape about what happened to a woman in the legal system after she reported a rape. When Mulligan graduated, UCV hired him as a part-time producer for the new series. "It was either going to Ottumwa, Iowa, to chase ambulances with a bolex or stay there and work half time," he explained. The choice was easy: stay and teach classes, produce documentaries, and work on a unique and innovative series for public television.[7]

In the summer of 1974, Greg Pratt came to Minneapolis as a graduate journalism student. With a few courses in photography and film behind him, he began his degree determined to do something more than sit in classes. He discovered UCV by way of the campus radio station, which was also housed at the Rarig Center. When he walked into Studio A, he found Kulczycki, Mogulescu, and cohorts madly scrambling to put a show together. Pratt started going out on some of their productions, carrying lights and cameras, observing the little whirlwind that became more and more interesting.[8]

During the first two years, everyone from the engineer to the office manager was involved in producing tapes. Everybody did everything, from making coffee to teaching classes to answering phones to editing to helping whoever walked through the door produce and edit a tape. It was part of the "allegedly" democratic nature of UCV, according to Mulligan. Although it could be frustrating, it did mean everyone felt involved. It also provided fledgling producers with an incredible technical education—learning sound, lighting, camerawork, editing—the sort of thing one rarely mastered in graduate school journalism programs. Producers were thoroughly immersed in every aspect of field production and postproduction, then passed that knowledge along to students and community members in workshop courses and production groups.[9]

The Center was constantly abuzz with talk about other documentaries seen on television or in the movie theaters. Staff would gather to watch the latest film by Fred Wiseman, a big hero, eager to see how he would lace together his stories. And they would always watch TVTV tapes, which probably had the biggest influence on their coverage of the King of Sweden's 1976 visit to Minnesota. Mostly, though, UCV distanced itself from the "tongue-in-cheek" view of America that TVTV came to represent. Their work had much more in common with the tapes of the Downtown Community Television

Center, which they followed enthusiastically because their documentaries were also broadcast nationally through the Television Lab at WNET/13. Such work always provoked discussion about the merits of documentaries as compared with what was being communicated on television news, and the ongoing debate helped to define UCV's own alternative style and content.[10]

Because UCV's ace producers were also trained journalists, they brought with them an approach to storytelling influenced by the classic television documentaries of Edward R. Murrow. More than most videomakers at the time, they started off by imitating what they thought was best in broadcast journalism, bringing a deliberateness and a professionalism to the editing process that was largely based on words. But when two producers from New York, Cara Devito and Jeffrey Kleinman, joined the staff, a new interest in "video vérité" style was added to the mix. People began experimenting with different visual styles, and all the producers went through a non-narrative phase exploring what one could do with a camera and a microphone. Jim Mulligan was tremendously influenced by vérité and remembers leaving the "CBS Reports" style of documentary and moving towards a non-narrative style which valued the "little natural moments, which you don't get with interviews and narration."[11]

Mulligan's style was kiddingly referred to as "plain view video" because he came from a little village in southern Minnesota called Plainview and because his work offered straightforward glimpses of people and situations. Mulligan was able to find unusual angles and points of view that were not being expressed in the news,[12] and his extraordinarily beautiful yet understated camera work made for some of the most visually satisfying tapes UCV produced.

The first season of "Changing Channels" extended from October 1974 to early June 1975. All but one broadcast was a half-hour mixture of art and politics; the exception was an hour-long special on *Art and Politics* profiling three groups who successfully integrated both in their work.[13] For Ron McCoy, who discovered video when process was in, UCV's new "broadcast" era brought with it a product orientation that demanded methodical interviews, written scripts, transcriptions, and rough edits. He was forced to "justify" programs on visual art, dance, or poetry to staff who wanted everything to be socially relevant and saw no merit in the careful documentation of a dance performance. UCV's ongoing struggle to integrate these two opposing positions would provide a creative tension that fueled the series throughout its four-year run.

The first 17 episodes of "Changing Channels" covered such diverse subjects as the legalization of marijuana, midwifery, rent strikes, sex shops, nuclear power, kids on speed, women's media collectives, the fall of Saigon, involuntary commitment of the mentally ill, abortion, and the business of television news. Social praxis was leavened with interludes provided by regional singers, dancers, musicians, mimes, and humorists. Because Minneapolis was a lively center for regional theater in the upper Midwest, some of the best experimental theater groups also contributed short sketches for the series. A whole new influence was introduced when Timid Video Theater, an invention of a talented student named Jeff Strait, became a frequent contributor to the series. Parodying public and network television programs, Strait produced *The Descent of Man, Mary Tacky Moore*, and *Bowling for Tenure*, among other witty spoofs. "The Mary Tyler Moore Show," which began broadcasting in September 1970, was set in a Minneapolis TV newsroom, offering the perfect subject for a "Changing Channels" retort to television programming in all its banality. Timid Video Theater's parodies allowed a different kind of critical voice, couched in gentle satire and self-parody, to enter the program.

Although McCoy prevailed in securing a toehold for arts programming, "Changing Channels" became known for its documentary achievements. Highlights from the first season included *Spray Now, Pay Later*, a 17-minute investigative report[14] produced by Jim Mulligan that asked questions about the chemical 2-4-5-T, used by utility companies, railroads, and highway departments as the cheapest and easiest way to clear brush. The tape included statements by scientists, public officials, and farmers exposed to the spraying and presented evidence that the chemical caused birth defects and cancer. Mulligan was responsible for producing some of the first reports on pesticides broadcast in the region and his later tape, *Pesticide Politics*, was submitted as evidence in hearings held by the state legislature.

Also noteworthy during the first year were the many documentaries produced in conjunction with Native American groups. *Why Wounded Knee* was made with the Wounded Knee Legal Defense–Offense Committee and featured interviews with AIM leaders like Russell Means, Dennis Banks, and Clyde Bellecourt, among others. The tape included footage from the 1974 occupation, background on the issues, and inside information on the trials of the participants.[15]

Occasionally UCV ran into trouble with KTCA and had to defend its decisions. One such case occurred over the investigation of FBI practices. In early February 1977 a broad-based group of Minnesota citizens held their own investigation into alleged improper activities of the local office of the FBI. Testimony centered on the alleged harassment of Native Americans in South Dakota, FBI infiltration in a number of local political and labor organizations, and the Bureau's involvement in the death of Black Panther leader Fred Hampton. The tape summarized the findings and recommendations from four days of hearings. KTCA's president was furious with this "people's investigation" because, as an old school journalist, he wanted to hear the FBI's response to the charges. Kulczycki argued with him, insisting that they had asked for a response and been refused and that was good enough for UCV. The tape aired.[16]

UCV staffers had no idea how difficult it would be to produce a series for television, because they all were doing it for the first time. As far as they were concerned, it was fun and exciting and difficult. They were so busy producing the show that they were lucky if they remembered to get their listing into *TV Guide* in time. They would master each episode on Monday morning and deliver it to KTCA that evening for Wednesday night airing at 10 P.M. "It was all the pressure of a television show. Are we going to get it done? 'Oh my god, this piece is not workable.' Or 'Oh my god, it doesn't transfer.' Or 'They said they were going to deliver it, but they didn't!' " Kulczycki recalled, remembering the last-minute craziness. He also remembered being sick with worry on Sunday evenings wondering whether they would make their deadline, whether there would be a show at all. Few people wondered about who was watching or how many. According to Kulczycki, when the Nielsen ratings started coming out for the station, "Changing Channels" got a 1 rating, which was impressive because the station was below measurable standards the rest of the time.[17]

During the second season, UCV produced 33 episodes for "Changing Channels." They moved beyond scan conversion, finally able to transfer their half-inch edits to quad because the university bought them a time-base corrector that stabilized the video signal for broadcast. All the equipment, including a color switcher to supply color burst and color titles for each episode, was provided by the university's Media Resources. UCV advertised in *Televisions* magazine for a video producer/facilitator to join the staff in time for the start-up of the new season. The job called for "lots of experience in teaching, video/film production, and/or community organizing." Candidates were expected to have "political consciousness about using media for social change." Women applicants were particularly welcome, and the salary range was listed as $7,500 to $9,500.[18]

UCV staffers thought of themselves as different from broadcast because they took chances others wouldn't, Kulczycki recalled. If they did a story on abortion, they would show an abortion procedure and demonstrate what would happen. This would anger many people, but a lot more would write and say, "Thanks for doing that. I'm no longer scared by the idea."[19] They were different because they were crazier, willing to serve a different set of social values than mainstream media acknowledged even existed.

During the second season, Kulczycki and Kleinman produced an exceptional documentary for the series using the new low-light nuvicon camera. *Officers of the Law* was one of the first tapes in which producers discovered the use of drama in documentary. Kulczycki, who up until then had only produced reports, felt they had finally found some tension they could stretch a story across—a Latino officer filled with so much anger that he provided the main thread for the whole structure of the story.[20]

Jeffrey Kleinman submitted the tape to the Chicago Film Festival, where it won a merit award and was seen by an audience beyond Minnesota. A year later Alan and Susan Raymond, the film team known for their shooting of the controversial PBS documentary series, "An American Family," produced their first video documentary and used a low-light camera. *The Police Tapes* followed officers of the 44th precinct in New York City on their nightly patrols; it was broadcast nationally on PBS through WNET's TV Lab. Although there was no way of knowing for sure, rumor abounded at UCV that the extraordinary similarity in subject and treatment between the two tapes was no coincidence. The Raymonds' tape—which reached a national audience first on PBS and later on ABC, winning both the Peabody and DuPont–Columbia Journalism awards—subsequently became the model for other shows, including the award-winning network drama series "Hill Street Blues" and the docploitation hit "Cops."[21]

During 1975 and 1976 UCV began to experience some opposition from the student government, which wanted to know why all University Community Video's funding was coming from the university and none of it from the community. As a result McCoy became increasingly involved in grantsmanship and management functions, responsible to a board of directors made up of students, faculty, and community representatives. As McCoy became more involved in the Corporation and less involved in the running of UCV, staff roles at UCV started shifting. Until then Kulczycki had been in charge of programming, but by 1976 Mogulescu had taken over programming, Ellen O'Neil was responsible for public access and training, and Kulczycki had become general manager of the center.[22]

In 1976 UCV produced one of their favorite tapes. The group had bought half-inch color video and had begun to experiment with it. One day two Swedish "filmmakers" walked in and wanted to make a movie. No one was especially convinced that they had ever really produced a film, but they hung around and took some classes. When they heard that the King of Sweden was coming to town to celebrate the U.S. Bicentennial, one of the fellows, whose father was in the Swedish foreign service and had diplomatic connections, was able to secure press passes to cover the event. UCV producers Jim Mulligan and Cara DeVito organized three crews to cover the king's four-day visit, later relishing the luxury of having the summer to edit the tapes. Their half-hour color tape provided behind-the-scenes coverage of King Carl XVI being toasted, dined, escorted, photographed, and applauded. *The King and Other Swedish Subjects* was one of their most popular shows, providing a witty if cynical view of some Minnesotans' obsession with pageantry, heritage, and the pursuit of royalty.

During "Changing Channels'" third season UCV began to acquire material for the series produced elsewhere, inviting people to send "works alternative in concept or execution, primarily documentaries, anywhere from 30 seconds to 10 minutes in length." So "Changing Channels" included documentaries by TVTV, the Center for Southern Folklore, the Videofreex, Optic Nerve, and other independent producers. Part of the reason for acquiring ready-made tapes was that the strain of running a busy video access center and producing a weekly series for public television had begun to tell on the staff. In 1976, the series was being produced collectively by four staffers and a continually changing nucleus of students and community members. There were no researchers, production assistants, or engineers, just one resourceful office manager, Connie Churchill, who was able to keep track of classes, people, phones, production schedules— and essentially keep the place running, a thankless job which was never really appreciated until she left.[23] Kulczycki presided over weekly production meetings where new project and program ideas were made, along with critiques of past programs. Meetings often consisted of daydreaming out loud, asking whether anybody had heard about anything interesting.[24] The decision to cut the number of episodes back to 28 was met with welcome relief.

As time passed, the balance between staff- and community-initiated tapes on "Changing Channels" gradually shifted. During the second season the split was roughly even, but by the end of the third year, the preponderance of programs were staff produced. UCV was trying to build a regular audience for the show, and as staff became more experienced and their work became more sophisticated, both technically and conceptually, more time was alloted for their work as compared with the essays and offbeat, esoteric tapes produced by community people. What UCV sacrificed for trying to upgrade the quality of the show and its content was community participation.[25]

In their last season they produced only 13 episodes, but they were among some of the series' most distinguished efforts. Greg Pratt and Jim Mulligan collaborated on a typical UCV documentary during this season, *Rural Justice: How Do You Plead?* In it they explored two diametrically opposed approaches to justice. Judge Sigwel Wood believed that there was no room for interpretation: The law spells out the punishment for crimes and prescribes the fines and jail sentences. Following the letter of the law was a judge's moral duty, according to Wood. But Judge Denis Challeen believed in restitution. The reason a person breaks the law, he thought, was because the lawbreaker felt like an outsider in the community. By working for that community, he could be rehabilitated with no drain on the community's funds to house and board him in jail. Although the fascinating dual profile presented two opposing views, it was quite clear where the producers' sympathies lay.

The program for which "Changing Channels" received the most acclaim was made during the last season. John deGraaf had been working as a newswriter for public radio in Duluth, Minnesota, when he came upon the 85-year-old John Bernard, an immigrant coal miner on Minnesota's Iron Range who became a U.S. Congressman during the New Deal. Bernard had been the lone member of Congress to challenge Franklin Roosevelt's refusal to aid Republican Spain against Franco's fascist onslaught. So deGraaf came to Minneapolis and sought out Jim Mulligan. When he proposed to Mulligan the idea of doing a program on Bernard, Mulligan said, "Sure, sounds great." With little ado, they threw the video gear into the back of a car and drove to a little film festival in northern Minnesota where Bernard was being honored. They passed a hat around to cover their expenses, netting $140 that paid for their gas and meals. After recording several hours of interviews, they came back to UCV and edited a half-hour tape, slipping in some archival film. The tape was simply structured and extraordinarily inexpensive to produce; its total cost was approximately $2,500. *A Common Man's Courage* received the Corporation for Public Broadcasting's award for best locally produced program in 1978; "Changing Channels" won for best local magazine format show, and UCV programmer Ellen O'Neil was selected best local programmer of the year.

Collaborators Mike Hazard and Greg Pratt produced another portrait tape that proved historic. Mike Hazard became interested in video just before he got married; he was extremely nervous and had no idea what to do with himself, so in 1974 he enrolled in UCV's training classes where he learned from Jim Mulligan how to plug in a portapak. His first tape was a sampler of Minnesota poets. Greg Pratt had heard Robert Bly read when he was a student at the State University of New York at Buffalo. Bly had read on the steps of the student union building while a squad of city police in full riot gear chased Vietnam War protesters across the football field. It was a moment he would never forget. Pratt and Hazard talked about doing a tape about Bly, and the result, *A Man Writes to a Part of Himself*, was the last broadcast of "Changing Channels." It was also a first for UCV: the first three-quarter-inch color show. Were it not for bad time code, which forced them to edit on three-quarter-inch equipment to make the broadcast deadline, it would have also been their first CMX edit onto two-inch tape.

Bly was adamantly opposed to television and at first refused to cooperate. He had once agreed to have a BBC team come film him at his farm in northern Minnesota. They arrived on snowmobiles, took over his home for seven days, strewed it with lights, and otherwise made themselves thoroughly objectionable as far as Bly was concerned. Had it not been for Jacob Bronowski's PBS series, "The Ascent of Man"—which proved to him that television sometimes could do something right—Bly would never have agreed to work with these two video whiz kids. It took numerous meetings with friendly go-betweens to finally persuade Bly to take the risk. Pratt was interested in doing a portrait of Bly as a person, whereas Hazard wanted to do something that accented his poetry. Their resulting compromise and collaboration, which benefited from a small grant from the state arts board, netted "Changing Channels" some of its best ratings.[26]

What made UCV work was the energy of its staff, according to Kulczycki, and "a matter of chemistry," in Mulligan's words. It was the cumulative effect of a number of talented people coming together with exceptional skills in very specific areas, people willing and able to rise to the occasion and tackle more difficult or complex subjects with each new show. It also derived from a strong work ethic that drove people to keep the wheels of production always moving, always trying to tell stories nobody else wanted to tell, always looking at situations, institutions, and people in ways they felt no one else was doing. But as UCV grew larger and more people joined the staff, the special chemistry that marked the first years began to change.

13.

Furor Over Fugitive

TVTV moved from San Francisco to Los Angeles shortly after "Gerald Ford's America" was broadcast, ostensibly because the group was going to work on "Prime Time," an 18-part series for KCET, the Los Angeles public TV station. The series, "a fictionalized account of the history of television," would be used as fillers at the end of a series of original TV dramas. TVTV was restless to move on to new and different challenges, and Los Angeles and Hollywood represented a test of their professionalism. "Fictional TV is a new direction," Megan Williams remarked. "We don't want to be known just as a documentary group. We're already into something new."[1] But there were other reasons for TVTV's move.

TVTV members had enjoyed living in San Francisco, but they had established virtually no relation to the city. All their work had been done in Houston, Miami, New York, and Los Angeles. "San Francisco gives you style and that's it," Allen Rucker said. "Maybe in the Sixties it was a place to start out, but it's not in the Seventies. . . . The culture movers in San Francisco . . . rest on what they did in the past," he added.[2] Perhaps most irritating of all was the fact that San Francisco public television had never funded any of their work. "They've been a real hassle," Megan Williams complained. "They always express interest and then back down." "Public TV is a turkey limping along not doing anything," Hudson Marquez bitterly concluded.[3]

With the move to Los Angeles, TVTV members split off to work on individual projects, pushing decentralization even further than in "Gerald Ford's America." With success came a desire to explore individual interests, and the all-for-one camaraderie of earlier productions no longer proved TVTV's guiding spirit. At the time it did not seem to be a major shift, but rather a natural progression that allowed individuals a chance to work on their own projects with the support of the group. With a contractual obligation to provide WNET with three more hours of nonfiction programming and a deal with KCET to produce what would eventually turn into *SuperVision*, TVTV decided to divide up the work.

Michael Shamberg had long wanted to do a serious journalistic interview. He and Megan Williams had made wish lists of all the people they wanted to interview for a show they called "V.I.P."— people who were impossible to get like Marlon Brando, Greta Garbo, and Patty Hearst.[4] At that time, Hearst was living underground with the Symbionese Liberation Army, and Shamberg believed an interview with the elusive "Tania" would be a sensational journalistic coup. So TVTV put out the word that they would like to do an interview with a fugitive.

Abbie Hoffman reached Shamberg one evening in March 1975 at the home of a friend, but he did not identify himself on the phone. He just said, "I hear you want to do an interview. You know who this is, don't you?" Hoffman had gone underground in April 1974 after being indicted on charges of selling cocaine. As far as Shamberg was concerned, being underground for selling cocaine was not all that fascinating. But he knew Abbie from the 1968 Convention and from the guru tape, and he knew Abbie was operating in the same underground as Hearst. Shamberg calculated that if he did a good job with Hoffman, maybe he could then get a crack at interviewing Hearst. Besides, Abbie Hoffman was a media celebrity.

In the mid-'60s, at the point when the New Left turned over to the media the capacity to anoint its leaders, Abbie Hoffman "stumbled into the spotlight."[5] Movement leaders were selectively promoted by the media, elevated to celebrity because of their flamboyance and because they knew what the media would define as news, what rhetoric they would amplify. Abbie Hoffman was one of the most famous celebrity leaders. He was also one of the least attached to any organizational base and one of the least ambivalent about his star status. As Todd Gitlin later wrote, he "used the media to invent an organization out of high spirits and whole cloth, and formulated a theory of organizing through media."[6]

Reporters loved Hoffman—whether he was strewing dollar bills on the floor of the New York Stock Exchange, being arrested for wearing an American flag, or cutting up on a TV talk show—because he was always quotable and colorful, and he guaranteed good copy. "Recognizing the limited time span of someone staring at a lighted square in their living room," he later wrote, "I trained for the one-liner, the retort jab or sudden knock-out put-ons."[7] As a cofounder of the Yippies (Youth International Party), Hoffman enticed thousands of freaks to Chicago in August 1968 to create a "Festival of Life" against the "Convention of Death." He subsequently became a codefendant in the Chicago 7 trial, providing video guerrillas and straight journalists alike with bulletins from the countercultural frontline. At times Hoffman realized the media was far from transparent, distorting and muffling reality rather than reproducing it. He later wrote of his stunts: "The goal of this nameless art form—part vaudeville, part insurrection, part communal recreation—was to shatter the [media's] pretense of objectivity . . . rouse viewers from the video stupor."[8] But more often Hoffman collaborated with the media, performing according to the media's standards for newsworthy events, "trapped in a media loop, dependent on media . . . sufferance and goodwill, . . . destined to become a cliché."[9] By trivializing the issues they were attempting to dramatize, media guerrillas like Abbie Hoffman did unintentional damage to the movement for radical social change.[10]

Michael Shamberg was a fitting match for Abbie Hoffman; Shamberg was himself a leader within the alternative video movement, with a keen sense of how to sell himself and his group. But despite his clear-sighted view of the limits of television and the necessity of creating an alternate broadcasting system, Shamberg nonetheless had committed himself to working within the broadcast world, albeit the outer circle of public television. He was determined to prove he could produce investigative journalism on a par with the networks, but on his own terms. Caught up with the celebrity status accorded TVTV's brash documentary video group, Shamberg lost sight of how dependent TVTV had become on media sufferance and good will.

Hoffman instructed Shamberg to go to a phone booth on Sunset Boulevard and Las Palmas at noon. When the phone rang, they conducted a lengthy discussion about the terms of the interview. Ron Rosenbaum, a print journalist for *New Times*[11] magazine whom Shamberg had never met, would be part of the interview, and Shamberg was to notify him. Shamberg, who was an awful camera operator, wanted to bring someone else from TVTV, but the idea was vetoed by Hoffman. There were three basic demands. Hoffman wanted $5,000 cash—$2,500 from TVTV and $2,500 from Rosenbaum and *New Times*. He also wanted a video cassette recorder from TVTV, and he wanted to keep the tapes of the interview for two weeks to review them. TVTV eventually agreed to pay the $2,500, but Rosenbaum offered only $500. They put together a package deal—$3,000 plus a video player, and left it fuzzy who would keep the tapes. The bargain was for three to four hours of tape. Shamberg insisted they be able to tell whatever transpired. If the FBI interrogated them, he did not want to have to hold anything back. And how the interview came about was part of the story, so one of the conditions was that if there was anything the underground did not want the journalists to see, they should not let them see it.

Rosenbaum and Shamberg went back to the phone booth on Sunset and Las Palmas at 7 A.M. on the appointed day. A call came telling them to go to a nearby phone booth. Shamberg was asked if they were recording the call, then he was told to instruct Rosenbaum to go down the street to a dumpster next to a motel. Their instructions would be there. In the dumpster were two airline tickets from Los Angeles to Sacramento in an envelope marked Jerusalem Travel Service; the tickets were made out in the names J.E. Ray and A.D. Bremer. James Earl Ray had assassinated Martin Luther King Jr. and A.D. Bremer shot Governor George Wallace of Alabama. "I guess," Shamberg commented later, "that's revolutionary humor."

Shamberg had kept all the negotiations secret. On D-day, Allen Rucker called Megan Williams to tell her that Michael had to go to San Francisco and would not be home until the following night. She knew by the sound of Rucker's voice that something was going on. It never occurred to her that her husband was interviewing a fugitive. Maybe he was having an affair. In all the excitement of setting up his cloak-and-dagger rendezvous, Shamberg set off without having discussed any format for the tape and without a strategy for editing it.[12]

The code name for Hoffman and for all the other underground members was Harlow. When Shamberg and Rosenbaum arrived at Sacramento airport, they were met by a couple who called themselves "Bruce and Marilyn Harlow." Both were very prim and proper looking, not noteworthy in any way. (Much later Shamberg identified them from pictures as Bernardine Dorn and Bill Ayres.)[13] When Shamberg and Rosenbaum left the airport building, they were given sunglasses that were opaqued on the inside to prevent them from seeing anything. They were then led around the parking lot, escorted into a van and asked to take off their clothes, leaving on only their underwear. Their clothes, bags, and selves were searched for transmitters, and only when they had been thoroughly inspected were they allowed to put their clothes back on. They were driven on highways for approximately three hours, finally arriving at a house where they saw only the room shown in the tape. Three other people were present but Shamberg was allowed to videotape Hoffman only.

When Abbie Hoffman went underground in 1974 he left behind the prankster concept of revolution as a lifestyle in pursuit of the pleasure principle and entered the Weather Underground, the radical splinter group of the Students for a Democratic Society. Hoffman had finally aligned himself with a group that embraced violent revolution and spelled communism with a capital C. Despite the survival of his trademark wisecracks and one-liners, Hoffman had changed. He claimed to be disguised, asserting he had had plastic surgery and was now wearing a wig and putty nose, which he touched frequently during the interview. His new physique was so convincing, he said, that he had been able to lead a middle-class life: he attended night classes, held a job, and even bribed a cop into releasing him on a minor charge. Although his appearance and mannerisms seemed unchanged, it was his attitude that seemed radically different.

Early on during the three-hour interview Rosenbaum called Hoffman's attention to a copy of *Prairie Fire*, a revolutionary tract issued by the Weather Underground the previous year. Hoffman pronounced it the most valuable theoretical contribution of the Left in the United States. Shamberg countered that *Prairie Fire* was irrelevant since few people knew about it. Hoffman then quipped he doubted few people knew when Samuel Adams, John Hancock, and the Sons of Liberty put out the *Massachusetts Spy*, joking that he was doing an ad campaign for *Prairie Fire*. Claiming that what happened in Chile could happen here, he talked about organizing cadres, which he likened to extended families. Cadres could do anything from pulling off a rent strike to bombing a building to kidnapping somebody. The next stage was the formation of an American communist party, adding that we need to defuse the word and its associations with the devil. Not only did Hoffman speak as a pawn for an extremist organization, he also acted like one, frequently interrupted by people behind closed doors who were apparently monitoring the interview and advising him on what he could say. "Some people who had known Abbie as the free-wheeling anarchist who disdained party discipline and party rhetoric," Rosenbaum later wrote, "found it disturbing to see Abbie acting like . . . a disciplined mouthpiece for tired and stilted Marxist slogans."[14]

After the interview Shamberg negotiated with the collective about their keeping the tapes for two weeks and then delivering them to him in Los Angeles. The journalists were then dropped off at the San Francisco airport. Several weeks later a woman calling herself Harlow said he could have the tapes if he erased portions of them. Shamberg met her in a motel room in Los Angeles where he had to erase three apparently insignificant sections: one where Hoffman moved his wig (because they felt it betrayed his disguise), another when he referred to being remarried, and finally Hoffman's reference to being a romantic: "I could never be a shoe salesman from Sheboygan." It was erased, Shamberg claimed, because it was ideologically offensive to shoe salesmen from Sheboygan.

Shamberg then handed over the tapes to Megan Williams and Eleanor Bingham, who transcribed and edited them. Williams found Hoffman wonderful, a real TV personality, but she was less sanguine about the structure Michael devised for the tape: having her interview him about the perils of doing the interview. "It was this whole mess, the worst," she later reflected.[15] It may have been crude and even embarrassing, but it was the only way of incorporating into the final tape Shamberg's experience of getting the interview without resorting to voice-overs. As far as Shamberg was concerned, the best part of the story was his experience of it. He had been disappointed with the interview, largely because he had been unprepared for Hoffman's manipulating it exclusively as a propaganda platform. Shamberg had expected to give Abbie some advertising time, but wrongly assumed he would cooperate and answer more direct questions about his life.[16]

In Hiding: America's Fugitive Underground—An Interview with Abbie Hoffman is a tape about the making of a tape. It is punctuated by Williams's interview with Shamberg, who explains the process of taping the interview, and by her frequent comments questioning the veracity of Hoffman's statements (such as, did he have plastic surgery?) and suggestions of alternate explanations. This doubtful posture was essential if TVTV was not to look like a shill for the radical underground.

Shamberg was committed to the idea that TVTV's work was journalistically sound and nonjudgmental. As video guerrillas, TVTV appeared to be aligned with the Left and the counterculture, and yet closer scrutiny of tapes like *Four More Years* and *The Lord of the Universe* demonstrate that the counterculture was subjected to TVTV's jaundiced eye as much as, and maybe even more than, members of the establishment. "There was Shamberg: businesslike, professional, terribly serious, hedging his bets, and generally playing the heavy," wrote Ingrid Wiegand, "the perfect foil to Hoffman's loose, light, fast, clever, intuitive image—a contemporary version of the free spirit on videotape."[17] Shamberg came down especially hard on Hoffman at the end of the interview. Hoffman had frustrated all attempts to get him to answer direct questions. He surmised that the FBI now would redouble their efforts to find him, and Shamberg asked him point-blank: "Do you think anybody cares if you're a fugitive?" Hoffman glared at him, then replied, "How do you want me to respond? Hostilely? You care. What the fuck are you sitting here? You just risked your life."

This burst of venom was uncharacteristic for Hoffman. Seen in hindsight, his precarious mental state is discernible in comments during the interview. When Rosenbaum asks if he is addicted to being a fugitive, Hoffman protests, saying he wasn't happy in his former life and had his bags packed since 1970. "I had a fucking amulet with cyanide that I wore for a necklace for about three months." But then he makes a joke, adding, "There's a dybbuk inside, you know, greased with chicken soup that says 'survive, survive.' " Shamberg wondered about Hoffman's insistence that he had never felt better and was not surprised to learn a year later, reading an interview with Hoffman in *Playboy*, that Hoffman had a mental breakdown after their cloak-and-dagger interview, screaming from a motel room in Las Vegas that he was Abbie Hoffman.[18]

David Loxton and one WNET lawyer were the only people who knew about the project.[19] Shamberg had made an executive decision when he negotiated with Hoffman, but he had conferred with Loxton and had left the decision with the executive producer whether to cancel the program at that stage. Loxton gave him the green light but insisted that all the terms be revealed in the tape to avoid having it become a "smoking gun issue." They were all aware of the potential risk of seeming to be aiding a fugitive, but WNET's lawyer assured them they were on safe ground. They kept all knowledge about the tape to a minimum to forestall the FBI from descending on them before the show was aired; as a result no one at the station was prepared when all hell broke loose after news of the financial deal between Shamberg and Hoffman was made public at the press screening on May 16, the Friday before airdate.

The press screening generated tremendous excitement for the show, and Loxton and Shamberg were sure of praise for a journalistic and television coup. The following Monday, both the Associated Press and United Press International ran news items on the interview, highlighting some of Hoffman's more witty one-liners and sensational statements. UPI emphasized Hoffman's claim that he could find Patty Hearst[20] and AP underscored his preference for life underground.[21] *The New York Times* ran a news story by Paul L. Montgomery headlined "Abbie Hoffman Speaks of Life in 'Underground.' "[22] The item squeezed details of the financial arrangements for the interview into the eleventh paragraph. In that same issue was John J.

O'Connor's review of *In Hiding*,[23] which proved consistent with all his reviews of TVTV's work: disinterested praise ("the result is complex, often fascinating") tempered by pointed criticism. O'Connor was the first in print to link the tape with charges of "checkbook journalism," but he made a special case for TVTV's handling of Hoffman and the issues posed.

Calling the tape "one of the more bizarre journalistic undertakings of recent times," O'Connor branded the payments and censorship arrangements as "highly suspect," raising basic questions that "demand serious examination and debate." "Is television—no matter how cautious or well-meaning—being used for the purposes of self-styled fugitives?" O'Connor asked. Yet earlier in the review he had written: "The great ripoff artist has himself been ripped off by this documentary. Mr. Hoffman has been reduced to a bit player in a production that is clearly more interested in making a statement about something that might be called the 'video process.'" Finding Shamberg's recapitulation of the interview scenario "the most interesting section of the hour," O'Connor concluded that, "given its multitextured format," *In Hiding* could probably "muster an impressive case for the defense" of all charges brought against it.

When Fred Friendly, former CBS news director and broadcasting consultant at the Ford Foundation (one of the funders of WNET's TV Lab), learned about the payments made to Hoffman, he "screamed bloody murder," Loxton later recalled.[24] Friendly expressed "revulsion" at the Ford Foundation's identification with the program and sought assurance that no Ford monies had been used to pay Hoffman, "which, if not illegal, is unethical for a broadcaster to do," he told reporters.[25] Network officials quickly joined Friendly in publicly denouncing the payment, claiming ignorance of the terms until the press screening. The issue of "checkbook journalism" rapidly deflected any further discussion of the journalistic merits of the actual interview, which few of its detractors appeared to have seen. *In Hiding* was yanked from the network schedule at the last minute and a rerun of a United Nations concert was plugged in for the national feed. The reason given to WNET was that there was not enough time to "work through" the Hoffman show.[26] In the end, the only stations to air *In Hiding* were WNET in New York and KQED in San Francisco, which chose this moment to demonstrate support for TVTV.

George Page, WNET's director of program administration, leveled the blame at TVTV for having failed to inform station officials of how this program came about. Page ominously stated: "What this obviously does, regretfully, is color our future relations with TVTV." Curiously the name of David Loxton, director of WNET's TV Lab, never appeared in any of the news stories. Shamberg shouldered responsibility for the decision to pay Hoffman, commenting:

> We didn't want to pay anything, because we don't believe in paying for a story. But I began to question whether this was different from any other kind of program packaging, which the producer exploits and for which the participants are paid their fair share.
>
> Lectures, consultancy and performance are usually valid grounds for payment in our TV culture, and that was what we got from Hoffman. Some of the money went to defray his expenses in connection with the show.[27]

What fanned the flames of the "checkbook journalism" charge was the recent controversy over Mike Wallace's payment of $50,000 to H.R. Haldeman for a two-part interview on "60 Minutes." Haldeman was former White House chief of staff in the Nixon administration. Les Brown, writing in *The New York Times*, explained why the analogy between the two cases did not hold and not just because of the discrepancy in sums of money.

> Mr. Hoffman received his money from a freelance production company anxious to be noticed while Mr. Haldeman made his deal with a major news organization with specific policies against buying news exclusives. . . . CBS News justified paying Mr. Haldeman on the ground that it was purchasing a memoir by someone of "historical importance."[28]

Needless to say, Brown's bias is readily apparent in his "objective" report.

Both Shamberg and Rosenbaum defended their decisions. Shamberg stated:

> We wanted the Hoffman interview because we have always chosen to cover what does not normally get on the air. Whether we like it or not, there's a fugitive underground in this country that keeps the FBI busy, and that's a subject that seems worth some exploration on television.

Rosenbaum added, "It is possible to do a story on Haldeman by talking to his neighbors and friends, but you can't do that kind of story with a fugitive, so we did what was necessary to get it.[29]

WNET's lawyer Gregory Ricca explained that the station paid Hoffman just as it paid other people to appear on programs. "The honorarium is the oldest thing in the book," he commented. "Based on available case law, we were satisfied that we were not aiding and abetting a criminal, even with the payment of money."[30]

But the controversy raged on and drew in new players. Senator

James L. Buckley, a Conservative from New York, demanded that the Federal Communications Commission and the Corporation for Public Broadcasting investigate the $2,500 payment to Hoffman. Buckley, in a letter to FCC chairman Richard E. Wiley, claimed the sum enabled Hoffman "to continue to escape justice." His letter to Henry Loomis, president of the Corporation for Public Broadcasting, which distributes federal monies to public television stations, called for an inquiry into whether any of the $2,500 came from CPB's annual authorization to WNET.[31] In response, WNET officials emphasized that the money used was from neither the Ford Foundation nor the Rockefeller Foundation (which also was given a donor's credit). Nor would they agree that any "public money" had been used, claiming it came out of the station's "discretionary fund," which comes from various sources including corporate grants and public subscriptions.[32]

Fred Friendly, who (according to *Variety*) "blew his top" over WNET's airing of the interview, threatened to reconsider the Ford Foundation's outstanding grants—totalling several million dollars— to WNET.[33] Friendly was also quoted as calling the tape "a nonstory" and labeling Hoffman "an electronic pickpocket who is ripping off the medium."[34] Although he claimed that his anger over the payment did not enter into his judgment that Hoffman was not a newsworthy subject,[35] Friendly's self-righteous views on journalistic standards clashed with the Public Broadcasting System's own "Document of Journalism Standards and Guidelines" (1971). These standards recognized "the obligation to reflect voices both inside and outside society's consensus," noting that "Today's dissent may be tomorrow's orthodoxy . . . [and] to re-examine these ideas critically is part of the broadcaster's role; he cannot fulfill it if he does not conscientiously attempt to understand those ideas—and the forces that created them."[36] John Jay Iselin, then president of WNET, played politician, seemingly concurring with Friendly when he said the program was more "a happening than a news piece," but going on record to support Shamberg as "a very promising guy." Iselin also told reporters he encouraged department heads to take chances and "be daring," indicating that he believed those executives who knew about the project acted properly, in a veiled reference to Loxton's role.[37]

Ironically, the reason *In Hiding* was scheduled on such short notice was because WNET needed a replacement for a Swedish documentary, "Harlem: Voices, Faces," which was withdrawn a week before airdate in response to pressure from African-American groups. The Swedish documentary was later shown with a neutralizing wraparound panel discussion to "balance out" the negative aspects that stirred Black ire.[38]

Not everyone was convinced the reason for pulling the Hoffman interview revolved around "checkbook journalism." Ingrid Wiegand, writing for the *Soho Weekly News*, praised Shamberg's work and suggested that Hoffman's promo for the revolutionary Left was far more persuasive than public television or the American public could bear.

> Most of all . . . Hoffman implied a sense of true family: a sense of closeness, mutual concern, real responsibilities, seriously fulfilled authority and purpose evenly distributed among peers. . . . What they [channel 13 and the Ford and Rockefeller Foundations] are really crying about . . . is that their real enemy—not merely Hoffman—had a major propaganda victory . . . by displaying . . . a fully-lived way of life with clearly a minimum of material goods on a major television station.[39]

Wiegand, herself a video artist, was the only observer to suggest that the meaning of life underground was really about a new concept of family. Her analysis betrayed an unsophisticated grasp of the political ideologies that separated the Weather Underground from earlier experiments in collective lifestyles. During the '60s, the counterculture had offered many lost souls a sense of belonging to a collective family as a diversity of groups flourished. For nearly ten years, video freaks had created extended nontraditional families that often served as the principle reason for an individual's joining the video scene. If anything, this cultural impulse toward collectivity was about to reverse itself, a reality that was just beginning to be evident in TVTV's own relaxation of its identity as a collective entity. Wiegand's theory that the establishment was afraid of the dangerous power of the far Left's message remains unconvincing. By 1975 the allure of the counterculture and its one-time media celebrities had faded as the media moved on to new subjects and the new Left witnessed its gradual disintegration.

Wiegand reported that Shamberg had received death threats from the Left "for ripping Abbie off." Scorned by the media establishment and by the Left, Shamberg was badly shaken.[40] His ambition to prove himself a hard-nosed, serious, investigative journalist was extinguished by the tempest stirred up by Friendly's attacks. Shamberg, the driving force behind TVTV's aspirations to be journalistically sound, never tried journalism again.

14.

Living Newsletter?

Broadside TV was vulnerable to any changes in the communications environment, and in 1974 a change was forged that ultimately announced Broadside's demise: the FCC rescinded its requirement that CATV operators provide locally originated programming. Since this mandate had been the only incentive for the local cable industry to cooperate with Broadside's grand scheme, the ruling wiped out narrowcast programming virtually overnight—not just in Appalachia but throughout the nation. New rules went into effect on January 6, 1975, eliminating the local-origination ruling and adopting new rules requiring any cable system with 3,500 or more subscribers to have equipment for local cable programs, including non-operator production—what was commonly called public access.[1] Within a year, Broadside's funding from CATV operators was cut in half, and in two years it was gone.[2]

When the FCC was considering revising its rulings on local origination and public access, little was said in support of local-origination programming by citizen groups which opted to defend public access. The FCC had issued a strongly worded attack against public access, noting demands for "excessive" amounts of equipment, programming and engineering personnel, and funds for programming were "franchise bargaining chips rather than serious community access efforts." The National Black Media Coalition responded by noting, "The Commission seems terribly concerned with the burden that access may put on the cable systems, but unconcerned with effectively promoting and safeguarding meaningful access to cable for the citizens who are its users and viewers."

Ninety percent of those filing comments rejected the proposition that cable operators should be required to produce local programming. Cities and states opposed the rule, because they argued it was not a matter for federal jurisdiction. Among the "public interest" filings,

RAND Corporation staffers and officials at the Cable Television Information Center filed as individuals and called for elimination of mandatory local-origination provisions in favor of requiring access. Also in opposition were the Office of Communication of the United Church of Christ and the Consumers Union; both groups urged that origination be allowed only when a system provides competitive access to channels. Among the few groups favoring local origination were the National Black Media Coalition, the Philadelphia Community Cable Coalition, and the cities of Somerville and Pittsfield, Massachusetts. Without adequate understanding of how local-origination requirements could be used to further community cable productions, little support was marshalled to counter the greed of the cable operators.[3]

Carpenter had targeted July 4, 1976, as Broadside's date for financial independence.[4] It had seemed realistic; in 1974 Broadside had a budget of more than $12,000 from each cable system and Carpenter expected to double that amount in 1975. Instead, 1976 saw Broadside begging for grants and contracts, anything but independent. Carpenter formed a board of directors to help raise money, and in the audio recording[5] of that first board meeting Carpenter's voice was strained as he explained the financial picture.

Broadside's original two-year seed grant from the Appalachian Regional Commission had run out, and a grant from the Lily Foundation—given at the prompting of the Ford Foundation—had been spent quickly on new equipment. Carpenter had spent nearly half of the first two year's income on equipment, since none of the federal support could be used for this essential and costly staple. Once the cable support evaporated, the Ford Foundation provided a two-year recoverable grant of $40,000; however, that money was virtually untouchable, because it went straight into the bank to help Broadside handle its cash-flow problems, and technically it was supposed to be returned to Ford. Were it not for that Ford money, Carpenter grimly confided to the Board, "we wouldn't be meeting here today." Carpenter soberly announced he anticipated a $30,000 deficit for that year.

Under the new FCC ruling, cable operators no longer had to develop local programs or buy them, but they were required to provide community producers access to system equipment, and they had to make time available for community tapes to be shown. Forced to depend on this revised public access clause, Carpenter explained to his board that the cable operators could not charge Broadside for channel time because it was a nonprofit organization, but they could make a modest charge for use of their equipment. This complete reversal of fortunes must have proved awfully bitter to the entrepreneurial Carpenter, who not long before had the cable operators at his beck and call. Having scorned access, Carpenter ironically was now dependent upon it if any of Broadside's work was to be narrowcast.

Without economic and programming clout with the cable systems, Broadside now had to grapple with censorship. No longer required to carry local productions, some cable operators began objecting to Broadside's programming, singling out individual shows on the basis of their content. One cable operator in Bristol censored a tape on a community grocery co-op, calling it a socialistic, communist activity. The co-op was funded by the local Human Development Corporation and was an Office of Economic Opportunity project. Carpenter confided to the Board that part of the reason for the man's objection was that he was in a bad mood that day, but Carpenter still had to fight it out with him in order to get the program on.[6]

Demoralized, Carpenter left Broadside in 1975 to head the newly formed National Citizen's Committee for Broadcasting in Washington, D.C., and work with former FCC Commissioner Nicholas Johnson.[7] Carpenter kept in touch with Broadside for a time and was deeply distressed that with his departure, many of Broadside's funders withdrew their support. Having laid the foundation and framework for an innovative institution, Carpenter wanted that structure to endure without its being tied to his personal involvement. He made that argument with the funders before he left, but it was not heard, and he came to resent the foundation world for its fickleness and shortsightedness.[8]

Carpenter had been a benevolent dictator, according to several Broadside staffers. After him, no one had the vision, the administrative ability, or the clout with funders to be able to run Broadside as it had been designed to function. Succeeding directors[9] managed to keep Broadside's doors open three more years. A few projects still had money, like the SAVES project, and for a time Broadside simply functioned around it.

Broadside affected the lives of most of the people who worked there, and they in turn affected others. Jo Carson had grown up in Johnson City but left after college and lived in New York. When she returned to the region, she knew little about her own culture. Working at Broadside and discovering Highlander "changed her life." Watching tapes about strip mining's destruction of the Cumberlands at a Highlander video workshop, she began her education in the issues of her region and what she could do about them. "I don't know anywhere else I would have gotten the education so fast," she recalled.[10]

As Broadside's school coordinator, Carson taught teachers and students how to make video. A slight woman, she never was physically strong enough to be a very good cameraperson herself, but she made an impact of a different kind. She remembered a child with poor grades who hooked up with the school's video club, proving to be, at the age of ten, an extraordinary videomaker. She worked with him on most Saturdays for about a year and a half, collecting him at home and bringing him to Broadside where together they would edit. It never mattered what they worked on. "He simply excelled at editing, and there had never been anything that he excelled at before. To find something you excel at and then not be allowed to do it," Carson recalled, pausing, "well, it is really crushing. So I just felt like that was really important."

When things got financially tight at Broadside, it was harder for staff like Carson to pursue Broadside's original philosophical goals. She was working on a tape about country historians, shooting it on weekends because the feeling at the time was that staff should be working on what was going to pay. She was able to interview two elderly historians within months of their deaths. But the videotapes were "lost"—stolen from her desk by another staffer who routinely rifled desks looking for tape to recycle for use on paying jobs.

Despite the presence of women on staff like Carson, director Gregg, production manager Darlene Mastro, and producer Phyllis Scalf, Broadside resembled many other video collectives of the era, basically a "good ole boy" organization in which a few women worked hard but were rarely acknowledged for their contributions.[11]

By 1977 Broadside's equipment was nearly shot and there was no money for its upkeep. Broadside had made the big move from half-inch to three-quarter inch, and refurbishing would have required a huge investment. Fixing things was like putting Band-Aids on Band-Aids, according to part-time camera operator Ray Moore. Moore, a native of East Tennessee, had been in the Peace Corps in Africa and with the teacher corps in Shelby County, Tennessee. He recalled how poor the control room equipment had become and how the cable line from Broadside to the head end would frequently short out. Broadside was tied to project-oriented funding, and the money just did not go far enough to take care of all the necessities. In a desperate search for paying projects, Broadside even resorted to taping Sunday services at a local Baptist church for $50 each week. Beset by numerous problems, Broadside struggled on.

Although unrestricted blocks of funding had allowed Broadside flexibility in following the newspaper model—which could encompass

Friday-night wrestling, regional music, and issue-oriented social documentaries—without ample cable monies the concept eventually devolved into something more expedient than high minded. When money came in, regardless of its source, it was spent on whatever was needed—rent, salaries, equipment repair, and so on. This triage approach to budget management eventually backfired, because when it came time to deliver on a contract, the resources often were gone. Grants posed another problem: For example, Broadside would ask for, say, $30,000 and the grant would be awarded for $15,000, half the sum. Broadside could not afford to do the work for half the money, but it also could not afford to turn it down, so the grant would be taken while Broadside cut corners to find a less expensive way of realizing the project. (Broadside was not alone in this predicament, since chronic underfunding haunts most nonprofits to this day.) Moore eventually became concerned about Broadside's growing lack of accountability to its funders and brought his concerns to the board. "Things decrease at an increasing rate," Moore tersely observed.

At the end Broadside's sole priority was getting on cable every night, with project funds "milked" to insure this. People in the community were puzzled. They did not understand nonprofit organizations, and wondered about where the money was coming from and what was in it for the sponsors. Some may have thought Broadside was a front for some dubious enterprise. And long hair was not looked on kindly by many people from Appalachia's rural and conservative communities. Even Broadside supporters like George Stoney were confused by its neutral role in helping people tell their stories, regardless of their points of view. When Broadside produced a program on prison reform for a conservative community group, liberals like Stoney were bewildered by Broadside's apparent betrayal of progressive values.[12] Anyone sporadically viewing Broadside's programs would have gotten a very skewed idea of what views it represented. Although Broadside remained highly visible on cable and in the surrounding communities until the very end, no scientific polling of audiences was ever done, so it is not clear how many people actually watched Broadside or understood what it was all about.[13]

One of Broadside's last acts was a serious, though unsuccessful, bid for the allocation of a public service broadcast channel in the Johnson City area. Broadsider intimate and longtime observer Ski Hilenski insisted this act left the Tennessee Educational Television network "quaking in its boots," but Broadside camera operator Ray Moore recollects it differently, asserting that the local press opposed Broadside's bid, publishing derogatory editorials that typified them as a bunch of amateurs who were incapable of handling broadcast channel business. Perhaps the worst dismissal was the charge that they did not represent the community.

Broadside's demise was the result of a number of factors. Apart from obvious problems posed by the fluctuations of cable fortunes, fickle funding sources, and erratic staffing was a fundamental philosophical problem inherent in the folk society model on which Broadside was built. According to Hilenski,[14] the model depended on the notion that economic and cultural specialization—the dominant characteristics of urban–industrial society—was absent in folk societies. This then perpetuated the false notion of Appalachia as a homogeneous culture and society, denying the region's historical pluralism and the dynamics of biculturalism. Ironically, while Broadside was propounding this theory, it was participating in events that contradicted the validity of these assumptions. If mountaineers had ready access to "experience, language, and ideas when it comes to their own vital interests," then there would have been no need for Broadside to function as mediator between city officials, area residents, city planners, senior citizens, and housing officials in a Johnson City urban renewal project or to present the views of farmers, coal miners, mine owners, and TVA spokespersons to legislators in Washington, D.C. As valuable as such interventions were, they were not examples of mountain people participating in their own learning. This was not a case of people of the region sharing experiences with people like themselves; rather, quite the opposite was occurring. And in some instances, racial differences also played a key factor in such exchanges. Additionally, the funding Broadside received largely involved the pitching of a curriculum, message, or some form of enlightenment other than self-enlightenment. Even programs produced expressly about folkways, crafts, and lore, such as the SAVES productions, were recorded and preserved not for regional people to share with each other but rather for scholars, students, and nebulous future generations of Americans. To what extent this inconsistency between underlying philosophy and actual practice served to undermine Broadside is impossible to gauge. The irony is the Alinsky model that Carpenter repudiated (in which outside organizers forcefully martial a community behind its program, only to discover that, once they leave and the original funding dries up, the model collapses) describes Broadside's tactics better than the folk school approach of self-sustaining self-empowerment.

Broadside TV's "electronic folk school" experiment may have been a chapter in the history of outsider benevolence toward Appalachia, which in the end was defeated,[15] but it was an honorable chapter. Were it not for the change in the FCC's cable rulings, it is possible that Broadside TV could have become a thriving example of decentralized, community-based, alternative media today. If it failed to achieve a naive and perhaps romantic view of folk society enlightenment, it nonetheless succeeded, however briefly, in aligning all the resources of the region—a social alignment of individuals and institutions never before assembled in Appalachia. Through the agency of portable video, cable television, creative thinking, and entrepreneurial leadership, Broadside TV offered a powerful vision for a new community and culture in Appalachia.

15.

The Good Times Are Killing Me

While Michael Shamberg was preoccupied with arranging cloak-and-dagger adventures underground, Paul Goldsmith was at work realizing a long-standing dream. The veteran documentary film cameraman had been trying to raise money to do a film about Cajun music when he first met up with TVTV. Goldsmith, who spent summers as a boy in Louisiana, had shot a short documentary on Cajuns for French TV in 1972 and was convinced there was a richer, deeper story to tell. When WNET offered TVTV the contract to make five hours of programming, the understanding was that Goldsmith's Cajun project would be one of those hours. Not only was it agreeable to David Loxton, who was attracted to the idea of doing a music program in color, but the station was pleased with TVTV's interest in something other than politicians.[1]

TVTV members were also excited. After four months of wearing neckties and dresses, begging for meetings with Washington bureaucrats for "Gerald Ford's America," TVTV was ready to take off for the country. Shamberg, the supreme strategist, was not interested in the show. "He doesn't like to hang out with country people; he doesn't like music; he isn't interested in something that isn't the center of power—so he didn't feel that he was missing anything," Goldsmith remembered.[2] But Hudson Marquez, who grew up in Louisiana,[3] had his bags packed and so did Wendy Appel and Allen Rucker.

In February 1975, TVTV went on location in southwest Louisiana to cover the music and lifestyle of Cajun culture. They conceptualized the program as an experiment combining high-quality music with color documentary videotape in an entertainment format. Pioneering technological innovations had become a matter of course for Goldsmith as TVTV's ace cameraperson. But here his first concern was music. Goldsmith originally thought of doing a stereo simulcast and approached Mal Albaum, WNET's head engineer, with the idea. But since WNET had limited postproduction audio facilities, TVTV was told they would need to transfer video to film to do the multitrack audio mix. The cost and technical complexity was prohibitive, so instead they chose to upgrade and mutate their new color production system.[4]

TVTV took a new Sony color camera and a 31-pound cassette deck that produced a higher quality video signal than half-inch and offered two-track audio. For low-light shooting, TVTV installed a black-and-white nuvicon tube in one camera, an improvement over the tivicon that had been used in Washington. Sound was recorded on a Nagra tape recorder with a variety of sensitive microphones, the first time crystal synch sound was used with portable video.[5] Goldsmith also designed a modification for the camera, adapting the viewfinder so that the camera could rest on the cameraperson's shoulder; this made it easier to hand hold by centering the camera's weight over the operator's body. This not only allowed TVTV to mount a heavier zoom lens on the camera, but it also enabled the cameraperson to face the subject instead of being obscured behind the rig. Having adapted their equipment, TVTV was now prepared to take it to the musicians, not the other way around. This seemed important because Cajuns were not recording-studio musicians.[6]

The Cajuns of southwest Louisiana were the descendants of French-speaking Acadians exiled from Nova Scotia by the British in 1755. Over the years their cultural vitality had been enhanced by intermarriage with Indians, Black slaves,[7] and later immigrants to the region. Geographically isolated, the Cajuns had maintained their cultural traditions and distinct language, but after World War II inroads of mainstream American culture threatened their survival, and the term "Cajun" became synonymous with "hick." Music was the "glue" of Cajun culture, played in dance halls, bars, and homes and at holiday celebrations like Mardi Gras. With new interest in American folk music in the '60s, appreciation of Cajun music had led to a reappraisal of Cajun traditions and respect for their endangered heritage.[8]

TVTV spent the month leading up to Mardi Gras in Cajun country, living in cabins in a trailer camp which were rented for $25 a week.[9] They gathered with a group of Cajuns every Thursday night to eat homemade food, drink, and play cards. TVTV deftly used the local media to familiarize the community with them, appearing on local radio programs and even writing a profile of themselves for a local newspaper. They represented themselves as interested in Cajun culture, which they characterized as "highly evolved."[10] Unlike outside media which "usually mishandled and exploited Cajuns,"[11] according to TVTV, they had no particular point to make, but rather wanted to "capture the feeling of the community and the way people live," allowing people to "speak for themselves."[12] Despite such disclaimers, when the production was completed, a WNET press release declared TVTV's production was "a bittersweet impression of proud, poor people caught in an isolated, unassimilated culture that now seems stopped in time."[13]

TVTV arranged big outdoor dinners of gumbo or sauce piquant for any musician they were interested in taping. After wining and dining them, instead of trying to get good footage of them, TVTV set up monitors so that people could watch themselves while they played their music into the night. Using a tried-and-true method to break the ice and enlist community support,[14] TVTV employed video's instant feedback to ingratiate themselves in the Cajun community. When TVTV was about to leave the region, they hired a dance hall for a "good bye, thank you" screening, showing eight hours of unedited tape to the 250 people who turned out for the event.[15]

"Essentially we went down there to record the music of the Balfa Brothers, Nathan Abshire (Mr. Accordion), and Boissec (a black Cajun musician)," Wendy Appel told critics later. "We also wanted to capture the local Mardi Gras festival, which is a country Mardi Gras as opposed to the one we're all familiar with down in New Orleans."[16] When they encountered Abshire, they realized they had found "an archetypical American folk hero" and the central character for the tape. They felt "Mr. Accordion" was outgoing and intuitively musical, with a natural presence that telegraphed "star" video material.[17] He reminisced about the beginning of his musical career when, at the age of six, he disobeyed his uncle's orders and played his accordion until he was caught and whipped. "That was a long time ago," said Nathan, laughing and shaking his head, "a long time ago."

Behind Abshire's lively music and jovial demeanor lay a sad story. Abshire was a fabulous musician and songwriter who had never made it, even though his music was known around the world. He had to support himself by working as a watchman at the city dump, an increasingly arduous job for a man in his sixties. But that was not the real problem. His adopted son, the joy of his life, had been arrested for robbing a drugstore and was in jail. After 18 years of sobriety, Abshire had started drinking once again. "I've never been in jail in my life," he lamented. "All the time I try to make a strict living. If it's not mine, I don't want it. My life is no more."

Critics pronounced Abshire's story the stuff of American tragedy,[18] "a sobering antidote to the manicured 'real-life problems' of the soap-opera folk."[19] *Washington Post* critic Tom Shales captured the poignancy of Abshire's disillusionment along with a fine feeling for TVTV's approach:

> Not until the end of the program do we find that Mr. Accordion is a truly troubled man. . . . Nathan himself says he is tired of his music and doesn't understand the way the world is going. He breaks down, weeping, at a local bar. . . . Earlier he seemed satisfied, especially when glimpsed on his ramshackle front porch, playing his music, an old washing machine sitting in the front yard and a cat sauntering by. One is struck by the beauty of this image and by the fact that television is capable of such beauty. Suddenly, it also seems that journalism has the potential to be art.[20]

Goldsmith invited his old film partners, Petur Hliddal and Robby Kenner, to work on the tape; he also asked Dave Myers, a "legendary" film camera operator who joined the crew to tape during Mardi Gras week. More than any other TVTV tape, *The Good Times Are Killing Me* bore the imprint of filmmaking, including several scenes scripted in advance. For example, the opening consisted of a series of edits which begins with an aerial shot that zooms into a car on the highway, dissolves through a driving shot that arrives at C.C.'s Lounge, zooms in and dissolves through again to Dewey Balfa who is broadcasting a live music show on the radio.[21]

During their stay, each crew member was responsible for "hanging out" with one character and keeping track of his or her story. While the guys hung out in bars, Wendy Appel and Suzanne Tedesco (the only women in the crew) took their camera to Priscilla Fontenot's beauty parlor, the only one in Basile. They taped there every Thursday and Friday as women came in for their weekly appointments.[22] The ladies let their hair down while Priscilla teased it up, telling ribald jokes and confessing their secret desires. "I was brought up real strict, but it never did any good," confided Priscilla. "Elvis! He's beautiful! He's the onliest man I ever wanted beside my husband. He really tempted me. I want to lock him up and attack him every five minutes! Gets my husband mad when I say that." Branded a riotous and hilarious sequence, Priscilla's beauty parlor was relished by critics like Judy Flander, a *Washington Star* staff writer, who wrote: "a few four-letter words are bleeped out, but the raw and free language expressed in melodious Cajun and the sexual overtones of everyday life are the strongest I've ever heard on television."[23] "We get plenty of barbershops and saloons on TV but no beauty parlors," wrote Phil

Perlman in *Millimeter*. "It's refreshing to see the ladies in their own environment and find out that they, too, can tell bad dirty jokes, be quite frank with one another about their love life, and at the same time mother the children who're waiting while 'Mommy' gets her hair done."[24]

The search for material led TVTV to Mardi Gras organizational dinners; during one of these events Paul Goldsmith met Louis, son of the co-owner of Mamou's only bank, who was planning to dress up as a black female nurse for his Mardi Gras costume.[25] If Abshire evokes Faulkner, then Louis comes on like a character from Tennessee Williams. Immediately after being introduced as "The Banker's Son," TVTV takes us into Louis's bedroom at his parents' home, where he is stepping into a 42C brassiere and being made up and fitted in a wig by his mother. Although it is a dress rehearsal for Mardi Gras, TVTV withholds this detail for so long that some viewers wondered whether transvestism was an everyday event. Subsequent scenes of actual Mardi Gras festivities, which included chasing and strangling chickens, wild horseback riding, and drinking until paralyzed, painted a portrait of Cajuns that was far from glowing, leaving room to question TVTV's reasons for failing to make certain basic facts clear.

Seven weeks after they arrived in the bayou towns of Mamoo, Eunice, and Basile, TVTV departed with 80 hours of tape. They traveled to New York with an unfinished rough edit and spent an unbudgeted six weeks polishing it before going into the final quad edit, which was done in segments and assembled with musical interludes connecting them. TVTV principals like Michael Shamberg also helped structure the tape. Not only was the tape slick in its sound quality—the music tracks were Dolbyized and dubbed to quad in sync with the video—but new special effects equipment now available for video editing allowed them two-color titles, black-and-white colorization, shot reversals, and slowmotion. They also used a Rutt/Etra synthesizer to fade into a map of Louisiana. The final edit was done in a 29-hour marathon that finished hours before the scheduled press screening. The total cost of the show was about $45,000. Direct production costs in Louisiana came in at $21,000; $11,000 went for TVTV's personnel salaries and overhead; and the balance, $13,000, went to WNET for postproduction, which was the only part that went significantly over budget.[26]

The program was aired first in New York on Monday, June 23, with a national feed scheduled for Wednesday, June 25. After the harsh reception given *In Hiding*, TVTV needed a critical comeback if they were to maintain their good standing with PBS and stand a chance of getting renewed funding for another year of programming. John O'Connor devoted only a portion of his *New York Times* review on Monday to *The Good Times Are Killing Me*, but his response was favorable. Calling Nathan Abshire's story "gently moving," he judged that "the documentary captures something of pure, intriguing experience." Curiously, after leading the review with a reference to the wall of criticism that greeted TVTV's prior tape, O'Connor ventured to suggest that: "Tonight's portrait of some Louisiana cajuns is not likely to trigger a similar uproar, although a prefatory note warns that it is 'recommended for a mature audience.' "[27] O'Connor's prophecy proved way off the mark.

Although a number of critics were enthusiastic about the show, an outraged review by Arthur Unger, the esteemed television critic of the *Christian Science Monitor*, attacked the program:

> In a series of interviews which on the whole constitute insulting and belittling intrusions, the camera crew managed to demean just about every person with whom it came into contact. All in all, the program proceeded to record a people whose major activity seems to be drinking and carousing, telling dirty jokes, dressing up in grotesque costumes for the Mardi Gras and, for good measure, killing chickens—all on camera.[28]

Unger's ire was so potent that, on the strength of it, many public television stations in the South declined to air the program. *The Good Times Are Killing Me* reportedly never aired in Louisiana, so the Cajuns never saw it themselves.[29]

Some critics excused the excesses shown as a necessary outlet from the repressions of Cajun society.[30] Tom Shales, who was largely enthusiastic about the tape, offered this criticism of the tapemakers:

> The basis of the TVTV approach is selective information, of course: this is not all there is to know about the Cajuns and their culture, but is a haunting, moving and profound impression. Unfortunately, the program risks just the sort of "over-interpretive" approach it is trying to counter by failing to make certain basic facts clear, by occasional cutesy editing and by cluttering the screen with irritating titles, subtitles, and superimposed introductory material.[31]

Having called attention to such flaws, Shales dismissed them by attributing them to "daring, not lapsing into the safely trite or of underestimating the intelligence of an audience." He went even further to predict that "what TVTV is doing looks and feels very much like the television of the future. The prospects are exhilarating."[32] By excusing TVTV's flaws, Shales shifted attention from further scrutiny of the intentions of the tapemakers. What was TVTV's attitude toward the people they had lived with, drunk with, and made music on tape with for seven weeks?

Paul Goldsmith told Phil Perlman in an article in *Millimeter*: "Usually TVTV deals in topical issue-oriented trips. This is the first tape in which the subject was one that we really loved."[33] Elsewhere, Goldsmith commented more bluntly: "We had always made shows about people we didn't like: it was a put-down. The Cajuns we really liked. This was important after the Ford ["Gerald Ford's America"] show: we had to show that we didn't just put people down and that we weren't cold people."[34] Goldsmith's "love" for Cajuns was probably more complex than he was willing to admit even to himself, influenced by early experiences as an urban kid transplanted to a rural environment where he did not fit in. Surprised by the negative criticism, Goldsmith expressed "concern" that the program did not show the affection the crew felt toward the community.[35]

Wendy Appel commented for publication at the time of the broadcast that "the Cajuns are totally unconscious of the media. They're completely up front. When you watch them on tape, you get no sense that they are performing for the camera, which is unusual in a country such as ours with its heavy media exposure."[36] TVTV relied upon the trust and naiveté of the isolated community much as they had depended earlier on media superstars' lack of familiarity with the video medium to capture them unawares; here, however, TVTV was equally naive in failing to calculate the effect public exposure would have on these "ordinary people." Years later Appel observed,

> We loved the ladies in the beauty parlor. We never dreamed of the repercussions exposing their women's environment would have. They told dirty jokes, gossiped, and they felt very safe in doing it in their closed environment. When the tape was broadcast, they got a letter from the governor of Louisiana or the mayor of someplace saying these women had "defiled their community." We had no idea of the damage we were about to do. We were so naive about the cultural difference.[37]

Not everyone involved was chastened by the criticism. Hudson Marquez told *TV Guide* writer Dwight Whitney a year later that "the Cajun show represented a softer, subtler aspect of our work," and Whitney concurred, referring to its "sensitive evocation of Cajun life in rural Louisiana."[38]

Having concentrated until then on public figures—political candidates, antiwar protesters, TV reporters, gurus, radical fugitives, admen, and actors—TVTV had never focused on people who had not chosen to thrust themselves before the public eye. The Cajuns had not asked these hip urban journalists to make a tape about them, and TVTV, accustomed to winning plaudits for exposing the silly side of pompous people with their satire, never stopped to consider the impact their "wise ass"[39] perceptions might have on unsuspecting subjects.

David Loxton was disappointed because *The Good Times Are Killing Me* lacked the journalistic edge of the earlier shows.[40] TVTV still had another hour to deliver on their contract and the prospects for another year's renewal hung precariously in the balance. Loxton had gambled a lot on TVTV's ability to prove that nonfiction video could become an exciting, significant addition to public broadcasting programming.

Loxton embarked on his adventure with TVTV at a time when PBS was scared of controversy and nonfiction production was at an all-time low. The TV Lab had been created to facilitate high-technological video experimentation by artists who were exploring various kinds of image-processed video art. Loxton was going out on a limb to prove that doing something with nonfiction video fell within the Lab's mandate to be on the cutting edge of video programming. Having discovered a way to broadcast half-inch video, Loxton believed he could slide nonfiction through the back door under the guise of experimentation, thereby reviving public television's interest in documentary. Video breathed new life into the documentary for PBS, but when that new life turned rambunctious and controversial, "experimentation" became very risky.[41]

The odd thing was, even as TVTV was being criticized for being unethical and unprofessional, some critics were beginning to question how different TVTV's work was from mainstream TV documentary. A Rockefeller Foundation seminar on independent producers in public television was interrupted by a flareup over TVTV's journalistic practices. TVTV was attacked by a traditional documentary producer who claimed " 'a trained journalist' would not have made such a mistake." They were defended by video partisans who resented the implication that alternative video lacked seriousness and ethical standards. Carey Winfrey,[42] executive producer of a more conventional documentary series for PBS, commented,

> It seems to me as I've watched the development of the work of such groups as TVTV that it has come more and more to resemble conventional network documentaries. Now, as the technology becomes available,

conventional network documentarians like myself are borrowing some of the techniques, and certainly the videotape look, of the groups working with half-inch tape. So, in a way, we're all meeting in the center, or at least coming closer.

Writer John O'Connor partly agreed with Winfrey, citing *The Good Times Are Killing Me* as an example of how TVTV was moving toward that broadcast center described by Winfrey.[43]

Was TVTV becoming increasingly indistinguishable from conventional television? Speaking about *The Good Times Are Killing Me*, John O'Connor observed:

> It still remains a safe distance from the standard commercial product, but it reflects some basic changes or trends in TVTV production. The tone and point of view are less condescending. The program is filled with "characters," some rather bizarre, but they are presented with a minimum of editorializing. In addition, some effort is made to indicate that this particular portrait is not necessarily definitive, that it has limits.

Clearly O'Connor disagreed with Unger about the degree of condescension in the tape and the limits set on its portrayal. TVTV had always peopled their tapes with bizarre characters. Their "editorializing" had never been overt or verbal, but rather expressed through wide-angle lens distortion or a telling juxtaposition in time. Just what was different?

O'Connor concluded with this analysis:

> Technology, finally, is pushing some of the videotapers and some of the traditional documentarians toward a shared center. At present, the ultimate product is only dimly perceived. The bystanders can probably assume that it will be serious and complex. One can only hope that it will also be able to remain offbeat, irreverent and questioning.

What had changed was not TVTV, but its context—broadcast television. As mainstream television adapted the technology of video, it also began absorbing the innovations in style and content of guerrilla TV, and the cutting edge began to appear duller, more familiar, more centrist.

Perhaps the most striking evidence of this shift in perception appeared in a *TV Guide* essay by Benjamin Stein, a writer for the *Wall Street Journal*, who offered suggestions for rescuing the public television system. Stein praised TVTV as a vital source of "new and unexpected viewpoints" for documentary production, proof that PBS was getting away from the dullness of conventional formats and the same old faces that had sunk most of their public affairs programming. Rather than giving large sums to the Washington PBS affiliate, WETA, to cover the 1976 political conventions, Stein urged turning money over to groups "off the beaten track" like TVTV for more "exciting and offbeat documentaries on political conventions."[44] In an article that mainly urged more Congressional oversight of PBS programming for bias and lobbied for more conservative spokespersons on public television, Stein's championing of TVTV's work revealed the extent to which their "offbeat" work had come to appear politically neutral and acceptable.

Although many continued to defend TVTV from criticism, there was no united front for a variety of reasons. TVTV enjoyed a privileged position within PBS, and their unique, autonomous relationship with WNET's TV Lab had become a source of jealousy within the independent community, especially among filmmakers who considered that the funding and broadcast time given to video slighted the established film medium and its practitioners. Loxton was a devout believer in tape rather than film for television,[45] and his mandate at the TV Lab was to develop experimental video programming. Although television may have had an all-electronic future, most filmmakers at the time were unwilling to face that fact.

Shamberg believed that TVTV provided a foot in the door for independent producers, and he publicly urged the creation of a regular national time slot for independent producers with a policy, funding, and method of access for producers.[46] At the time, however, public television had a limited pot to support independents and TVTV received the lion's share. Prospects for new independents to make any headway in the PBS system looked bleak, partly because the costs of programming at $30,000 per half-hour ruled out increased support for independent productions and partly because of public television's innate conservatism, opting for blandness over controversy at all costs. "Virtually every outside production on the air is an exception to the rule," declared Howard Klein of the Rockefeller Foundation.[47]

Parenthetically, prospects for independent video producers to sell their news documentaries to network television were even more unlikely. Participants at the Rockefeller Foundation seminar held in March 1975 indicated that their networks would continue to adhere to strict policies against using documentaries produced outside their news divisions. There was no chance of commissioning work by independent documentary producers. Although there were a few programs that did buy film from outside sources, it was always in short segments. A year later the networks did purchase what they considered "hard news" from independents, but reserved the right to edit and select what they would air. In December 1975, "The CBS Evening News" ran less than two minutes of a color portapak tape shot inside San Quentin by Marin Community Video, which had been documenting prison conditions for months. CBS used only the portion showing guards killing inmates.[48] When given the chance to buy outstanding video, "60 Minutes" rejected Downtown Community Television's documentary *Cuba: The People*, the first all-color video documentary, which aired in its entirety on PBS in December 1976. The only one optimistic was TVTV's Michael Shamberg, who opined that "technological inevitability is on our side." After five years of experimentation to develop technological compatibility with broadcasting and comparable craftsmanship to the point where TVTV could become an ongoing news service to the networks, he was convinced "that different material, well done, will create its own acceptance."[49] Shamberg's confidence, however, was before the ill-fated broadcasts of *In Hiding* and *The Good Times Are Killing Me*.

Competition was not the only factor to turn video independents against TVTV. Idealists were repelled by TVTV's cavalier treatment of "real people" in the Cajun tape. Video activists who had been laboring in America's heartlands, making community tapes with local populations in cities and towns around the country, expected respect for the community to come first, and TVTV had offended against the prime directive. Although they might continue to look to TVTV for stylistic and technological innovations, many community video producers lost their admiration for guerrilla television's most successful group.

No matter which way TVTV turned they were bound to lose. Blamed for a lack of journalistic integrity and attacked for being insensitive and condescending, the group was also accused of losing their countercultural edge as irreverent and provocative producers. Although Paul Goldsmith told writer Catherine Twohill that TVTV was "never going to abandon hard journalism," the evolution was already underway.[50] The shifting tides of opinion that greeted TVTV's last two tapes had a debilitating effect on their resolve to produce more hard-edged, or even soft-edged, documentaries. In addition their lack of progress in finding a niche in American televison had begun to eat away at their collective soul. By the mid-'70s their friends at Second City, "Saturday Night Live," and the *National Lampoon* crowd had begun to make it big. There was no similar vehicle or outlet for TVTV. As Allen Rucker later observed, there was no HBO, MTV or Fox Network to offer their edgy, off–the–wall sensibility a chance to flourish while making four or more big documentaries each year.

Instead, TVTV offered two series to PBS's station programming cooperative; their 1976 entry, "The Seventies,"[51] failed to interest stations and was withdrawn after three of 12 rounds.[52] How they fulfilled their year's contract with WNET demonstrated the extent of their growing disaffection with the worlds of nonfiction programming and public television. TVTV was losing the "grrrr" in guerrilla TV.

16.

Super Video

In the fall of 1975 TVTV was working on several projects simultaneously and had to hire two people to help with the work: Karen Murphy as secretary and Steven Conant as equipment manager. The staff was earning $150 a week while the seven partners pulled salaries of $175. With investors like the Point Foundation, the Vanguard Foundation, and family members, TVTV was able to meet their basic operating costs of $10,000 to $12,000 a month. They owned $26,000 in equipment, which included three color cameras, a portapak camera with a low-light tube, a brand new three-quarter-inch cassette editor and various portable decks, cassette recorders, editors, playback machines, and monitors.[1]

No longer a small group, TVTV began to experience problems associated with their growth. Hudson Marquez complained:

> It used to be four people with some other people. Decisions were real easy to make. We knew each other so well through tape, and we knew ourselves. It was non-verbal. We could do it blind-folded. We were very tight. We had no money, just ideas. We used to run the whole scene. Now we have people to do the typing. And there is creeping democracy. Now to make decisions, we have to have two-hour meetings.[2]

Some people wanted to do hard journalism, others soft journalism, and still others nonfiction. Rucker explained that they were afraid they were becoming too serious and locked into a professionalism that lacked innovation. It was dedication to experimentation that linked the group together as TVTV turned a difficult transitional corner.[3]

To accommodate the diversity of the group, TVTV members decided the next step was to go off in different directions. Some people were working on "Super Vision," an original 90-minute drama which offered a retrospective history of broadcasting from the vantage of the year 1999. Others were developing new PBS proposals. In addition, everyone was producing a "quick tape" of about twenty minutes on a variety of topics. Michael Shamberg was examining the recent wave of political bombings; Megan Williams was following the career of Randy Shields, a 19-year-old professional boxer; Allen Rucker and Paul Goldsmith were documenting the senatorial campaign of antiwar activist Tom Hayden; Wendy Appel was producing "L.A., L.A.," a musical tribute to Los Angeles; and Elon Soltes was following former President Nixon in exile.[4] The idea behind the quick tapes was to experiment with the new portable color equipment, in a return to the casualness of early video production. The result was to be a magazine-style program that would also fulfill their year-long contract with WNET. One jaundiced writer explained it as an "antidote" to TVTV's recent prosperity, a chance to recapture the "hey-wanna-go-out-and-shoot-some-tape spontaneity of the good old days before tiresome preproduction meetings and galloping postproduction costs set in."[5]

None of the tapes were broadcast as TVTV tapes, largely because the strategy was mistaken. As Rucker later explained, the decentralized concept "dissipated their energies and frustrated everyone."[6] According to Williams, the TVTV style of producing tapes was hard to duplicate individually.[7] Shamberg—who had been the natural leader for the group, its strategist, salesman, and businessman—had become more interested in developing fiction projects and neglected his usual role as executive producer.[8] Without a united effort under the guidance of a leader, TVTV and their quick tapes faltered. Rucker became bored with his subjects (Tom Hayden and Jane Fonda) and ran out of things to shoot, although the tape eventually ran in abbreviated form on the Los Angeles PBS channel, KCET. Megan Williams's profile of Randy Shields was, according to Rucker, the best of their separate efforts but it was never completed. Elon Soltes's tape, *Nixon in Exile*, finally aired but after Soltes and TVTV parted company.[9]

Soltes's idea was to track down the elusive ex-president at his San Clemente retreat and interview him. But numerous efforts to capture Nixon on tape proved unsuccessful, invariably foiled by the elaborate maneuvers of Secret Service men guarding the former president. Soltes relied upon a *Los Angeles Times* photographer, Deris Jeannette, who had become obsessed with tracking Nixon in the 13 months following his resignation. Paul Goldsmith, who helped with this tape, recalled fantasizing that Nixon would stroll over to them on the beach and say, "Hi, there. I've got some things I wanna get off my chest. You guys got any sound?" What happened was considerably less interesting, but at least it was not the standard meaningless newsclip

that network camerapeople shot. At a Monday morning TVTV planning meeting, Goldsmith ventured that what the piece needed was "a
little more theater. It's such a non-story we'd be better off scripting
it."[10] Soltes eventually added a fictional character, who he claimed
protected the identity of a source.[11] The decision to experiment with
fiction in a nonfiction situation revealed how much fiction was becoming intertwined with TVTV's identity.

TVTV had worked exclusively in nonfiction formats for four years,
Shamberg recounted. "We've explored one facet of what is possible,
i.e., nonfiction or documentaries and special events," he said, "now
it's time to get into new explorations." Allen Rucker explained
TVTV's drift toward entertainment programming: "We always followed the edict that it had to happen to put it on tape. But there is
a nonexistent line between fact and fiction. We see no reason not to
mix the two." Other TVTV members added that "editing removes the
whole idea of reality"; in building a narrative, the reporters become
actors. After all, Skip Blumberg had become a "personality" when he
interviewed Roger Mudd at the Republican convention. As far as
TVTV was concerned, adding fictional characters in the context of an
actual event gave viewers something they could relate to as "television." It also introduced a self-reflexive element that appealed to
TVTV's concept of process-oriented video.[12]

TVTV submitted a major proposal to PBS to do series coverage
of the Bicentennial and the 1976 presidential elections which would
mix fictional characters with real people and real events. They went
on record saying 1976 was too important to leave to the commercial
networks. In thirteen half-hour programs budgeted at roughly
$333,000, they proposed to cover: the candidates, the campaign op-
erations, the voters, the Bicentennial operations (including both the
official American Revolution Bicentennial Administration and its unofficial counterpart, the People's Bicentennial Commission), and
events like state primaries, national governors' conference, Liberty
Day, the conventions, and the presidential race.[13] Despite the advice
of TV critics like Benjamin Stein who encouraged support for TVTV's
"unexpected viewpoint,"[14] PBS turned down the project.

For a year TVTV had had a sweetheart deal with WNET, which
provided them with financial support and regular access to national
prime time audiences. But that was coming to an end. Stepping into
the breach came Paul Klein, who was then buying programming for
PBS. He commissioned TVTV to do a show on the Super Bowl.[15]
TVTV would borrow on their expertise with event-oriented coverage
while experimenting with mixing real and fictional characters. Once

more it was all-for-one-and-one-for-all as TVTV alumni like Skip Blumberg, Nancy Cain, Anda Korsts, and Tom Weinberg reassembled in Miami for the big blowout game of the national football league season.

Super Bowl was "the Woodstock of corporate America," the American sports event that had become big business. "The Super Bowl weekend is the ultimate expense account arena," writer Roger Angell had said. "A place to meet and gratify one's true friends, to put on the company dog, to do it up right, to flaunt it. . . . The Super Bowl is an invention of American business."[16] By following rich fans like Dallas millionaire Ed Krump, who flew his friends to the game on a chartered airplane, TVTV hoped to skewer big business along with sports' sacred cow.

WNET's David Loxton managed to get together a little more money for the group by allocating some funds for programming from the annual PBS membership drive.[17] TVTV had a budget of $55,000 to produce the tape—$175,000 less than what CBS was charging for one minute of advertising during the game. CBS had 150 people, 18 cameras, numerous record and instant replay decks, and 60 microphones. As far as Allen Rucker was concerned, how CBS covered the game was TVTV's main story.[18] Tom Weinberg's access to CBS's Tom Wussler was to have provided the inside CBS story as the spine for the show, but TVTV's CBS footage really did not work. CBS gave TVTV complete access, including technical rehearsals, interviews with the executive producer and on-camera sports personalities, plus exclusive coverage of an intramural touch football game with such former pro stars as Johnny Unitas. But it just did not happen as TVTV envisioned.

Super Bowl X was held January 18, 1976, but TVTV began their coverage at the American and National Football Conference playoffs where they developed rapport with the players. The crew assembled in Miami three weeks before the event, living in a genteelly peeling rental on Miami's Palm Island during pro football's annual "Armageddon."[19] Returning to Miami "was sort of a homecoming for us," Allen Rucker, who produced the tape, told reporters at the time.[20] Like people in a failing marriage, TVTV had returned to the site of their honeymoon tapes to recapture the excitement of their early successes. Four years later TVTV was now working with slick, all-color equipment and mixing improvisational humor with six or seven real stories.

"We're interested in the players as people, not just helmets with heads under them," Shamberg told *TV Guide*.[21] He explained:

There were the two teams, of course—the Steelers and the Cowboys, and the NFL itself, the business end of the event. There were also the media, the players' wives, and of course the fans—six or seven layers in all. Then we assign different teams—usually two people, a camera and a sound person—to a story, and then we work with whatever these crews get.[22]

TVTV followed their approach to event coverage, but it did not work as planned. In a mad rush they spent four weeks rough cutting the 110 hours of tape they shot, a process that several observers felt was less than smooth and led to "over-editing."[23] David Loxton recalled the state of disorganization that prevailed which, at the time, seemed part of TVTV's communal process. It might have worked providing they had months to try everyone's different version, but TVTV was working under tremendous time pressure; they had only seven weeks between the Super Bowl and their airdate during PBS's "Festival '76."[24] *Super Bowl* was supposed to be 52 minutes but came in at 47 because, according to Megan Williams, "the editors got carried away and tightened it too much."[25] Rumors of cocaine in the editing suite remained unconfirmed.

Another factor was that Allen Rucker's first child was born three days after the Super Bowl, sidelining him during much of the editing process. Michael Shamberg, who had been peripherally involved in the tape, was recruited to salvage the edit, bossing people around and stirring resentment.

The critics appeared united in their enthusiasm for the tape, even when they were acknowledging its flaws. "Leave it to pioneers to make the most exciting mistakes" was the opening line of Tom Shales' *Washington Post* review, entitled "Bringing Video Vérité Closer to Art."[26] "The visual organization of 'Superbowl' is occasionally confusing. Specific identifications tend to be cursory, and the football outsider will find it impossible to determine which player, or even which team, is being displayed on screen," *New York Times* critic John O'Connor wrote. "But the overall occasion . . . is projected clearly and quite delightfully."[27]

Most writers were wholehearted in their endorsement. *Houston Chronicle* TV–Radio Editor Ann Hodges branded the tape a "rib-tickling delight,"[28] and *Newsday* TV critic Marvin Kitman proclaimed "the underground has produced what I feel is the best reporting of the year." He wrote,

"I'll tell you why I enjoy playing football," explains Ernie Holmes, the defensive tackle of the Pittsburgh Steelers in a contemplative mood on the eve of Super Bowl X . . . "I enjoy kicking ass. I'm an ass kicker." I always sort of suspected that something like that might be the case. But in all the years I've been watching football on television, I've never heard anybody put it quite so well. . . . This one line, I submit, probably says more about the American spirit today than 13 hours of the "Adams Chronicles."[29]

For Kitman, the game was the skeleton on which TVTV hung the real story. As the cameras toured locker rooms to interview the players or went out to the swimming pool where the wives were "in training," Kitman found TVTV's camera discovering what Cartier-Bresson called "the decisive moment," or what Howard Cosell used to call "telling it like it is." TVTV wandered from locker rooms to hotel suites, from barrooms to yachts, from practice fields to the playing field. They captured a man in a gorilla suit dancing on the beach, a charter plane full of well-oiled Dallas fans, players in pain, cheerleaders wiggling their behinds, and wives complaining about how much money it cost to feed their husbands. They also found a team owner with a mechanical monkey he called 'Ed Garvey' (head of the NFL Player's Association), who not only let them photograph him playing with the toy, but insisted they do so.

Contrary to what TVTV may have thought at the time, it was the players who were the heart of the story. Several proved to be natural performers. Dallas Cowboy Jean Fugett introduced his teammates with charm and good humor in the opening scenes of the tape. Pittsburgh Steeler Lynn Swann obliged with a rendition of "Moon River" and emceed a black-and-white tape shot by the players in their hotel rooms. The stand-up comedy they captured of autograph hounds arguing pre-game strategy surpassed the "improvised" humor TVTV contrived. Cowboy John Fitzgerald and Steeler Lynn Swann—who proved to be the hero of the game—offered the camera a tour of their scars and injuries. Swann's lack of affectation provoked admiration from several critics[30]; others were surprised and impressed by the diffidence of men trying to make a living in a dangerous occupation.[31]

Ingrid Wiegand later praised the intimacy TVTV was able to capture which network coverage of sports events never achieves. When Fuguett stood on the sidelines before the game began, Wiegand noted, he answered TVTV's question about how he felt. "I feel fine," he says quietly. "Real good. Very physical." He pauses and then adds: "Listen to that crowd. Sounds like a fight crowd, doesn't it?" He scanned the crowd, punching his fist into his palm. "Feels like there's gonna be some blood on that field before the game's over. I'm sure of it."[32]

Marvin Kitman was equally struck by what he called these "moments of truth." His favorite occurred after a Steeler scored a touchdown: "Rather than the instant replay or expressions of joy expressed by the booth men on CBS, TVTV cuts to the reaction of a player on the Dallas bench. 'Shit,' he says. This, I somehow know intuitively, is really accurate reporting."[33]

Tom Shales was the only critic to comment on TVTV's fictional characters and improvised comedy, branding them a flop. Holding TVTV up to high standards, Shales called the tape "terribly imperfect" and faulted TVTV for the "bad habit of cluttering the screen with useless print information while at other times omitting seemingly essential identification." He continued:

> Repeatedly, just when the show is running at a good zip, it stops for unnecessary or ill-timed interruptions—sudden fades to yellow or player interviews signalled with overly cute bubblegum card logos. It's ironic that the TVTV gang, of all people, still doesn't trust the visual.

Nevertheless, Shales concluded that *Super Bowl* was "a flawed epic," "a dazzling tape," and "pretty rare television."[34]

Some critics argued about where TVTV's work belonged. "TVTV . . . is so good that it should be making shows for the large networks rather than the limited audience of PBS," opinioned *Wall Street Journal* critic Benjamin Stein.[35] But Tom Shales differed: "Unfortunately the TVTV people are contemplating a break into commercial television, where they will have much less latitude for experimentation and goofing off. They . . . are exactly what public television needs. Fresh perspectives are a chronic scarcity in TV, public TV included."[36]

Poised between the allure of network television and the old, familiar terrain of public television, TVTV was tilting more and more toward the former as the subjects of its tapes and the new interest in dramatic and comic material moved the group increasingly into the arena of entertainment programming. On the strength of their Super Bowl coverage, KCET signed TVTV to produce a documentary about the Academy Awards. TVTV had come a long way from its beginnings as a countercultural group of alternative video producers. These long-haired hippies in jeans were about to don tuxedos and gowns and mingle with movie stars and Hollywood producers. The alternative video group had taken a detour and was traveling in the fast lane on quite a different course than it had once charted.

17.

Intermedia

After years of calling themselves an alternative video magazine, the producers of "Changing Channels" began to suffer from a peculiar form of anxiety that comes from not knowing what you are, only what you are not. According to Stephen Kulczycki, it had worked only as long as they were immersed in the culture that had formed them. But in the late '70s, baby boomers who grew up wanting to believe they were something more complex than the 7-Up Generation discovered they were buying a hell of a lot of 7-Up. One day they woke up thinking, "Dammit, I deserve more than three or four minutes a show. I'm not going to do all this work for just a four-minute piece. I could make a ten-minute or a twenty-minute or a two-hour piece."

The producers—in particular, Mulligan and Pratt—had burned out after four years of full-time, nonstop producing for "Changing Channels." They felt they were too drained creatively and personally to sustain the show. Their decision to leave, announced during an annual planning retreat, was the source of heated debate. UCV staff were split on their views of how important "Changing Channels" was to the Center. Some felt the show had diverted UCV from its primary mission to serve as an access center for the university and local community. But others, including the university fund-raiser, insisted the series was the carrot that led community people to the center; and, without the highly visible and successful series, it would be more difficult to raise money to run the center and justify its importance. The debate was moot, however, because without the commitment of "Changing Channels'" core producers, there would be no series.

UCV's decision to cancel the series was overshadowed by an even more compelling event; KTCA had reorganized, and, in re-evaluating its policies, had decided to abandon its practice of selling airtime to anyone. After years of grumbling about "Changing Channels," the new administration was eager to do business with UCV, but only if they could have control over the program. All bets were off, and the reasons were many.

About this time Stephen Kulczycki decided to leave University Community Video. "Ultimately, the principle of access in its pure form became less and less interesting to me as I practiced it more. Basically it became the indulgence of a limited number of people, not the democratic institution that I had always dreamed it would be," he later observed. As "Changing Channels" became more highly crafted, access work was siphoned off into a show called "Everybody's Television Time," and UCV ran whatever anybody brought in. Sometimes this was interesting; mostly it was, in Kulczycki's reckoning, "some guy's super 8mm film of his girlfriend smoking a cigarette for twenty minutes."[1]

UCV had grown over the six years Kulczycki had been there; their budget mushroomed from $30,000 in 1973 to $120,000 in 1978. The staff had swelled to 20 with a large number of new, younger people brought in with money from the Comprehensive Education and Training Act (CETA). Over the years Kulczycki had assumed the "patrone character in the game." Part of that was his own need to control things, and part of it was everyone's need to have someone else assume ultimate responsibility. But the newer people were frustrated with having a patriarch as boss; they were unfamiliar with past events that had shaped this role, and they felt distant from the "old timers" who had made UCV and "Changing Channels" what they were. Sensing this displeasure, Kulczycki decided to hire an organizational psychologist from the university to sit in on their staff meeting. When the staff, prodded by the professional, finally let loose with their complaints, Kulczycki was unprepared for the personal attack and his own defensiveness. Not long after, during a testy negotiation with the new president of KTCA over programming a controversial tape in "Changing Channels," Kulczycki was offered a job, and he decided to take it.

With Kulczycki working at KTCA, UCV staffers assumed they had an inside man who would make it easy for them to continue to broadcast their tapes. During the first year, Kulczycki was instrumental in seeing that several hour-long documentary specials by UCV producers were broadcast, but his involvement with UCV changed when he crossed over and became a broadcaster himself. And when he called UCV, someone new would answer the phone who had no idea who he was. It was as if the past had never existed.

"What I thought I was doing was building an institution, and I was completely wrong," Kulczycki soberly recounted, using words remarkably similar to those of Ted Carpenter, who faced a similar disappointment:

> Organizations are combinations of people's energy and input in time, and that's what you've got. It's not something you can leave on to the next group. You just give them what you started with; they'll probably want to change it for their needs anyway. That was a very important lesson. I'd never try to leave behind an institution. Just leave behind a body of work.[2]

In 1979 Greg Pratt produced an hour-long documentary, which Kulczycki broadcast as a special on KTCA. *In the Midst of Plenty* offered a sobering view of what it is like to be "the invisible poor" in rural America. The Kellers evoked the Joads and the farm families photographed by Dorothea Lange and Walker Evans during the '30s. The irony was that they were living in a land of seeming abundance. Pratt presented them as a hardworking, proud, close-knit family whose home, land, and very lives were endangered by forces over which they had little control. Through the eyes of one family, Pratt was able to disclose the face of widespread rural American poverty and some of the political and economic reasons for its existence. *In the Midst of Plenty* won Pratt a radio and television news director award.

Not long after, another UCV producer, Mark Frost, produced a feature-length documentary about James Beattie, a boxer ravaged by drug addiction who was making his own personal comeback by helping others in a drug rehab program. *The Road Back* was shot in black and white and departed from UCV's straightforward style. Frost was a dramatist captivated by the pathos in Beattie's life. What he set out to do was create a moody, dramatic character study, so he chose to present Beattie in the best possible light, providing a purposeful, happy ending that was more illusory than factual. "If you're a boxer, and you're in there getting your head beat up by other people, and you're trying to do the same thing, there's something underneath that drives you to that, to duck that kind of hate," Kulczycki recalled, explaining the dark side of Beattie which Frost deliberately left out. The tape featured original music composed for it by a local singer and songwriter, providing an emotionally-charged blues background for the haunting images of the lonely ex-boxer. Greg Pratt directed the sensitive camerawork, which was brilliantly edited by Frost so that close-ups of Beattie were followed by long shots, isolating him from himself as well as the world. Though strikingly different from UCV's forthright journalistic style, *The Road Back* suggested new directions UCV's video documentaries might take.

At KTCA Kulczycki discovered public television was very different from the Video Access Center. "The pressure on you as a broadcaster in a company where you have all these contributors and all these individual subscribers and all these large philanthropists and others interested in what you're doing is a very different kind of political game than we had at the Video Center." He got more and more involved in programming television and understanding the marketplace: "How to position a product—a television product or service (it's both in a marketplace)—and have a solid business structure keeping it going." He eventually moved on, becoming an executive at the PBS affiliate in Los Angeles, a long way from Minneapolis and a social experiment in public access television.

After Kulczycki left the center, Sallie Fischer was hired to replace him as general manager. Under Fischer's leadership, the four aspects of UCV's activity were ranked as: equipment and facilities access; training; production; and distribution. Approximately 500 groups and individuals were using the center's equipment and facilities each year in 1979, and roughly 650 people were attending workshops in production, editing, and technical matters. UCV's access equipment still depended on portapaks, although two color three-quarter-inch systems were available. In 1979 they were planning to add a second three-quarter-inch editing booth. The staff included five producers, an engineer, an equipment manager, and a number of part-time access, clerical, and graphics personnel involved mainly with teaching and production.

Fischer, in a profile of the center she wrote for *Community Television Review*, expressed optimism that UCV would resume some form of regular series for KTCA in the future, although the basis for her optimism was never clearly stated.[3] In 1979 and 1980 UCV organized the Minnesota Independent Film and Video Festival/Showcase, which was broadcast on KTCA sequentially over the course of a week during the first year and then in a five-hour broadcast the second year. Mike Hazard organized the festival and Stephen Kulczycki, still at KTCA, supported the broadcast. But Kulczycki was disappointed with the work and had a hard time drumming up an audience for it. After two years, the showcase was dropped.

When Sallie Fischer announced to her staff that UCV's facilities were moving to a larger space housed in a former church, she was met with mock cries of "Holy Video!" from young staffers.[4] The church was located across town on the East Bank, far from the old Rarig Center on the West Bank. The West Bank had been a rambunctious neighborhood embroiled in a big housing fight when UCV started up. Staffers actively participated in the community association, producing a number of early tapes on housing issues in the high-density neighborhood. When UCV moved to the church on South Ontario, they were caught between a freeway and dormitories, removed from the bustling atmosphere where community and university had so fruitfully intersected in the early' 70s.[5] No amount of community devotion on the part of UCV's leadership could change the fact that a neighborhood community was no longer the context for UCV's day-to-day existence.

With the sudden influx of nationwide attention for UCV's work, staff began to think about what it meant to have a national reputation. "UCV was more concerned about taking care of things at home, about developing services that would meet the needs of its community, and basically, just doing the best job that it could," one staffer remarked.[6] Now that the center had "proven itself" by wining national awards, Fischer believed they could begin to think about how they fit into the national video scene.

With the installation of a woman as head of the center, women producers assumed a stronger presence at UCV. Kathy Seltzer, who worked as equipment manager, and producer Elle Anthony were among the younger staffers whose work began to carry women's issues and causes to the forefront. Although Cara DeVito—whose video portrait of her grandmother, *Always Love Your Man*, became an early feminist classic—had been a mainstay of "Changing Channels," it was not until the early '80s that women producers exerted a visible difference on program content at UCV. In 1979 Kathy Seltzer and Ann Follett formed the collective Iris Video in response to the need for television programming produced by women about their own issues and concerns. Three years later they produced an award-winning documentary *The Fear That Binds Us* on the history and extent of violence against women and the underlying reasons for it.

In 1980 Elle Anthony was a producer at UCV, where she wrote, shot, edited, and narrated *Stay With Me . . .* , a portrait of Karen Clark, a nurse, activist, and lesbian, whose successful Democratic campaign for state representative created unprecedented coalitions between tenants, senior citizens, and gays and lesbians. Because the subject was a politician running for election, the tape was not broadcast until 1983 on KTCA. In the fall of 1982, Anthony joined with Karen Lehman and UCV stalwarts John deGraaf and Jim Mulligan to produce *Dairy Queens*, a half-hour documentary on the politicalization of three farm women who stood up to defend their land and their values. Two of the women held their ground against a utility company that wanted to run a power line across their dairy farms; the third organized a "tractorcade" to Washington, D.C., to protest federal farm policies. Funded in part by a grant from the CPB, *Dairy Queens* was selected for broadcast in the national PBS documentary series "Matters of Life and Death." By that time Anthony had left UCV and was working as public affairs director for a PBS affiliate in St. Cloud, Minnesota.

UCV's alumni is like a who's who in television, covering broadcast news, documentary, and entertainment. Barry Morrow encountered a mentally retarded man while he was a staffer at UCV and went on to write *Bill*, an acclaimed made-for-TV movie starring Mickey Rooney. Morrow then wrote the screenplay for *Rain Man*. Mark Frost moved to Hollywood and became a writer for "Hill Street Blues," later teaming up with David Lynch on the TV series, "Twin Peaks." Miles Mogulescu works for Edward R. Pressman Films managing start-up ventures in interactive media. Greg Pratt became a documentary producer for the Minneapolis CBS affiliate, WCCO, at times collaborating with Kulczycki on documentaries for KCET in Los Angeles; he later moved to a PBS affiliate in the West. Stephen Kulcycycki was promoted to Vice President and General Manager for KCET. Jim Mulligan opened his own production facility, hiring out as a camera operator for the networks, PBS, CNN, and foreign broadcasters; he continues to be a one-man UCV for independent producers who need his talent and expertise in developing their own documentaries. Ron McCoy still runs his own corporate-sector video production businesses in Minneapolis. And the list goes on.

Staff changed quickly during the transitional years between the '70s and the '80s. In 1981 Sallie Fischer left UCV and Tom Borrup was hired to fill a new job, Executive Director. Borrup was well identified with community access and had been honored by the National Federation of Local Cable Programmers for his leadership in advancing community television. But if his selection was a response by the board of directors to Fischer's more national ambitions for UCV, Borrup's plans outstripped Fischer's as he steered a course that would lead UCV away from community access and social documentary production.[7] Borrup knew that the university support was destined to end, because the long-range picture included declining enrollments and less interest in what UCV was about. Separating was a matter of survival. Hence the refocusing on video as an art form that included documentary but did not make it a priority. He came with the idea that cable, which was just about to be laid, would influence UCV's future, only to discover that the cable landscape really didn't include UCV. For UCV to survive it seemed to Borrup that the surer bet was the regional media arts center route.

When the National Endowment for the Arts designated UCV a major regional media arts center, the pull to compete in a national arena was publicly confirmed. In 1982 UCV launched a major membership campaign, raising funding from members' fees as it began to free itself from financial dependency upon the university. More and more video art was stressed in UCV press releases and literature, and new equipment was purchased with the production and postproduction needs of experimental artists in mind. In 1981 UCV referred to itself as a video *arts* and access center.[8] In time, "access" would be dropped altogether. Curiously, Borrup had little idea that the origins of UCV involved a comparable struggle between art and politics. That juggling continued but the balance had tilted dramatically. In the Reagan '80s, no one could pull the two together as Stephen Kulczycki had once done. The forces were larger than personal differences, and an era hospitable to community organizing, social activism, and documentary production had come to a sudden end.

In 1984, University Community Video changed its name to UC-Video. In 1987 it became Intermedia Arts Minnesota. Gone were the strong ties to the university and the community. Gone was the focus on video. Gone too was the concept of a "regional" center. Although production classes were still given to members, exhibitions now stressed art—video, film, performance, and music—by national figures. The provincialism that had once been UCV's source of pride was temporarily abandoned as fierce competition for federal funding dollars and national priorities in the '80s made the cultivation of regional richness at video access centers a thing of the past.

18.

Hooray for Hollywood?

TVTV's acceptance was due largely to their ability to "polish the rough but vital ethos of 'guerrilla video' to a marketable gloss."[1] But despite a track record that included more boosts than knocks, TVTV still waited for a firm commitment for future work. Independent producers were all clamoring for a bigger presence in public television, having formed a Coalition for New Public Affairs Programming in February 1976, and competition among filmmakers and videomakers to get their work aired on PBS threatened to become livelier and tougher. Larry Grossman, new head of PBS, had promised to introduce innovative projects like a weekly news show with input from independent producers as well as a weekly evening of independently produced documentaries, but nothing as yet had come of it.[2]

With the conclusion of *Super Bowl,* TVTV's relationship with WNET had ended, and they had no idea what they could expect from KCET, the Los Angeles PBS affiliate that signed them to produce a program on the Oscars.

Beginning with the announcements of the nominees, including a young Steven Spielberg doing a comic lament at being passed over yet again, this time for Best Director (*Jaws*), TVTV travelled to the homes of nominees, interviewed them, zipped up their dresses, and rode with them to and from the ceremonies, recording their reactions. Goldie Hawn, Jack Nicholson, and Ronnee Blakely, among others, gave star turns as themselves; Lee Grant, who won the award for Best Actress (in *Shampoo*), provided TVTV with candid interviews before, during, and after the affair. TVTV also traveled to Oregon to interview Ken Kesey, whose novel *One Flew Over the Cuckoo's Nest* was the basis for the Best Picture. The interview offered a perfect TVTV moment, focusing on a countercultural hero speaking about being ripped off by the crass commercial people of Tinseltown.

At the center of *TVTV Looks at the Oscars* is Lily Tomlin, nomi-

nated that year for Best Supporting Actress for her performance in
Robert Altman's *Nashville*. Tomlin plays two roles: herself—hilari-
ously decked out like the Queen mother for the awards ceremony—
and Midwestern housewife Judy Beasley, who watches the show at
home on TV. Judy's tight-lipped, droll commentary on the proceed-
ings are interspersed throughout the tape, ending when she drops off
to sleep on her sofa long before the big winners are announced.
Switching back to herself, Tomlin, dripping in fake jewels, grandly
descends a staircase and climbs into her rented limousine. When a
TVTV staffer asks her how it is to be a star, she gushed: "I have a
big blue house and all these trees and the '68 Pontiac I brought out
from New York. I guess you could say it's been a fulfilling life," as
the electric window slowly rolled up to close the shot. TVTV's comic
intermingling of real people—who were also actors and actresses—
with fictional characters worked terrifically well.

According to Elon Soltes, the idea of integrating actors into real
events arose out of TVTV's discomfort with being on camera.[3] They
had the right cast of characters to choose from (people like Bill Murray, John Belushi, Lily Tomlin, and Harold Ramis) but they still did
not have the expertise to direct actors in a documentary situation.
Although other documentary makers often scripted and directed their
work, TVTV had never worked that way, relying instead on spontaneity. The success of the Lily Tomlin/Judy Beasley scenes in *TVTV
Looks at the Oscars* had to do with the fact that they were separate
from the documentary scenes. Earlier efforts with Bill Murray, Chris
Guest, and Brian Doyle Murray in *Superbowl* had been less successful
largely because TVTV had yet to find an elusive directorial approach.[4]
With *TVTV Looks at the Oscars*, TVTV made a leap into fiction that
it could not come back from.[5]

TVTV was disappointed with the mild reception accorded KCET's
local broadcast of the Oscars tape in September. *LA Times* writer Lee
Margulies seemed never to have heard of TVTV. Allowing for "plenty
of good moments," Margulies was not especially interested in the
show. "A briefly used narrator tells us early on that 'winning an Oscar
is a timeless experience.' Watching it, however, is not."[6] TVTV would
have to wait until spring 1977 for national response, because PBS
had decided not to broadcast it until the next Oscar ceremony.

TVTV's enthusiasm for public television had turned sour. Rucker
told one reporter at the time:

In public television, the payoff was always confusing. They gave you
money but you weren't sure whether they were giving it to you so you

could build an audience—and thus they could give you more money—
or whether they did it because they felt good about it. . . . They don't
promote programs, and they still don't know how to do television in
terms of scheduling and audience flow. . . .

You would end up right at the same place where you started every
time you made a program. You'd get stacks of reviews, but only two or
three million people in total would see it because PBS didn't promote
it, they didn't slot it right, and they didn't plan it. You ended up right
where you started because they no longer had a commitment to you.[7]

With broadcast television completing one of its dullest seasons,
according to both the critics and the ratings, the time was right for
TVTV to make its move, and they began by talking with commercial
stations and the networks. In the spring of 1976 *Village Voice* writer
Ingrid Wiegand predicted that "TVTV credentials will make it the
first independent to break the documentary barrier on network television or to get a full-season program commitment from PBS."[8] It
was the networks, not PBS, that wanted TVTV.

Allen Rucker told Wiegand that

We're still committed to information, to showing how groups and situations in the American culture actually work. But we're trying to do
that outside the documentary label. If people hear that something is a
documentary, they feel they have to learn something, and you've already
lost them. That's why we call what we're doing nonfiction entertainment.
Real people acting naturally are the best kind of entertainment.[9]

Shamberg added:

When you create a really effective fictional character, you have a much
bigger impact than with a documentary. There have been plenty of documentaries of the working class which have been forgotten, but Archie
Bunker is on every T-shirt in America. So we've decided that we're going
to do fiction TV as well. But that doesn't mean we're going to stop doing
nonfiction work, because people are entertaining per se. What we're trying to get to in our work is to treat people in an entertaining way, to
make portraits rather than deal with issues. In a sense, this is a soft-
ening of our work.[10]

TVTV's first foray for the networks actually turned out to be a
documentary of a concert by the legendary folk singer Bob Dylan.
Paul Goldsmith had been moonlighting, shooting film of Dylan's
"Rolling Thunder Review" on tour. Dylan had a contract with NBC
to do a special and was given complete artistic control. Burt Sugarman, producer of NBC's "Midnight Special," had shot one of Dylan's
concerts in Clearwater, Florida, but Dylan had not liked how glitzy

it looked.[11] He liked Goldsmith's style of shooting and called him suddenly in the spring to ask if he would shoot another concert. "Well," Paul said, "we can produce it." And Dylan agreed.[12]

It was TVTV's first all-quad shoot, and they pulled it together with only 48 hours notice. Since they did not have enough equipment, they borrowed and rented whatever they could get, wherever they could find it. They used Fernseh, Ikegami, and RCA cameras plus their own handheld cameras, but only one of the portables was working when they arrived, a glitch that limited their coverage and affected the final look of the tape. They flew to Fort Collins, Colorado, and went to work.[13] Originally TVTV thought they would produce a few songs to be inserted into the earlier concert tape, but the Fort Collins concert surpassed the one taped earlier in Florida. It was held during a downpour that soaked the performers, TVTV's camera crew, and the 23,000 people out in the audience—so the title, *Hard Rain*, had as much to do with the weather as it did with Dylan's signature Vietnam era protest song, "A Hard Rain's Going to Fall."

According to Paul Goldsmith, TVTV screened a rough cut of the tape for Dylan at his home in Malibu. Also invited to the screening were the competition: Burt Sugarman and Dick Ebersol,[14] both from NBC. The network biggies arrived in a Rolls Royce and a Mercedes, while TVTV drove up in an old Dodge Van with Vermont plates and Hudson Marquez's $200 nondescript American car with the dead snake on the dashboard. Both groups screened their footage. "I'd never been in an experience where we were so clearly the coming aesthetic and they were the old one," Goldsmith remembers, savoring the collision. "The more nervous they got," he continues, "the more they unbuttoned their shirts," flashing gold chains to no avail. Their stuff was awful, recalls Goldsmith, while TVTV's was so raw, "it was gonna jump out of your TV at you."[15]

Reviews for *Hard Rain* were mixed. Charlie McCollum, writing in *The Washington Star*, repeatedly referred to the show as "startling." "The difference between the way TVTV approaches Dylan and the concert and the way network television normally handles such specials is startling," he wrote. "From original conception to actual execution, TVTV's production is almost a total reversal of what one expects to see on the Big Three." McCollum had some reservations about dizzying fast pans and some tight out-of-focus closeups, but overall he appreciated the spareness of the production. McCollum wrote:

No stage announcements are made and there is no chit-chat between Dylan and the audience. At least 80 percent of the camera work consists

of tight close-ups done on-stage by handheld cameras. . . . Some are startling. Dylan possesses one of the most striking faces in music and the
changes that come over him while singing . . . is something not even rock
concert audiences get to see. . . . The lack of clutter also allows Dylan's
music to be the main focus of attention. . . . The music is tough, hard,
clear . . . [it] is allowed to speak for itself, which is quite enough.[16]

Chicago Daily News writer Eliot Wald agreed with McCollum,
claiming that the tape "is a refreshing change from the standard,
hyper-slick fare that generally inhabits our phosphor screens." Wald
praised the "live" feel of the handheld cameras, although he found
TVTV's direction and camerawork treaded a fine line between "vérité
and amateur."[17]

Not everyone was prepared for TVTV's low-keyed, intimate difference. *Los Angeles Times* writer James Brown found it "devoid of
all visual trickery" and thus "static and one-dimensional." Brown was
equally underwhelmed by Dylan's music and performance—finding
the opening number "a stultifying choice"—and that antipathy may
have been more influential on his review than TVTV's video style.[18]
Hollywood Reporter Morna Murphy was thrilled neither by the music
nor by the video. "This is actually nothing more than a taped concert," she complained, dismissing the camera work as "more wor-
shipful than workmanlike" and the editing as "overindulgent."[19] In
the end, TVTV decided that opinions about the show lined up according to whether viewers liked Dylan's music or not.[20]

TV Guide did a profile of the group, which ran in conjunction with
NBC's airing of *Hard Rain*. Writer Dwight Whitney presented TVTV
as wild and crazy kids, opening his article with a description of their
headquarters that stressed its unconventionality:

The funky old stucco house in West Hollywood is high-fenced and ivy
covered. There is a crumbling outside stairway, a lumpish piece of fiber-
glass car sculpture, cracked and fading, in the front yard, and a three-
story rubber tree leaning crazily into the building. Over the front door,
a sign says "Elevators Are For Award Winners Only," a cardboard
remembrance of a videotaped documentary that TVTV . . . shot last
spring . . . [21]

Whitney pursued the zany, frantic activity of "furious" creativity
all over the house. "Ideas ricochet off these old walls like balls in a
handball court," Whitney explained. Upstairs, Megan Williams was
editing "The Video Asylum" sequence from *Super Vision*. "David
Sarnoff invents the TV set and sells it to a family," Shamberg ex-

plains. "The family is delighted. Other families buy sets. Pretty soon we have to have video asylums where addicts go to take the cure."[22]

Downstairs, Whitney reported a constant flow of people discussing the "videotape aesthetic" and how it differed from what Craig Gilbert had done, concealing the presence of the camera crew when making "An American Family."[23] Talk was about the limitless future and about the impact of TV on its first generation. "Fictional characters attending nonfictional events. Nonfictional characters attending fictional events . . . Wild? Insane?" Whitney asks. "Not to the people at TVTV."[24] TVTV had spent more money on their video clubhouse on North Robertson than they did on their salaries, creating a media salon where all sorts of people dropped in—John Belushi and Bill Murray even lived there for a time.

To conventional broadcasters, TVTV continued to look funky and insane, but to countercultural holdouts, TVTV had departed the fold and were on their way to broadcasting hell. TVTV got one indignant letter from an outraged video guerrilla, who wanted to know what had happened to the '70s and the revolution. He had been part of the whole video scene in New York, and he felt TVTV had let the movement down. When Megan Williams telephoned him, it turned out he was living in Los Angeles and running a video dating service.[25]

TVTV's next work to air was *Super Vision*. The program began as a 90-minute original drama for the PBS's anthology series "Visions." But KCET's Barbara Schultz, who was in charge of the project, asked TVTV to change the script and develop short segments—three to fifteen minutes long—to serve as fillers for the series. Adjusting a 90-minute script to be aired as 10 segments drove them nuts, according to Megan Williams, but they did it.

Super Vision was to be a retrospective history of broadcasting seen from the year 1999. The satirical "recalls" integrated a number of TVTV concerns about broadcast policies: corporate control, power of sponsors, fear of risk by network execs, consumerist ethic, among others. It also included a brief history of alternative video, plus predictions for the future of television. No aspect of television was ignored—from the immense global network of the future (Super Vision) to video art (we "witness" the purchase from C.T. Lui of the first portapak sold in New York). The episodes include carefully detailed reenactments of events such as the invention of one of the first television cameras (featuring Philo T. Farnsworth and Dr. Vladimir Zworykin) to fantasies like "Chroma Key Lane," a children's show of the future. TVTV borrowed archival materials, including an Eisenhower campaign spot and an excerpt from "I Love Lucy," and mixed them with recreations of early programming.

"Off Now" is perhaps the most revealing and autobiographical segment. In it Gerrit Graham and John Belushi play video guerrillas who stage a takeover of the global network Super Vision, proclaiming "Death to the corporate media mongers! Power to the individual! Free the videosphere now!"[26] With Belushi looking on, his eyebrows expressively pumping up and down, Graham points a gun into the camera and says, "I hereby terminate the video dictatorship of Super Vision." But then Belushi interrupts him, whispers in his ear, and suddenly the video guerrillas settle back, smile, and introduce themselves, saying "It sure is great to be here." Their co-option is imminent. TVTV's satiric depiction of television's irresistible seduction of even the most radical video guerrillas can only be seen as arch awareness of their own transformation.

With *Super Vision* TVTV tried to reinvent the wheel. They had no clue about how to do a dramatic production. Here they were in the entertainment capital of the world. When they were doing documentaries, they were inventing a form and a style of working that did not exist in television; and they were using the equipment to define a new way of doing journalism. But they came into TV drama without having done their homework. They would show up on the set—but there was no set because someone had not finished it in time—and there were 25 actors waiting for the day to begin.[27]

Nevertheless, the script contained some Orwellian prophecies of TV history to come. When Ted Turner began CNN2 on New Year's Day 1982, the event and its staging had an uncanny resemblance to Super Vision's Sara Arkoff and Global One channel. TVTV (and Nam June Paik) also speculated on *TV Guide* becoming as thick as a phone book, a joke that is not far from today's truth.

TVTV had proved they could write, direct, and produce dramatic vignettes with their installment series *Super Vision*.[28] Now, through *Hard Rain*, they had a foot in the door at NBC, and it was just a matter of time before TVTV had a contract to do a pilot for the network. Borrowing upon the talents of friends like Harold Ramis and Bill Murray, TVTV ventured into deep, new waters with *The TVTV Show*.

The decision to write comedy was a pivotal one for TVTV. Up to that time, their strength had come from their improvised, spontaneous coverage of real events—whether political conventions or a live music concert. Writing and producing television comedy was a whole new ball game, calling for different talents, different equipment and expertise, and, in the end, a different organizational style. Shamberg had been inching more and more in that direction ever since the checkbook journalism charges dampened his journalistic zeal. His old friend Harold Ramis had been a member of Chicago's "Second City" and of "The Prime Time Players" on Howard Cosell's "Saturday Night" program on ABC. Borrowing on talent like that, "The TVTV Show" seemed a sure thing to Shamberg.[29]

The TVTV Show was the first show negotiated between a network and "survivors of the 'video freak' generation." It was also, according to *Videography*'s Peter Caranicas, "the first time broadcast television consciously sought to satirize itself."[30] NBC had liked the "Shoot Out" segment of *Super Vision* with its wry take-off on network news, and Paul Klein signed TVTV to do an expanded version.[31] TVTV took the dramatic style and thematic approach of *Super Vision*[32] and fashioned a 90-minute program that featured an average American family immersed in television images and trivia. *The TVTV Show* was designed as media satire with a purpose: to show how television affects the lives of its viewers.

The show opens explosively as a home viewer is blasted off his sofa by a bullet from his TV set as the announcer proclaims: "It's the TVTV Show!" Appropriately enough, Michael Shamberg played the gunman. The story draws on a number of television formats—the family sitcom, action news, police action drama, commercials, and variety shows—and skewers them all. It follows a day in the life of the WTKO Action News team. Clad in peach polyester suits, Mary Kay Fass (played by Mary Fran) and Ralph Buckler (played by Howard Hesseman) can't stand each other. Mary Kay is more concerned about her luxurious coiffure and Ipana smile than her journalistic ethics, and Ralph is tormented with jealousy—he's so eclipsed by Mary Kay that even his dry cleaner doesn't recognize him. When Bonnie-and-Clyde terrorists break into the home of a typical TV family, Mary Kay is on the scene, interviewing the police captain fresh from his backyard barbecue and offering herself as hostage, to Ralph's evident glee.

Cast in the roles were a number of then unknown actors who would later make their names in television and film: Debra Winger plays Wilma "Dusty" Upstrum, terrorist and psycho girlfriend; Annie Potts is Nancy, the teenage daughter in the TV family; Ed Begley, Jr. is WTKO's competition at WHAM-TV; and Rene Auberjonois is WTKO's news director. Bill Murray was orginally slated to play a key role, but because "NBC's Saturday Night" objected, his part as WTKO's cameraman Jerry had to be kept to a minimum. Instead of

TVTV intimate Harold Ramis, Allan Myerson was hired by NBC to direct the show, an unfortunate choice since Shamberg and Myerson never got along.

John J. O'Connor was generous in his praise for their last program, which aired April 29, 1977, in the 11:30 P.M. time slot usually reserved for "NBC's Saturday Night." Shamberg had sent what appeared to be a form letter to selected reviewers, explaining that the show was uneven, to which O'Connor gamely replied: "But so is 'Saturday Night.'" Insisting that the show scored frequently and devastatingly enough to merit encouragement, O'Connor judged the action news team—the comedy core of the show—"near enough to the startling truth to be appallingly hilarious."[33]

O'Connor asserted:

> The co-anchor team of Mary Kay Fass and Ralph Buckler are just about perfect. . . . Loathing each other with undisguised relish, they fight for air time and camera exposure. She dreams of making a "Geraldo Rivera kind of move," perhaps going so far as to host a national telethon for unwed mothers. He is waiting for the day when Edwin Newman breaks a leg. In a final "live report," Mary Kay, gleefully promising her viewers what "may be a violent conclusion to a massive manhunt," gets to cover a bizarre police raid on a private home and to offer herself, on camera, as substitute hostage.

In addition to this "scathingly on target" send-up of action news, O'Connor added: "For good measure there is a commercials satire, this one for 'Perpetual Life' and featuring a blandly malevolent youngster wondering if his daddy has purchased enough insurance to take care of him when he grows up." O'Connor admitted the show was terribly uneven—"and terribly funny."[34]

O'Connor's even-handed review was not echoed by others, including TVTV's own staff and intimates. Paul Klein, TVTV's mentor at NBC, said: "Even by standards of 'Saturday Night,' it was terrible. It didn't do what it set out to do . . . to be an examination with humor and wit of TV's effect on American life . . . it didn't do anything. It laid there." Even TVTV's own staff recognized that much was wrong with the show. Allen Rucker, co-producer of the show, found the pacing off. "The situations were good but there weren't enough laugh lines," Rucker observed, attributing the problems partially to the writing and partially to the directing. Rucker later admitted TVTV blew it creatively. "We bit off way more than we could chew and didn't have the luxury—like, say, 'SCTV'—to develop a comic style outside of the need to make it big on NBC. We knew it was dicey going in, and we knew we had to score—so we went way into debt to make the edit, and it still sucked."[35]

TVTV intimate Skip Blumberg was blunt in his criticism at the time.

> As a satirical analysis of TV news, the show rarely got beyond the personalities of its characters and it avoided industry and management issues entirely. In one section, when the news director of the station (the only management character) lectures the squabbling news show hosts— "I don't decide (what should be on TV), the people who own the station don't decide, the public makes the choice!"—it was difficult to determine whether it was satire or propaganda.[36]

TVTV had been publicly confident about the show, telling *Videography* that "if the NBC program is both good and popular, NBC will make a very long-term commitment to TVTV. We'll have more stability than we've ever had."[37] They had been working directly with the head of variety programming in Los Angeles as well as head of late-night programming in New York. With Paul Klein as their rabbi at NBC, TVTV thought they were at the beginning of a whole new era. They wanted to walk the line between fiction and fact because "that's where the near future of television is."[38]

TVTV was right about television's future, but wrong about their place making it. NBC decided not to turn the pilot into a series. Had TVTV been given more time to develop *The TVTV Show*, some insiders thought it might have become a commercial success.[39] Shamberg felt that, had he been stronger willed and stuck with the method they had devised for *Super Vision*, it could have been extraordinary work. But TVTV caved in to all the network pressure: "We like you because you're different, but make it like everything else."[40]

Working with the networks demanded a hierarchical structure that flew in the face of TVTV's heterarchy. Up to that point, TVTV's leadership shifted from one area to another. On location, there was no producer, so it was up to the crew to decide what they were about. Editing a segment was up to the editor. Once TVTV got into commercial television, they needed a new organizational structure. "You needed one or two people to talk to their business guys," Shamberg recalls. "Some of the group thought, 'that's where the power has gone,' and they wanted to be there too. The group was organically, emotionally, and psychologically unsuited to do it."[41]

Skip Blumberg offered his own view of TVTV's changeover. By adopting the conventional hierarchical structure of television production, TVTV "essentially cut themselves loose from any obligation to work in a collaborative, organic, democratized production process. . . . They're not working especially with friends; it's on a pay-as-you go basis, and if they've got the bucks, they'll work with the most talented Hollywood professionals."[42] Blumberg, whose many contributions to TVTV documentaries over the years included the memorable interview with Roger Mudd in *Four More Years*, judged that TVTV would have to return to the independent producers and artists who had been the source of many of their ideas if they were going to succeed again.

TVTV had produced tapes for cable, public television, and now network TV, garnering praise for most of their innovative work. In five years they had emerged from the video underground and metamorphosed from countercultural radicals to commercial television producers. But, with the failure of their NBC pilot, TVTV was stalled.

They could no longer count on public television support. They had sent new proposals to the Corporation for Public Broadcasting's Revolving Fund—one about high school kids' life style and another about a Coast Guard Captain in Newport, Oregon—and both proposals were rejected. "It's really a painful process the way they [PBS] develop ideas," Allen Rucker observed at the time. "There's no system for dealing with producers on a continuing basis. They don't seem to be interested in nonfiction series, and that's the only way we can build on what we've done. We can't sustain ourselves on a 'specials' basis."[43] Moreover, TVTV had crossed the line by working with actors and directors, and mixing genres was even more trouble when it came to enlisting public television support.

Although Shamberg and Rucker reported at the time that they were working on another prime-time comedy deal at NBC, nothing came of it or of a made-for-TV movie for CBS about the '60s. They were broke and living on credit cards, moving more and more into the world of commercial entertainment, and distancing themselves from former friends and video colleagues.

19.

The Big Chill

TVTV died very slowly, enduring a long and agonizing death ritual. They had incurred serious debt in producing the NBC pilot and tried to salvage things by bringing someone in to handle their financial affairs, only by then it was already too late. For Wendy Appel, *The TVTV Show* marked the end.[1] Allen Rucker suggests it happened the day Hudson and Megan were let go. He and Michael had decided that they could no longer afford to pay anyone, so the best thing was to cut salaries and expenses by shrinking the staff. They closed down the house on North Robertson and moved to an office on Santa Monica Boulevard, renting out their editing equipment and their tapes, stripped down to almost nothing so they could try to deal with their creditors. "It was impossible, bullshit," he mournfully remembers, recalling the time as a period of sitting in a windowless room, smoking cigarettes all day, having no money coming in and no sense of what he was doing in Hollywood. TVTV existed this way for a year or so until one day they announced a meeting, decided not to file for bankruptcy, and let it all go by walking out the door.[2]

"When all this soul went out of the room, we still maintained the offices. I held on to it for years," Allen Rucker recalls. "I knew it probably was irreplaceable, and I just didn't want it to die. People yelled and sued each other and hated each other. Everyone made mistakes. We handled it badly. We didn't know how to manage ourselves. . . . Michael didn't skip a beat. I skipped a beat—the music stopped. And it took me a long time to recover."[3]

Many date TVTV's end to the broadcast of the 1979 profile of the group made by KCET's Senior VP Charles Allen. *TVTV: Diary of the Video Guerrillas*[4] was a lame documentary that was TVTV's equivalent to the Beatles' "Let It Be" sessions, when everyone hated each other but came together one last time before the inevitable dissolution. The difference was that TVTV appeared together via tape only; the interviews were conducted seriatim since no one was talking to the other. Allen Rucker, in his last official act as a TVTV producer, selected all the excerpts from their tapes for a show that provoked bitter controversy because the credits did not acknowledge a number of people who were key to TVTV's success. "That wasn't what caused TVTV to disband, but it was a fitting end," Megan Williams recalled. "We'd organized to rebel against hierarchies and had ended up fighting over credits. But that was way after it had ended."[5]

She remembered:

> We were all in debt, all getting married and having babies. We needed money. We were tired of working that way. We got the Big Chill. Our needs changed. When we were in San Francisco and thinking of moving to LA, Hudson said, "Don't move to LA, LA will make you greedy." I always wondered if that was what had happened. Not for material things. You want to achieve your own things and be recognized.
>
> I don't think it was any one thing that tore us asunder, but we didn't share any one goal. In the beginning we did. It takes guts to shoot for a week and turn tapes over to someone else to edit. Interesting people were willing and able to contribute in that way. To have that trust, you had to share a goal.[6]

Most of the partners agree that TVTV's unity fell apart when they got into fiction. "You could never write it the way it happened" was what Hudson Marquez always said.[7] But TVTV's demise might have happened anyway, because there was virtually no market at the time for their nonfiction work. Despite their notoriety, good reviews, and considerable track record, they were making practically no money. The group had worked together for six years. "It was just such a different world," Shamberg recalls. "It seemed better, more romantic, to leave it at that point with a lot of pride in what we had done."[8]

Allen Rucker's nostalgic view was that, had they held on a little longer and reconfigured, they might have become an independent production company—if they had stayed in nonfiction and expanded to music instead of going into fiction entertainment. With spinoffs of TVTV like George Schlatter's "Real People" and the rise of magazine format TV shows, TVTV might have been able to turn itself around.[9]

Shamberg said,

> If people had been prepared to deal with how hard it is out there, the fact that the novelty value was gone, that it was being done partly for money, that you might have had sponsors, that you had to fight for network time—you still could have done it. If we had reconfigured our-

selves as a group working in commercial television and applied the same energy and stuck to it, we would have succeeded. But at the time we were just not emotionally equipped to do it. The emotional center was gone from the experience, at least it was for me.[10]

TVTV was a superorganism, drawing on the talents of its various members. It depended upon the careful balancing of personalities and abilities to thrive as long as it did. Perhaps because most of the men in the group had not had fathers around in their childhood, they invented for themselves strong father figures. Some likened the twin leadership roles of Shamberg and Rucker to the contrasting figures of God in the Bible: Shamberg was the wrathful Old Testament father, bullying and ordering people about, invariably asserting his leadership in the public eye; Rucker was the charitable New Testament father, a moderating force holding people together, working behind the scenes to get things done. Not everyone subscribed to this divine metaphor, however, preferring to view Shamberg as a demon riding roughshod over people. Shamberg was a born producer, a master strategist and visionary with all the requisite skills for organizing and packaging and promotion. His journalist's ability to speak effectively in sound bites, appearing spontaneous while planting carefully considered quotes, was essential to TVTV's success. Equally essential was the hardworking, genial Rucker who mollified injured feelings within the group and smoothed over the rough spots. Without both "fathers" driving and stabilizing the group, TVTV could not survive.

Michael Shamberg began pulling away from the group as early as 1975, when he began working on a film project in the wake of the *In Hiding* fiasco. When NBC vetoed the pilot of "The TVTV Show" in 1977, he was out trying to sell his script. By 1978, when TVTV was folding in earnest, Shamberg began production of his first Hollywood feature film about Neal Cassidy and Jack Kerouac, a project that would be Shamberg's own, not a TVTV production. *Heart Beat* (1980) was not very successful, but it established his credibility as a film producer. He went on to produce a number of box-office hits, several of them critically acclaimed. His first big success was Larry Kasdan's *The Big Chill* (1983), a film that could have been about TVTV. In it one character says, "Just because we look alike and we had the same experiences, doesn't mean we're all the same." That was the Big Chill, Kasdan told Shamberg, "when you think you have a common background with somebody and you realize you have nothing in common."[11] Shamberg, of all people, understood.

Shamberg founded TVTV as the embodiment of the guerrilla television theory he articulated in his 1971 book. Roughly ten years later, he was producing movies in Hollywood, having used TVTV as a springboard into the entertainment industry he once disparaged. Many guerrilla video veterans felt betrayed by his apparent defection from the cause. Some of them were members of TVTV who were shocked to discover how smoothly Shamberg had transformed from countercultural leader to Hollywood mogul. But how radical was that transformation?

Shamberg and company were stolid McLuhanites who were more interested in the people who were "fucking with the definition of political reality" than with those who were trying to create political and social change.[12] They were postpolitical media mavericks intent upon sabotaging the media from the inside, pointing to the Emperor of the Air and announcing he had no clothes. In *Guerrilla Television* Shamberg argued that you could not pump alternative programming over the commercial airwaves: you needed an alternative system, because trying to reform broadcasting was like trying to build a healthy dinosaur. But when those alternative channels—cable TV and videotape distribution—proved nonviable in the early '70s, TVTV pragmatically set about working within the belly of the beast, producing programs first for cable, then public television, and finally network TV. When television spurned them, as it undoubtedly would, they had become so much a part of the world they had tried to revolutionize that there was no turning back.

Wendy Appel suffered that she could not change network TV, idealistically believing TVTV could. She had not understood TVTV as Shamberg did—as a stepping stone.[13] Shamberg, who appeared to be an idealist, was a shrewd pragmatist who always remained one step ahead of the game. When the zeitgeist favored countercultural radicalism, Shamberg was a master of guerrilla television rhetoric, an inspired critical observer of the media scene, and a deft producer of lively, satirical video documentaries. He knew how to package the counterculture so that it appealed to jaded television viewers, and he knew how to choose the right subject matter for tapes.[14] When the "music changed," Shamberg had positioned himself to assume a powerful role in the lucrative world of feature film production. Shamberg was the only TVTV principal who, in Rucker's words, "didn't skip a beat."

On March 7, 1992, TVTV commemorated its founding twenty years earlier. Organized by Allen Rucker, the reunion was held at the old North Robertson house, TVTV's headquarters during the halcyon

Hollywood era. The night was warm, the champagne flowed, conversation spilled out of the downstairs rooms and into the little courtyard where Ron Kovic held court from his wheelchair. People flew in from all over the country to attend, not just TVTV members but an array of people involved in one way or another with TVTV's career, including critics Michael Dare of *Billboard* magazine and Tom Shales of *The Washington Post* and writer/performers like Brian Doyle Murray of "Saturday Night Live." Reporters for National Public Radio and a newspaper syndicate wove in and out, interviewing people on tape. Nancy Cain circulated with a palmcorder, capturing the event in the most fitting TVTV way. A home video release of four of TVTV's "greatest hits" was on display, distributed by the Chicago-based company, Subtle Communications.

The tension and acrimony that marked TVTV's last days was virtually absent, or perhaps the champagne only masked it. Beneath the cocktail party buzz was the constant question, "What are you doing now?" Maureen Orth, ace reporter of the convention tapes, was writing for *Vanity Fair*. Tom Weinberg at Chicago public television station WTTW was producing "The '90s," the realization of a series TVTV had proposed in the '70s. Paul Goldsmith had become a highly successful cameraman for commercials and Hudson Marquez was now a Hollywood sound engineer still making his own art. Steven and Roger Christiansen had become, respectively, a professor of screenwriting at the University of Southern California and the video director of "Murphy Brown." Karen Murray, a former TVTV secretary, had produced *Spinal Tap* and *Drugstore Cowboy*.

Absent from the party was Skip Blumberg, who had stayed in New York to edit a new video documentary. Permanently absent were two people who played critical roles early on: David Loxton of WNET-TV in New York had died of cancer, and Anda Korsts had died after a fall, never recovering consciousness.

Allen Rucker was now successful writing comedy for television, most notably as author of the award–winning "White People in America" cable specials with Martin Mull. Wendy Appel had continued working in cable, pursuing both entertainment and documentary projects. A long-term project she had been developing with Lily Tomlin had recently fallen through, leaving her uncharacteristically quiet. But it was Michael Shamberg who had the lowest profile. His marriage to Megan Williams had ended in divorce four years earlier, and he had not yet recovered. Despite more successes like *A Fish Called Wanda* (1988), his fortunes in Hollywood were in flux and he looked older, more brittle, and more evasive than the one-time powerhouse who drove TVTV's creative engine. Megan Williams, by contrast, was full of vitality and no longer Michael's wispy wife. She had left mediamaking some years earlier to establish a school for the deaf, inspired by her own child's physical challenge.

Over dinner after the party, Allen Rucker marvelled that there was not a lot of bitterness or ill feeling left, just an assessing of lives and looking over shoulders. It was, in his generous view, a "re-union."

Two years later I flew to Los Angeles again and met with Shamberg and Rucker to review this manuscript. Allen Rucker was thick into production on "George and Alana," a new talk show for cable, and simultaneously editing a Martin Mull special on the Iowa State Fair for Comedy Central. He had read the manuscript and had lots of notes. Snatching time from his busy schedule, Rucker met me for breakfast in a favorite local coffee shop, waxing enthusiastic once again about TVTV. What he was doing today, he observed, was merely an extension of what he had been doing back in the '70s. TVTV had always had one foot in the entertainment industry. The line dividing fiction and reality was fluid; TVTV and "The History of White People in America" were just on either side of that line. Dashing out the door, Rucker let this thought hang in midair: Hollywood may have seduced them or maybe it just genuinely connected with them to do what they do best.

Shamberg's offices at Sony Pictures were located in the Frank Capra Building. Walking the studio lot through a maze of movie-set facades, I wondered what version of Shamberg I would find. When I had interviewed him in 1983, he had a small office with a standing desk and memorabilia on the walls. He was no longer a young man dashing about like a Roadrunner cartoon, spewing rhetoric effortlessly while commanding video guerrillas in a frontal assault on Media America. He had been dressed casually in polo shirt and slacks, looking very much the picture of a successful Hollywood producer. While he took numerous phone calls, I remember glancing at a framed cocktail napkin scribbled with a quip and signed "John Belushi." Curiously, there was nothing visible that connected him to TVTV. Our conversation had begun very formally but as time passed and Shamberg became more engaged in recalling TVTV's history, he became more animated and finally told his secretary to hold his calls.

Today Jersey Films has a large and sprawling office befitting a joint venture between Shamberg and Danny DeVito. Large theater posters hung on the wall for their recent films, including *Reality Bites* and *Pulp Fiction*, which had just won the Palme d'Or at Cannes. Shamberg was still working on the cutting edge, but having offices at

Sony Pictures only seemed to point up the irony between Shamberg's past and present. I wondered if the fast-talking, energetic advance man for guerrilla television could still be found. Eventually he emerged from a meeting and directed me into his office, which possessed the familiar standing desk but was easily four times the size of the office he had occupied ten years earlier. Informed by one of his assistants to take any seat but Michael's, I sank into the down plush sofa and waited for him to return. When we had spoken on the telephone to arrange the meeting, he had expressed appreciation that I had devoted this time to telling the TVTV story, but explained how busy he was, adding he would try to read the manuscript over the weekend.

Dressed all in black and shoeless, Shamberg moved stiffly into the room and took the hardbacked seat I'd been told to leave vacant. Speaking slowly and flatly he announced that he had not read the manuscript, casually apologizing, and asked what my deadline was. The only moment his affectless demeanor altered was when I mentioned my students still read and appreciated *Guerrilla Television*. A hint of a smile curved his mouth and light flickered briefly in his eyes. He was surprised to hear that people still read it. Promising to take my manuscript on his next cross-country flight—*Pulp Fiction* was opening the New York Film Festival so we might meet there—he stood and ceremoniously shook my hand. The interview lasted all of ten minutes. I never heard from him again.

20.

Epilogue

As many have noted, our national memory is meager: if the Fifties
and even Vietnam seem as remote as the Peloponnesian wars, it is
partly because each American generation neglects to pass on its
experience to the next; outside of the university, we don't respect our
history, as Europeans do. Our talent is for living in the present: that
elation is beguiling during spells of relative calm, but each new crisis
sends us reeling—because it seems unprecedented, and because the
past itself is suspect: arthritic as well as old.

—Nora Sayre[1]

Guerrilla television's failure to create a viable alternative to commercial television was not due merely to the shortcomings of individuals.
Larger forces operating in society influenced and ultimately prevented
the dream from becoming reality. Born out of the counterculture's
clash with establishment values and institutions, guerrilla television
was subject to the counterculture's disillusionment and disintegration.
Guerrilla television's future was also conditioned by its technology, by
rapid developments in the recording and broadcast transmission of
video that transformed the medium from an oddity to a novelty to a
banality, altering its power to challenge the status quo almost overnight. And, perhaps most important, guerrilla television existed within
the shifting landscape of American television: the boom–bust–boom
of the U.S. cable industry; the contentious rise of public broadcasting
and public funding for the media arts; the transformation of network
television from a powerful tripartite monopoly industry to struggling
competitors within a multichannel world; and changing federal policies toward broadcast regulation. Although guerrilla television was a
player in determining the outcome of certain of these changes, it was
only a pawn in a larger game.

Guerrilla television was part of the social, political, and cultural changes that swept through the '60s and into the '70s; thus it was vulnerable to the reactionary rise of conservative values that followed the '60s' liberal wake. As part of the counterculture, guerrilla television helped raise a critique of American society that went beyond the bounds of the political Left, even if it missed essential leftist insights about power, economic exploitation, and class. The counterculture's confrontation with the complacently monolithic, liberal–conservative establishment in the mass media, universities, government, and big business provided models for a new world, but they were too often based on a naive belief that the inverse of anything that existed must be better.[2] The video underground, in tilting swords with Television, believed they were creating an inherently revolutionary alternative to a monolithic system. They believed themselves to be outside of time and capable of transforming existing institutions. Unfortunately, they existed within a distinct time, and their fate was tied to that time and the fortunes of the counterculture that sheltered them.

The New Left emerged in the early '60s as a student movement working for university reform, civil rights, and community organizing and working against the war in Vietnam and corporate domination of foreign policy. They had to contest the culture of corporate capitalism—which relied on the sophisticated, pervasive shaping of values and images of the world through mass media, advertising, commodity consumption, and prolonged education—to focus its discontent and organize for a new society.[3] But every evening millions of Americans watched Walter Cronkite and more than 60 million people bought daily papers with news derived from two international wire services. The New Left countered with its underground newspapers and entered into an unequal struggle with corporate media, as its image and its agenda were rapidly transformed through a mass media campaign that portrayed it as a menacing single-issue antiwar movement with a communist slant.[4]

The early video underground attempted to provide alternative images to the mass media's view of this cultural and political ferment by documenting oppositional events and the appearance of the New Left's media-anointed celebrity leaders. But at the peak of confrontation between the political establishment and the radical Left, alternative video was still an underground movement of disorganized hipsters, and video was still a fringe medium that offered little chance of countering the pervasive negative television images of political contest. Efforts by videomakers to distribute more positive images of

protest to the broadcast networks during the late '60s invariably
failed to get on the air, and when they occasionally were used, they
were still framed by the networks' own agendas.

The counterculture shared many of the themes of the Left: a desire for community; a faith in spontaneous and direct action; a vision
of total social and personal transformation; a distaste for things big,
impersonal, and bureaucratic; and a hostility to the America of the
Corporate '50s. The quest for community was of paramount importance; in part this was a response to a widely felt sense of homelessness and personal isolation experienced by baby boomers, who were
faced with the postponement of adulthood brought about by extended
education and delayed entry into the labor force.[5] For video guerrillas
who had been raised in front of a flickering TV screen, the vicarious
site of childhood communion exerted an ineluctable pull, and the outlaw gangs celebrated in the Westerns that were a staple of '50s' television held sway over their imaginations. Forming an outlaw video
group determined to undermine and reinvent Television seemed to
fulfill some childhood fantasy of challenging authority, replacing conventional television with a new televisual reality and "our gang" sol-
idarity.

The counterinstitutions initiated during the '60s included communes; co-ops; free clinics; schools; counseling centers; day-care centers; encounter groups and other forms of collective therapy and
consciousness raising; grassroots community organizations; public interest lobbies and law firms; peace, environmental, consumer, and
women's civil rights groups; and alternative media. These counterinstitutions often depended for their survival on inherited wealth and
lacked economic self-sufficiency; thus their life span was often short
and membership turnover was high. Community often proved ephem-
eral, less a family than a home that can be left without guilt or grief.
Communes served as a retreat from the larger economy, whereas cooperatives attempted to compete with it. As a result, cooperatives
tended toward convergence with the established institutions. Some
alternative video groups opted for a communal existence, like the
Videofreex (later known as Media Bus and Lanesville TV), who moved
together to a rural setting in upstate New York, were supported by
state grants and trust funds, and produced a weekly low-power television show for their small community. But most others—like TVTV,
Broadside TV, and University Community Video—functioned as co-
ops, with members loosely organized and working in a relatively stable
financial environment dependent upon contracts with broadcasters
and investors. Co-ops were started with the hope of substituting com-

munity for private ownership, paying workers decent wages, holding open meetings and making decisions collectively, and abolishing all forms of discrimination. The reality proved rather different. When the leadership became less than egalitarian and democratic, groups revolted and stability eroded.[6]

Since rejection of bureaucracy and hierarchy often lead to suspicion of all structure, counterinstitutions favored a lack of organization on principle. Early on, alternative television had fought the establishment of centralized organizations, best exemplified in the strident opposition to the creation of "The Center for De-Centralized Television." Since strong leadership and professionalism tended to be viewed as elitist, this distaste for hierarchy often lead to disorganization rather than reorganization along more democratic principles.

Most of the counterinstitutions experienced high turnover because they could not offer members much of a career. They provided way stations for middle-class young people who were not yet established in families and professions. Some organizations offered a point of entry into careers. As a haven for the disenchanted, they offered a more acceptable alternative than work in a conventional bureaucracy. In high intensity, low-commitment organizations, those who worked for them or lived within them often oscillated between moments of exhilaration and depression before they burned out and went on to something else.

Guerrilla television, while seeming to embody a political, adversarial agenda, was really exemplary and eventually aimed at reforming broadcast television by example. Grassroots or community video, by embracing video as a means to an end—social reorganization—was politically adversary in nature. But to the extent that community video activists also became involved in the "politics" of broadcasting—that is, producing broadcast-standard programming either for public, cable or network television—their political agendas often became sidetracked or subverted.

Whenever alternative video sought power over (or from) the structure of broadcasting, their more radical messages were co-opted, diluted, or absorbed into the wider system of values embodied in mainstream media. Whenever they set themselves outside this system, limiting their scope of influence and concentrating it by controlling their own modes of distribution (through closed-circuit screenings, public access cable, home video distribution, etc.), they succeeded in articulating "other" voices traditionally excluded by mainstream media. Their successes looked small and their reach puny compared to the vast audiences demanded for success in the world of broadcast television, but alternative television's "narrowcast" successes were real.

Since the '70s represented a long-term economic bust when compared to the boom of the '60s, it was even more difficult for alternative institutions to survive. With the fragmentation of the Left and the counterculture, there was no unifying movement with which alternative institutions could associate to reinforce their political characters or cultural agendas. In pursuit of respectability and wider audiences, the alternative media toned down their language, diversified their reporting, and tried to bring moderate views into their work. Some believe the alternative media that survived were those who found a way of making themselves useful to the rich, capitalist society they had failed to overthrow. The lesson of the '60s was not that counterorganizations failed but that, in the absence of general social transformation, they survived only in certain limited forms.

At the time *Guerrilla Television* was written, changes in the cable industry offered real hope that cable could provide the alternative distribution channels guerrilla television needed if it was to create a parallel system to network television. In 1970, Ralph Lee Smith wrote a seminal essay on "The Wired Nation,"[7] which chronicled the history of cable television in the United States, inspiring video activists with his blue-sky optimism about the future.

Nearly half the U.S. audience received no more than six channels at the beginning of the '70s, prompting social critics to complain that "never before in history have the most powerful channels to the people been so completely controlled by so small a segment of the national life."[8] Cable promised the elimination of channel scarcity and the sharp reduction of broadcasting costs, which would break the hold on the nation's television fare then exercised by a small commercial oligarchy. "Television can become far more flexible, far more democratic, far more diversified in content, and far more responsive to the full range of pressing needs in today's cities, neighborhoods, towns and communities," Smith promised in *The Wired Nation*.[9]

What had held cable from realizing this dream was the united opposition of broadcasters, congressmen (30 members were owners or part owners of TV or radio stations when Smith's report was written), and other special interest groups (such as theater owners, newspaper publishers, and telephone companies). For example, former President Lyndon Johnson's family owned the Austin-based Capital Cable Company and Texas Broadcasting Corp., which held multiple licenses for radio and TV stations. Influenced by political and economic pressures, the Federal Communications Commission (FCC) was compelled to restrain cable's growth. During the '60s the FCC assumed an increasing regulatory role, generally succumbing to broadcast pressures, although occasionally acting in the public interest, such as requiring cable companies to carry all local-broadcast programming, a regulatory step that protected local programming from being overwhelmed by cable-relayed network programs. It was not until the early '70s, when Richard Nixon was in the White House, that forces were realigned in Washington to support cable's entry into the competitive broadcast arena. Nixon was an unlikely ally of guerrilla television proponents, but given his distrust of the Eastern media establishment, he had an interest in seeing the cable industry move ahead and provide a counterweight to the power of the broadcast networks. More than anyone, Nixon influenced the change in the federal regulatory tide.

Public interest advocates like Ralph Lee Smith were concerned that cable, as configured at the time, abridged basic freedoms of speech, press, and assembly. Urging that no economic links exist between the cable companies, the equipment suppliers, and the program producers, Smith argued for cable's status as a common carrier and public utility. Since cable systems were natural and unavoidable monopolies providing essential service, they qualified as public utilities, Smith argued. "Common carrier status would end a tremendous denial of basic freedoms that has been inherent in American TV. No provision exists or ever has existed for public access to broadcasting facilities, exclusive control resting with a small group," he wrote.

In 1971 hearings were held at which advocates urged that some urban cable franchises be granted to local civic, educational, and community groups instead of to profit-making firms. The FCC proposed that public-access channels be required and be available without cost to noncommercial users. The broadcasters predictably denounced all the new FCC rules, but the public access requirement remained, opening the door for alternative programming on cable.

Early support of public access by the cable industry must be understood in the context of the bitter struggle between broadcasters and cablecasters over the future of television in the United States. Portrayed by broadcasters as a mercenary threat to "free" television, cable television needed to polish its image if it was to thrive. It was enlightened self-interest that prompted cable industry leaders to embrace public access as a means of legitimating cable as a more socially responsible medium compared with commercial broadcast TV.[10]

But changes in cable in the mid-'70s featured more than alternative visions in the new programming mix. Early efforts at pay television dated back to the '60s, although they had failed due to the efforts of theater owners and commercial broadcasters blocking its success. In 1972 in New York City a new program service consisting of live coverage of sporting events plus older movies became available on Sterling Manhattan Cable for a fee. Since it was unlikely such a service would pay for itself based on lower Manhattan subscriber fees alone, the service was transmitted by commercial microwave relay to various other cable systems in the Northeast. In this way, Home Box Office began operating in November 1972. In 1975 HBO approached Time Inc. and proposed using the relay potential of a domestic communications satellite, Satcom I, scheduled for launch by RCA that year. Time leased from RCA one transponder, or channel, transmitting the video signals of HBO programs and supplying cable systems throughout the country. By 1977, 262 systems were taking the service.

HBO galvanized the cable industry. In 1976, Ted Turner's WTBS began to relay its movies, sports and news via Satcom I. In 1978 Showtime and Spotlight started. In 1979, Warner Communications began the Movie Channel and Nickelodeon; Getty Oil Co. started the Entertainment and Sports Programming Network (ESPN); and Turner began CNN. In 1981, Warner Amex launched Music Television, better known as MTV.[11]

The entire world of cable television turned completely around in barely ten years' time, as the power balance shifted away from network television and the movie industry and toward cable. Once they were no longer dependent on social experiments like public-access or local-origination programming to buy community good will during franchise bidding wars, many cable systems vigorously struggled out of their earlier access commitments and lobbied to rescind federal regulations that mandated public-interest provisions. Those requirements were struck down, and the FCC abandoned the assumption that broadcasters had no property rights to the licenses they were granted, giving communications conglomerates what had been recognized as the property of the American people.[12] In the regulatory void, cable companies were free to run their local monopolies virtually unregulated, creating concentrated media empires that threatened to outstrip the former big three network monopolies. It was now up to individual communities to demand that public-access channels be provided and maintained in each new franchise agreement or renewal. That public-access channels continue to exist today is due to the foresight and hard work of enlightened community planners and public interest activists. When the battle was joined to defend the concept of public access to the airwaves, local origination cable programming was sacrificed, a loss which only folks like Ted Carpenter and Broadside TV could fully appreciate.

The proliferation of cable channels did not provide the diversity of offerings promised. Based on conventional TV marketing practices—hustling for the biggest audience at the most efficient cost to advertisers and allowing other potential audiences to get lost in the shuffle for profits—the cable industry demonstrated why the creation of channels alone could not solve the problems of concentration in the electronic media.[13]

As cable became indifferent to community-initiated media, public television seemed to offer guerrilla video activists an alternative broadcasting outlet. The dream of public television's founders was to serve the broader cultural, informational, and educational needs of a democratic society, needs that were not being served by the commercial television industry. Rather than fundamentally restructuring commercial television, communications reformers decided to create a parallel broadcasting system, an alternative to commercial TV fare—the public television system. And public television should have been guerrilla television's first choice had public TV been able to realize its founders' dreams. Created when portable video was inspiring a new movement for communications reform, public television was an aboveground revolution with aspirations as radical and potentially transformative as anything envisioned by guerrilla television theorists and a lot more likely to be realized.

In 1967 President Lyndon Johnson signed the Public Broadcasting Act, one of the last pieces of his Great Society program and its only communications legislation. The ease with which it went through the legislative process revealed a clear consensus at the time that the nation needed a healthy, federally funded, noncommercial television system.

The designers sought to avoid the European model of state-controlled television by developing a complicated administrative and financial structure. The Corporation for Public Broadcasting (CPB) was formed as the administrative structure handling funding for public radio and television, but the actual financing was left to Congressional appropriations. To avoid politicization of funding, advisors urged stable, long-term funding, which would have been enacted had Johnson not decided to withdraw from the 1968 presidential race, thus leaving public broadcasting up for grabs. Richard Nixon's arrival in the White House produced new problems, because Nixon viewed public television as a home for liberal journalists who produced biased news and public affairs programs with the help of federal funds. In 1972, Nixon vetoed the CPB's authorization bill, arguing that public television had become too centralized and was becoming a "fourth network." He was capitalizing on the confusing relationship among the CPB, PBS, and the local stations. His call for a return to localism was actually a cover for the real difficulties his administration had with public television's public affairs programs. By strategically focusing on the CPB instead of on particular programs, Nixon avoided charges of political interference and censorship while steering public television away from the production of controversial, nationally distributed, public affairs programs.

The struggle between Nixon and the CPB revealed how vulnerable public broadcasting was to political pressure, especially from the White House, and it served notice that public television would have to create mechanisms to protect itself from such pressures. A new, decentralized method for distributing production funds—the Station Program Cooperative—was created to help diffuse the potential targets of political pressure by shifting programming decisions away from the CPB. In addition, public television began to look for additional revenue sources from the private sector (corporate underwriting as well as foundation support) to reduce its dependence on the politicized federal appropriations process. Nixon thus provided the framework and political contest that have plagued the public television system to the present.

Public television's responsibility to provide public affairs programming and access to independent producers became a pervasive topic throughout the '70s. Despite Nixon's efforts to suppress controversial documentaries on public television, a number of works were aired, due in large measure to relationships forged between video groups and their local PBS affiliates: University Community Video in Minneapolis (KTCA); Portable Channel in Rochester (WXXI); Optic Nerve in San Francisco (KQED); and various artists and documentarists at the New Television Laboratory at WGBH/Boston, the Television Laboratory at WNET/New York, and the National Center for Experiments in Television at KQED/San Francisco. Still, independents were frustrated by the problems of finding local PBS sponsors for their work; instead they clamored for direct access to PBS.

Public television grew during Jimmy Carter's presidency, thanks to support from a Democratic Congress generally friendly to public television. In February 1976 a coalition of 15 video-producing organizations filed a statement with the CPB addressing a broad range of issues in public television programming, but focusing on the problems of public affairs producers independent of the commercial and public TV industries. TVTV, University Community Video, and Broadside TV were members of this group. Organizers went on the PTV industry circuit, promoting video independents and explaining that video producers needed to cooperate with public TV stations for access to editing hardware as well as funds and airtime.[14] Their argument rested on the charge to the Corporation in the Public Broadcasting Act of 1967: that it should administer its public money in a manner designed "to facilitate the full development of educational broadcasting in which programs of high quality, *obtained from diverse sources*, will be made available" (emphasis added).

Many policy experts believed PBS's alternative programming mandate would ensure inclusion of in-depth analysis of news and current affairs. But the situation proved otherwise, because PBS feared both political interference in controversial programming and withdrawal of financing from corporate underwriters who seldom support public affairs programming. More often than not, alternative programming was interpreted as the importation of high culture (such as BBC dramas) to insulate programming politically.

The lobbying efforts of the New York-based Association of Independent Video and Filmmakers picked up the rallying cry in support of access, shifting their emphasis from cable to independent access[15] to public television. The independents' complaints—about bureaucratic delays and indecision, unfair or inadequate compensation, physical destruction of film prints and tapes, content interference with programs, poor time slots and inadequate publicity, late payments, rejection of award-winning programs, etc.—reached a peak in 1977 in testimony before Rep. Lionel Van Deerlin's Subcommittee on Communications, which was examining public TV as part of its rewrite of the Communications Act. By joining together with public interest advocates, minority producers, critics of public broadcasting, and Hollywood producers, independents prompted a flurry of activity at PBS and CPB to insure they were not being overlooked.[16] The passage of the Public Telecommunications Financing Act of 1978 marked an improvement for both public television and independent producers; it was the first piece of federal legislation that included language directly including small independent producers. But for veterans like TVTV, it was already too late, as PBS ambivalence about their role in public television propelled them to look to other sources for funding and distribution of their work.

The CPB's attitudes may be discerned in remarks appearing in an official report on the corporation's support for independent producers between 1969 and 1978, written by David Stewart:

> The work of independent producers, especially those who are young and talented, is characterized by introspection, an earnestness about life (largely its injustices) and criticism of contemporary social structures. Their film and video material (most prefer not to think of their work as "TV programs") is rarely marked by a sense of humor; burlesque is occasionally present, but comedy largely absent. What the most inventive, but inexperienced independent producers have to offer are fresh appraisals of our lives and world. . . . what they bring—along with their iconoclasm and production inexperience—is the cultural news of the day, and perhaps more importantly, previews of coming attractions—a sense of the future.[17]

Stewart's stuffy and inaccurate assessments of their work, stressing "inexperience" and "iconoclasm," demonstrated the CPB's antipathy to and grudging acknowledgment of the need for independent participation in public television.

In answer to an independent coalition's proposal that a Public Affairs Programming Fund be created,[18] the CPB established a revolving independent documentary fund available to independents and stations. In addition, an Independent Documentary Fund was established at WNET's TV Lab with financial support from the National Endowment for the Arts and the Ford Foundation. David Loxton, head of the TV Lab at WNET/13 and early champion of guerrilla television on public TV, became director of this fund. Unfortunately, Loxton's earlier emphasis on innovative uses of video had to be set aside, given the Fund's commitment to film as well as video productions; the cutting edge quality and experimental nature of guerrilla television became lost in the mix as the majority of grants went to more established documentary filmmakers. Video producers had been quicker to focus their attention on broadcasters than filmmakers had, creating a revolution in public television in which independent filmmakers now wanted to participate.

In 1979 the Carnegie Commission on the Future of Public Television issued its recommendations, advocating the formation of a Center for Independent TV and increased support services and financing. The Commission's report, *A Public Trust*, envisioned public television as a trustee of diversity with interests that superceded marketplace demands:

Inevitably, the introduction of a new invention is accompanied by bal-
lyhoo promising untold benefits to mankind. But, as we have seen repeatedly, services that meet human needs and that benefit society are
readily expendable in a thoroughly exploited market. American radio and
television are not just instruments of the marketplace; they are social
tools of revolutionary importance. If these media are permitted to assume a wholly commercial character, the entire cultural and social apparatus of the nation will become transformed by what may already have
become the dominant mode of the electronic media in the United States:
the merchandising of consciousness.[19]

The authors ventured further to suggest that nothing short of the
future of democracy in America depended on public television's ability
to nurture freedom and diverse public discourse "against the monolithic outlook of all forms of totalitarianism."[20] *A Public Trust* concluded on this resounding call to action:

Unless we grasp the means to broaden our conversation to include the
diverse interests of the entire society, in ways that both illuminate our
differences and distill our mutual hopes, more will be lost than the public
broadcasting system. . . . Americans have the capacity to rebuild their
local communities, their regions, and indeed their country, with tools no
more formidable than transistors and television tubes. . . . We remember
the Egyptians for the pyramids, and the Greeks for their graceful stone
temples. How shall Americans be remembered? As exporters of sensa-
tionalism and salaciousness? Or as builders of magical electronic tab-
ernacles that can in an instant erase the limitations of time and
geography, and make us into one people? The choice is in our hands and
the time is now.[21]

After Ronald Reagan became president in 1981, public television
came under renewed political and economic pressures from the White
House. Documentaries produced under the Independent Documentary Fund's auspices came under increasing political attack even as
they garnered awards for journalistic excellence. Several national
PBS series created to showcase this work, such as "Non-Fiction Television" and "Matters of Life and Death," were canceled after only a
few seasons. Despite a healthy tradition of passion, moral outrage,
and indignation that went back to the earliest broadcasts of Edward
R. Murrow, serious documentary production remained an endangered
species on public television.[22]

FCC chairman Mark Fowler targeted the concept of the government's role as trustee of the public interest in the broadcast industries, including the assumption that the airwaves are as much a part

of the nation's natural resources as are its national parks and water-
ways. "If there's a marketplace need for public television, it'll survive,
and if not, it shouldn't," Fowler was quoted as saying to then PBS
president Lawrence Grossman.[23] Reduction of federal support for
public television and the simultaneous deregulation of commercial
television had far-reaching consequences.

Like network TV, public television proved vulnerable to the
changes effected by the newly powerful cable television industry,
whose proliferation of cultural channels in the early '80s weakened
perception of public television as a unique provider of serious cultural,
public affairs, and documentary programming. When the FCC later
broadened its guidelines for identification of corporate underwriters
of public television programs, the differences between commercial and
noncommercial television became increasingly blurred, setting the
stage for what is happening in the '90s: the privatization of public
television. With the dismantling of industry regulations, the entire
spectrum of broadcasting—public television included—has become
less and less accountable to any measure of the public interest beyond
audience ratings. The undisguised market orientation of all broadcasting has become one more evidence of the erosion of the public
sector in American life.[24]

With cable and public television turning their backs on guerrilla television, the next possibility was (gulp) network TV. In 1977, John
Culhane, writing in *The New York Times*, outlined the following "seven
deadly taboos" in the world of television documentaries:

> You will rarely if ever see documentaries on your home screen about:
> big labor, big business, big TV networks, the automotive industry, nu-
> clear power, the military–industrial complex, U.S. foreign policy. Most
> of these taboos have been violated at least once by one or more of the
> three major networks, but mostly in years gone by—and the violators
> paid for their courage by losing out in the ratings war . . . [25]

Culhane might have added another taboo, namely that of hiring an
independent producer to make any documentary for network television. Since the quiz show scandals of the late '50s rocked television
and revealed the extent of sponsor domination of network programming, the networks had taken special measures to protect public perception of their integrity by insuring that no news or public affairs
programs produced outside the networks were aired. In 1960, when
ABC purchased Robert Drew's *Yanki No!*, the first independently
produced documentary ever to be shown on television, the head of

news programming quit, arguing that the networks must retain control over all stages of news and documentary production, because federal regulations made them liable for anything they programmed.[26] Twenty years later a group of 26 independent documentary producers filed suit against the three television networks and the television stations owned and operated by them, charging that their monopolization of news and public affairs programming violated antitrust laws. They argued to no avail that the networks' refusal to allow independently produced public affairs programs and news access to the publicly owned airwaves constituted monopoly practice.

With few exceptions, there have been no significant changes in network policy towards independently produced documentaries. Fiscal conservatism, a tendency to prefer staff productions over outside efforts (self-preference), and fear of losing sponsor revenues not only have limited the quantity and quality of network documentaries but posed barriers to entry for independent producers. Network television was the last place where guerrilla television was likely to find an outlet to an audience. Yet it offered just such an outlet, at a time when commercial television provided a more flexible arena than the increasingly politicized world of public television.[27]

Network interest in inviting independent video journalists to join the club seemed to peak in 1978,[28] but only one independent producer was admitted: Jon Alpert, one of the most politically controversial documentary video producers to emerge from the guerrilla television era. Between 1979 and 1991, Alpert was the sole freelance video documentarist regularly featured on network television. His reports for NBC's "The Today Show" and "Nightly News" offered mass audiences a view of domestic and international affairs from a decidedly decentered perspective.

Alpert, with his wife Keiko Tsuno, had founded one of the first and longest-lived community video access centers, Downtown Community Television Center (DCTV). In addition to serving the information needs of the Lower East Side and Chinatown communities of New York City, DCTV produced a number of award-winning documentaries for WNET's TV Lab. Their hour-long documentaries were championed by David Loxton and included *Cuba: The People* (1974), the first half-inch color video documentary ever broadcast; *Healthcare: Your Money or Your Life* (1977); and *Vietnam: Picking Up the Pieces* (1978). By 1978 it had become apparent to Alpert—much as it had to TVTV—that public television did not offer a future for documentaries by video independents. Alpert struck a unique deal with NBC's "Today Show," parlaying his contacts, his daredevil adventurism, and his considerable talents as a documentary producer, venturing into global trouble spots and returning with stories network journalists would never get. During the Iran hostage crisis, Alpert's reports focused not on the American embassy compound but on what was happening in the countryside. His reports from the Philippines, after Corazon Aquino was elected president, presented a somber view of Philippine reality at odds with what was being broadcast by other journalists.

Alpert's cameraman–interviewer style and high-pitched "gee whiz" commentary clearly identified him as an interested observer—distinct from the conventional, supposedly objective and detached news professional. This angered critics on both left and right, who insisted he was not above staging sequences and entrapping subjects for dramatic effect, despite NBC's staunch defense of his journalistic integrity.[29] The Faustian bargain Alpert made in his decision to work within the networks demanded certain compromises, but it also allowed him to influence not only millions of viewers but key legislators and corporate executives who otherwise might not have had to take his messages seriously. But talent and daring were insufficient insurance when more powerful opposition was marshalled against Alpert during the Persian Gulf War. He was summarily fired from NBC on his return from Iraq in 1991, his report canceled sight unseen. The reasons were complex, including matters of internecine competition and jealousy within NBC's news division, along with the overarching fear that unflattering coverage of the air war would provoke the Pentagon to revoke NBC's press pool privileges when the ground war began.[30] After 12 years, Alpert's unique relationship to a network, which allowed him to shoot, edit and narrate his own documentary reports for national broadcast, ended abruptly and with it, the last broadcast trace of guerrilla television.[31]

Guerrilla television theory asserted that if the people had cameras, they could change the world, but access to cameras was not enough. Once consumer video became small and relatively inexpensive, video became a staple of middle-class life. The new miniature camcorders were marketed as the latest electronic toys, status symbols of consumer power and economic privilege. Understandably, there was nothing in the ad copy about the potential for this new technology to overturn the economic, political, and cultural realities that most camcorder purchasers were struggling to maintain. Instead, video recorders were marketed as the latest version of Super 8 or the Polaroid camera, an electronic version of home movies and the snapshot, a medium for nostalgia, sentiment, and private memories, but not for public discourse.

Guerrilla television's influences were quickly absorbed and transformed by commercial media into something antithetical to its original intentions. One can see a perversion of guerrilla television today in prime-time network shows like "America's Funniest Home Videos" and "Cops," examples of what is now familiarly referred to as "reality TV." This disturbing trend, which began in the late '70s with programs like "Real People" and "That's Incredible!," borrowed heavily on guerrilla television style. The clearest indication of this trajectory is evident in the history of Alan and Susan Raymond's 90-minute documentary *The Police Tapes* (a 1976 video documentary that won the DuPont–Columbia Journalism award and had national broadcasts on both public television and ABC). *The Police Tapes* became the model for the drama series "Hill Street Blues," which based its look, style, and characters on the original video documentary.[32] Later came "The Street," a short-lived black-and-white reality show about cops notable for its herky-jerky camerawork—a poor approximation of the Raymonds' fluid hand-held videography. And finally came the popular "Cops," which routinely serves up the domestic problems and minor offenses of a global underclass for the amusement and satisfaction of American middle-class TV viewers. Even more disturbing are programs like "America's Funniest Home Videos," which encourage people to use small-format video equipment not to change the world but to humiliate themselves and their friends, families, and pets for the amusement of mass audiences and the economic advantage of program producers. Guerrilla television's discovery that ordinary people are fascinating subjects for television programming was twisted into the exploitation of "ordinary people" on cheap shows that appeal to sadomasochistic audience interests. So-called reality TV is a long way from guerrilla television, from the dream of democratizing the media by giving ordinary people a voice of their own and access to the air.

How could guerrilla television succeed at doing what public television—which was authorized, funded, and protected by legislative mandates—has ultimately failed to do: provide an information alternative to commercially driven cable and broadcast interests. The political and economic forces arrayed in opposition to a free public exchange of diverse viewpoints have only gained in strength since portable video first arrived on the scene, which is what makes it seem a minor miracle that guerrilla television has been passed on to a younger generation of activist videomakers. The radical discourse embraced by *Guerrilla Television* endured even after the work produced by its theoreticians proved to be less than radical in its substance although consistently radical in its style. The authority of guerrilla television remained despite its own inner inconsistencies, passed on to a new group of media mavericks.

In 1989 ABC's "The Koppel Report" investigated the "new" video revolution—a revolution portrayed as occurring everywhere in the world but in the United States. Koppel noted that if VCRs, cassettes, camcorders, and satellite dishes had appeared 40 years earlier, George Orwell would not have written *Nineteen Eighty-Four*. The proliferation of small, lightweight, inexpensive video equipment had turned little brothers and sisters into producers who could only confound and exasperate Big Brother. Koppel praised the uses of video in foreign lands like Poland, where the same equipment used in the United States to record weddings had shored up spirits in workers' ranks during the years of martial law. Curiously, the report gave short shrift to comparable domestic uses of video for shoring up revolutionary morale, instead presenting as troublesome gadflies the camcorder guerrillas who witnessed police beatings of the homeless at Tompkins Square Park in New York City in 1988. *New York Times* TV critic Walter Goodman was even more blunt. In writing about the program, he called for "more information delivered by professionals" as our best defense against "the availability and effectiveness of these new tools for lying, distorting and evading."[33]

Video's potential to be a tool, a weapon, and a witness in the hands of ordinary people finally grabbed national attention when another savage police beating was captured by a bystander in Los Angeles in 1991, and the Rodney King videotape became an international icon, screened endlessly on television and in the trials that followed. Not only was the Los Angeles Police Department on trial, but the legitimacy of "unprofessional" video to serve as documentary evidence and the power of ordinary citizens to confront institutional abuses were riding on the outcome.

The return of guerrilla video tactics and idealism in the '80s was reliant on the widespread availability of consumer video equipment and the fervor of a younger generation of videomakers caught up in the political and social issues of a newer age—war in Central America, nuclear proliferation, homelessness, environmental dangers, reproductive rights, and AIDS, among others. A host of video collectives organized around such issues: groups such as DIVA-TV (Damned Interfering Video Activist Television), Not Channel Zero, Repro-Vision, and MAC (Media Against Censorship) Attack, to name a few.

Eclectic and pragmatic, young video activists incorporated into their tapes whatever worked. By mixing the slick sophistication of music video style with guerrillalike coverage of demonstrations, by juxtaposing the high-end quality of broadcast Betacam with the low-tech grit of home video camcorders and toy video cameras, they appropriated the full range of production tools and aesthetics and effectively rendered distinctions between low- and high-end documentary video obsolete, further democratizing the medium and opening it up for creative and political possibilities.

Today's version of guerrilla television can be found on the public-access channels of cable thanks to the hard work and vigilance of community activists who fought, and continue to fight, to keep some public channels of discourse available. When this newer generation took up the camcorder as an activist tool in the '80s, the hard lessons learned by the portapak generation were built upon: Don't succumb to the traps posed by broadcast and cable television, keep your focus clear on your social change goals, and produce work for targeted audiences using alternative means of distribution. Politically astute veteran videomakers like DeeDee Halleck provided the experiential bridge for a younger generation, so that video activists could take off from where early community videomakers had ended. What Challenge for Change was for the '70s, Paper Tiger Television became for the '80s, providing an influential theoretic model for video activism using public-access cable channels and, eventually, satellite distribution.

Paper Tiger Television started in 1981 as a weekly cable program critical of the mass media; it was produced for the public-access channel in New York City by an energetic collective of videomakers. Drawing on the more radical aspirations of guerrilla television, Paper Tiger Television invented its own funky, homegrown video aesthetic, demonstrating that energy, talent, modest resources, and public-access cable were enough to make revolutionary television. Initially, the show's hosts were articulate critics who analyzed the corporate ownership, hidden agendas, and information biases of mainstream media. As collective members have moved on, they have set up regional offshoots (from Maine to California) that continue to expose not only the hidden ideologies of the mass media but a variety of national and international social issues.

In 1986 Paper Tiger rented time on a satellite and began to transmit community-produced tapes to more than 250 participating cable systems and public TV stations around the country. The successful syndication of "Deep Dish TV"—the first national public-access series of community-made programs on issues such as labor, housing,

the farming crisis, and racism—has helped stimulate alternative documentary productions in the '90s.

During the summer of 1990, Paper Tiger worked with Deep Dish
to produce a TV teach-in on peaceful alternatives to war in the Persian Gulf. Aired on public television as well as on cable, "The Gulf
Crisis TV Project" offered the only national broadcast coverage of
dissenting opinion about the war before it began, demonstrating the
power of alternative video to reach a national audience and fulfill a
critical information need.[34] McLuhan's prediction that the next war
would be fought with television was proven true in the Persian Gulf,
and activist video was ready to engage in guerrilla warfare of the
airwaves.

Although guerrilla television has survived into the '90s, the scale
of opposition to the championing of diverse viewpoints and innovative
aesthetics has never been greater. Alternative videomakers in particular have been identified for special attack from rightwing legislators
and presidential candidates. Marlon Riggs—an accomplished video
journalist whose extraordinary video essay on being black and gay,
Tongues Untied (1989), became the target of numerous attacks in
Congress as well as censorship by public television and distortion in
the 1992 presidential campaign ads—spoke out against the bigotry,
race-baiting, and homophobia that often lurk behind attacks on alternative media in America today.[35] Attacks on the National Endowment for the Arts and public broadcasting are part of a larger
conservative agenda that threatens more than our freedom of speech.

The future of guerrilla television remains to be seen. But if the
powerful obstacles that foiled its visionary founders in the '70s did
not crush the impulse toward more democratic access to public channels of electronic discourse, then perhaps this current challenge will
only serve to sharpen the alternative media's tactics and resolve to
insure that a broad spectrum of ideas and voices may be seen and
heard in the information environment of the new millennium.

Appendix

Information on Tapes by Broadside TV, University Community Video, and TVTV (Top Value Television)

In 1983, my research into the history of '70s documentary video led me on a cross–country journey in search of historic tapes and their makers. This was my first brush with the already alarming state of video preservation. In New Orleans I excitedly located a tape I'd read about only to discover, as I opened the black plastic box, a sickeningly sweet smell emanating from the powdery white crust that covered the unplayable tape. The New Orleans Video Access Center had been inundated and their tape archive, housed in the basement, was flooded. It was the first of many such disappointments—tapes mislabeled, tapes gone missing, tapes that played for five minutes then developed into a series of black-and-white glitches, tapes made on machines that were unrepairable or nowhere to be found. Housed in garages, basements, in closets and footlockers, the precious record of an historic period lay vulnerable to fire, flood, heat, humidity, carelessness, and indifference.

I was part of the first wave of video historians, critics, and curators who uncovered the array of preservation problems confronting individual artists, media art centers, video distributors, funders, and exhibitors. Since then progress has been made in launching the vast effort at locating historic programs, cataloging them, providing archivally acceptable storage for these tapes and their playback equipment, developing reliable, low cost methods for cleaning, restoring and preserving tapes, and sharing information with others similarly engaged. (For further information, see my monograph, *Video Preservation: Securing the Future of the Past*, New York: Media Alliance, 1993.)

Since videotapes have come to replace snapshots, audiotapes, Super8 films, letters, and written diaries for recording the milestones of our lives, video has become the fabric of our family memories and, by extension, of our collective social history. Video has a limited life span. The manufactures of video tape and recording technology know this, but millions of people who own handicams and record Billy's birthday party, Jennifer's soccer game, and the children's wedding on tape do not know that their precious memories will fade in time to mere snow on a flickering screen. What does this mean to a culture that has become increasingly dependent on visual images for its self-image, its view of the world, and its understanding of what is true? What does this mean if our databanks of images—those public and collective as well as those private and personal—fade into oblivion? Without evidence of the past to re-examine and reconsider, we become increasingly vulnerable to the spin doctors of history who reshape the past to serve other agendas. The entire spectrum of video recordings—from those professionally recorded for cultural institutions like network television to guerrilla television experiments to tapes made to memorialize the events of our lives—demands our preservation attention and concern.

Some of the tapes made by the groups discussed in this text have been preserved, but many historic collections have yet to be tackled. From the viewpoint of the social historian and the student of American politics, communications and culture, the value of such material is immeasurable.

Broadside TV

The Archives of Appalachia, located at East Tennessee State University (ETSU), is a regional institution devoted to the collection and preservation of the documentary heritage of the Central Southern Appalachians. Broadside TV's archive of over 600 tapes was culled for deposit there by Richard Blaustein, director of the SAVES project and an ETSU professor of sociology, and Broadside TV engineer Tom Christy. A special supplement (July 1, 1981) to the Archives' *Newsletter* provided a guide to the collection's audio and video recordings. Regarding the Broadside TV collection, the *Newsletter* says: "Only those [tapes] deemed of substantial research value have been duplicated. . . . The original collection included duplicates, reels of raw footage, and programs produced for the cable networks . . . many of these were passed over." The Broadside TV collection numbers approximately 100 tapes and includes mainly folk subjects—interviews with craftspeople and midwives, performances by musicians and storytellers, and the like—as well as some social-issue documentaries, such as Ted Carpenter's *A Mountain Has No Seed.*

Researchers can obtan access to the tapes by visiting the archives. For more information and a list of titles in the collection, contact: Archives of Appalachia, The Sherrod Library, East Tennessee State University, P.O. Box 70665 Johnson City, Tennessee 37614; 423-929-4338.

University Community Video

University Community Video became UCVideo in 1983; a few years later the organization chartered a new course and in 1987 was rebaptized Intermedia Arts Minnesota, a still vital organization.

Preservation of part of University Community Video's extensive videotape collection was made possible when a selection of tapes were restored and deposited with the Minnesota Historical Society several years ago. There are 173 titles, the majority of which have been transferred from original half-inch open reels to SuperVHS cassettes. No catalog to the collection exists, but the tapes are available for viewing by the public at the Historical Society's headquarters.

A catalog of the UCV collection was produced in 1982. The effort of many volunteers, it includes brief, occasionally inaccurate annotations and credits for a videotape archive of over 400 titles; nevertheless, it is probably the most inclusive document of the work produced during the '70s when UCV was still a university-community video center. A reference copy of this catalog can be read at the Historical Society.

Although Intermedia Arts Minnesota continued to distribute a selection of tapes produced over the years through their facilities, the difficult decision to phase out distribution was made in the early '90s because it was no longer economically viable. Hardest hit was the extensive collection of Native American video. (The American Indian Movement was founded in 1968 to patrol the streets of Minneapolis to prevent police brutality against Native Americans.) Sadly there is no distribution source today for many of UCV's historic tapes, although the Chicago-based Video Data Bank has expressed interest in handling some titles.

For more information about University Community Video's archive, contact: Bonnie Wilson, Archivist, Minnesota Historical Society, 345 Kellogg Blvd., St. Paul, Minnesota 55102-1906; 612-296-1275. Other inquiries about UCV should be addressed to: Tom Borrup, Executive Director, Intermedia Arts Minnesota, 2822 Lindale Avenue South, Minneapolis, Minnesota 55408; 612-871-4444.

TVTV (Top Value Television)

The tapes produced by and about TVTV do not exist in one archival location; a number of TVTV's works, however, are still in distribution to the home market and to the institutional market (universities, museums, and broadcast outlets).

Copies on VHS of the following tapes are available for individual purchase from Subtle Communications: TVTV Classics includes: *Four More Years, Lord of the Universe, TVTV Looks at the Oscars*, and *TVTV Goes to the Superbowl*. For more information, contact: Subtle Communications, 1208 W. Webster, Chicago, Illinois 60614; 312-871-6033 or 1-800-522-3688; 312-871-5463 (fax).

Electronic Arts Intermix, a video art distributor, handles institutional sales and rentals on VHS and three-quarter-inch cassettes of the following: *The World's Largest TV Studio, Four More Years, The Lord of the Universe, Adland*, "Gerald Ford's America": *Win* and *Chic to Sheik, The Good Times Are Killing Me*, and *VTR: TVTV*. For more information, contact: Electronic Arts Intermix, 536 Broadway, 9th floor, New York, New York 10012; 212-966-4605; 212-941-6118 (fax).

Three video portraits were produced about TVTV, the first of which is available for rental or purchase from Electronic Arts Intermix: *VTR: TVTV*, for the "VTR (Video/ Television Review)" series at WNET (1975) 28 min.; *The Recording Revolution* for the BBC's series "Worldwide" (1977); and *TVTV: Diary of the Video Guerrillas*, produced by Charles Allen for KCET (1979) 90 min.

The credits and broadcast history—as well as they can be reconstructed—for TVTV's opus follows. Please note that the spelling of names for several TVTV participants changed from tape to tape. For example, Wendy Appel sometimes spelled her last name "Apple"; Jodi Sibert is listed as Jodi, Jody and Jodie; and Laura and Frank Cavestany are often featured as Cavestani. The early tapes reflected the nonhierarchical nature of early video collectives: at first names were listed in alphabetical order, but as time passed, roles began to be assigned, a trend that culminated in the bitter battle over credits that marked TVTV's demise.

The World's Largest TV Studio (1972) 60 min. b/w
- Credits: Wendy Appel, Skip Blumberg, Nancy Cain, Frank Cavestani, Steve Christiansen, Bart Friedman, Mike Couzens, Bob Devine, Stanton Kaye, Chuck Kennedy, Anda Korsts, Joan Logue, Chip Lord, Andy Mann, Doug Michaels, Jim Norman, Maureen Orth, Hudson Marquez, Martha Miller, T.L. Morey, Allen Rucker, Ira Schneider, Curtis Schreier, Jody Sibert, Michael Shamberg, Tom Weinberg, Judy Williams, Megan Williams. Edited by Allen Rucker, Ira Schneider, Jody Sibert, Parry Teasdale, Michael Shamberg, Tom Weinberg, Megan Williams.

- Cable history: Shown in New York City on August. 17, 1972, on Teleprompter and Sterling cable at 8 P.M. Also shown August 30 on Teleprompter at 9 P.M. and on August 31 on Sterling at 8 P.M.. In Chicago, cablecast on WSNS August 24 at 8P.M.

Four More Years (1972) 60 min. b/w
- Credits: Wendy Appel, Skip Blumberg, Megan Williams, Ira Schneider, Nancy Cain, Steve Christiansen, Bart Friedman, Mike Couzens, Chuck Kennedy, Anda Korsts, Chip Lord, Maureen Orth, Hudson Marquez, Martha Miller, T.L. Morey, Allen Rucker, Jody Sibert, Michael Shamberg, Tom Weinberg. Additional material: Marc Weiss, Barbara Kopple, Laurence Storch, Vietnam Veterans Against the War.

- Broadcast history: Shown on Teleprompter on September 27, 1972, during prime time and later that week on Sterling. Group W broadcast of a 90-minute version of both tapes: Aired during the week of October 25–31, 1972 on WOR-TV in New York; and on five VHS stations in Boston, Baltimore, Pittsburgh, Philadelphia and San Francisco. It was also shown on San Francisco's public station KQED. (See Chip Lord, "TVTV Video Pioneers 10 Years Later," *SEND*, Summer 1983, p. 18.)

TVTV Meets Rolling Stone (1973) 17 min. b/w
Produced for WNET series "Behind the Lines," producer Cary Winfrey. Aired in March 1973. (No credits listed, but TVTV staffers included Allen Rucker, Michael Shamberg, Hudson Marquez, and Chip Lord.)

Lord of the Universe (1974) 58 min. b/w & color
  For TVTV: Hudson Marquez, Allen Rucker, Michael Shamberg, Tom Weinberg, Megan Williams.
- Production: Wendy Appel, Skip Blumberg, Bill Bradbury, John Brumage, Steve Christiansen, Paul Goldsmith, Stanton Kaye, John Keeler, Anda Korsts, Harry Mathias, Doug Michels, Tom Morey, Rita Ogden, Tom Richmond, Van Schley, Jody Sibert, Akio Yamaguchi.
- Editing: Wendy Appel, Hudson Marquez, Rita Ogden, Allen Rucker, Michael Shamberg, Elon Soltes.

- For the TV Lab: Editor—John J. Godfrey; Assistant Editor—Philip Falcone; Production Manager—Darlene Mastro; Assistant to Producer—Diane English; Production Secretary—Lynn Hott; Producer—David Loxton.

The Television Lab receives grants from the Rockefeller Foundation and the New York State Council on the Arts. *Lord of the Universe* was funded by the Stern Foundation, the Corporation for Public Broadcasting, and Vanguard Foundation.
© 1974 by Educational Broadcasting Corporation.

Adland: Where Commercials Come From (1974) 60 min. b/w & color
- For TVTV: Hudson Marquez, Allen Rucker, Michael Shamberg, Tom Weinberg, Megan Williams.

- Production: Wendy Appel, Skip Blumberg, Anda Korsts, Chip Lord, Rita Ogden, Elon Soltes, Videofreex.
  Editing: Chip Lord, Hudson Marquez, Allen Rucker, Tom Weinberg
  Production in cooperation with WTTW/Chicago.

  Broadcast April 8, 1974, in Chicago on WTTW; and on August 31, 1974, on PBS Channel 9 in San Francisco.

"Gerald Ford's America" (1975) four half-hour programs, 28 min. each. b/w & color
  Part One: Win
  A Videotape Production of TVTV and the Television Laboratory at WNET

- For TVTV: Wendy Appel, Skip Blumberg, Bill Bradbury, Nancy Cain, Frank Cavestany, Wilson Chao, Steve Christiansen, Steve Conant, Michael Couzens, Mary DeOreo, Bart Friedman, Paul Goldsmith, Anda Korsts, Andy Mann, Hudson Marquez, Allen

Rucker, Paul Ryan, Michael Shamberg, Jodi Sibert, Elon Soltes, Megan Williams.

- Editing: Frank Cavestany and Michael Shamberg.

- Thanks to: Baird Brown, Laura Cavestany, CBS News, Jack Goldman, Albert R. Hunt, KOIN-TV Portland, Steve Kolpan, Moe & Tommy, David Obst, Judy O'Neil, Betsy Ross, Gunther Weill, University of Massachusetts Media Center.

- For the Television Laboratory: Supervising Engineer and Videotape Editor—John Godfrey; Production Manager—Darlene Mastro; Administrative Assistant—Carol Brandenburg; Associate Director—Judi Elterman. Special Assistance from WGBH New Television Workshop: Coordinator—Dorothy Chiesa; Engineering Consultant—Wilson Chao.

This program made possible in part by a general program grant to WNET/13 by the Ford Foundation and the Rockefeller Foundation. The Television Laboratory is supported by grants from the Rockefeller Foundation and the New York State Council on the Arts.

Producer, The Television Laboratory—David Loxton
A Production of WNET/13 New York
© 1975 Educational Broadcasting Corporation

Part Two: Chic to Sheik
A Videotape Production of TVTV and the Television Laboratory at WNET

- For TVTV: Wendy Appel, Skip Blumberg, Bill Bradbury, Nancy Cain, Frank Cavestany, Wilson Chao, Steve Christiansen, Steve Conant, Michael Couzens, Mary DeOreo, Bart Friedman, Paul Goldsmith, Anda Korsts, Andy Mann, Hudson Marquez, Allen Rucker, Paul Ryan, Michael Shamberg, Jodi Sibert, Elon Soltes, Megan Williams.
Editing: Wendy Appel, Frank Cavestany, Anda Korsts, Megan Williams.

- Thanks to: Zahidi Ardeshir, Betty Beale, Baird Brown, Laura Cavestany, Lydia Preston, Helen Smith, U. Mass. Media Center, Gunther Weill.

- For the Television Laboratory: Videotape Editor—Philip F. Falcone, Jr.; Production Manager—Darlene Mastro; Administrative

Assistant—Carol Brandenburg; Associate Director—Judi Elterman.

- Special Assistance from WGBH New Television Workshop: Coordinator—Dorothy Chiesa; Engineering Consultant—Wilson Chao.

This program made possible in part by a general program grant to WNET/13 by the Ford Foundation and the Rockefeller Foundation. The Television Laboratory is supported by grants from the Rockefeller Foundation and the New York State Council on the Arts.

Producer, The Television Laboratory—David Loxton
A Production of WNET/13 New York
© 1975 Educational Broadcasting Corporation

Part Three: Second Hand News
A Videotape Production of TVTV and the Television Laboratory at WNET

- For TVTV: Wendy Appel, Skip Blumberg, Bill Bradbury, Nancy Cain, Frank Cavestany, Wilson Chao, Steve Christiansen, Steve Conant, Michael Couzens, Mary DeOreo, Bart Friedman, Paul Goldsmith, Anda Korsts, Andy Mann, Hudson Marquez, Allen Rucker, Paul Ryan, Michael Shamberg, Jodi Sibert, Elon Soltes, Megan Williams.

- Editing: Paul Goldsmith, Elon Soltes.

- Thanks to: Max Barber, Dennis Johnston, Peter Lisagor, Sara McClendon, Judy O'Neil, U. Mass. Media Center, Gunther Weil.

- For the Television Laboratory: Supervising Engineer and Videotape Editor—John Godfrey; Production Manager—Darlene Mastro; Administrative Assistant—Carol Brandenburg; Associate Director—Judi Elterman, Robert Morris.

Special Assistance from WGBH New Television Workshop: Coordinator—Dorothy Chiesa; Engineering Consultant—Wilson Chao.

This program made possible in part by a general program grant to WNET/13 by the Ford Foundation and the Rockefeller Foundation. The Television Laboratory is supported by grants from the Rockefeller Foundation and the New York State Council on the Arts.

Producer, The Television Laboratory—David Loxton
A Production of WNET/13 New York
© 1975 Educational Broadcasting Corporation

Part Four: The Hill
A Videotape Production of TVTV and the Television Laboratory at WNET

- For TVTV: Wendy Appel, Skip Blumberg, Bill Bradbury, Nancy Cain, Frank Cavestany, Wilson Chao, Steve Christiansen, Steve Conant, Michael Couzens, Mary DeOreo, Bart Friedman, Paul Goldsmith, Andy Korsts, Andy Mann, Hudson Marquez, Allen Rucker, Paul Ryan, Michael Shamberg, Jodi Sibert, Elon Soltes, Megan Williams.

- Editing: Skip Blumberg, Nancy Cain, Jodi Sibert, [Elon Soltes].

- Thanks to: John Guiniven, Bill Sudow, Max Barber, Mike Michaelson, Baird Brown, U. Mass Media Center, Gunther Weil. Videofreex/Media Bus.
  The Friendly People of Lewis County, West Virginia.
  Soft Sculpture: "The Capitol: A History of the United States," 1974 by Michelle Gamm Clifton.

- For the Television Laboratory: Videotape Editor—Philip F. Falcone, Jr.; Production Manager—Darlene Mastro; Administrative Assistant—Carol Brandenburg; Associate Director—Tony Marshall.

Special Assistance from WGBH New Television Workshop: Coordinator—Dorothy Chiesa; Engineering Consultant—Wilson Chao.

This program made possible in part by a general program grant to WNET/13 by the Ford Foundation and the Rockefeller Foundation. The Television Laboratory is supported by grants from the Rockefeller Foundation and the New York State Council on the Arts.

Producer, The Television Laboratory—David Loxton
A Production of WNET/13 New York
© 1975 Educational Broadcasting Corporation

Broadcast nationally over PBS; shown in New York on WNET in January:

WIN, January 10, 1975
Chic to Sheik, January 17, 1975

Second Hand News, January 24, 1975
The Hill, January 31, 1975

In Hiding: America's Fugitive Underground—An Interview with Abbie Hoffman (1975) 58 min. b/w & color
For TVTV
* Production and Editing: Eleanor Bingham, Frank Cavestany, Paul Goldsmith, Allen Rucker, Michael Shamberg, Megan Williams.
* Production Support: Wendy Appel, Steve Conant, Hudson Marquez, Elon Soltes.
* For the Television Laboratory: Supervising Engineer—John J. Godfrey; Videotape Editor—Juan Barnett.

Broadcast Monday, May 19, 1975, 9 P.M. on WNET/13, New York.

The Good Times Are Killing Me (1975) 58 min. color & b/w
* Production: Wendy Appel, Paul Goldsmith, Petur Hliddal, Robby Kenner, Hudson Marquez, David Myers, Allen Rucker, Suzanne Tedesko.
* Editing: Wendy Appel, Frank Cavestany, Paul Goldsmith, Petur Hliddal, Andy Mann, Hudson Marquez, Allen Rucker, Michael Shamberg.
Production Support: Elon Soltes, Megan Williams.

Broadcast June 25, 1975 (according to KCET's "Diary" tape)

Super Bowl (1976) 60 min. (46 min?) color & b/w
Produced by TVTV and Great Balls of Fire.

* For TVTV: Wendy Appel, Steve Conant, Paul Goldsmith, Hudson Marquez, Roone [Allen] Rucker, Michael Shamberg, Elon Soltes, Megan Williams.
* For Great Balls of Fire: Billy Adler, Van Schley.
* Production: Tom Baker, Eleanor Bingham, Ned Belcher, Skip Blumberg, Nancy Cain, Cali Cerami, Wilson Chao, Pat Crowley, Alida Davidson, Bob Elfstrom, Bart Friedman, Alison Cebaile, Joel Gold, Petur Hliddal, Laura Jeffers, L.A. Johnson, Anda Korsts, Pepper Mauser, Michael Mead, Tom Morey, Harold Ramis, Rick Rosen, Leslie Shatz, John Walsh, Tom Weinberg.
* Performances: Christopher Guest, Bill Murray, Brian Doyle Murray.
* Editing: Billy Adler, Alida Davison, Alison Cebaile, Paul Gold-

smith, Hudson Marquez, Susan Martin, Billy Murray, Allen Rucker, Michael Shamberg, Megan Williams.

Shot January 18, 1976 at the Superbowl.
Broadcast during membership drive week, March 7-21, 1976: March 10 in Washington, D.C., on WETA. March 15 in New York on WNET; March 19 in Houston.

TVTV Looks at the Oscars (1976) 60 min. color
Produced by TVTV in association with KCET.

* For TVTV: Wendy Apple, David Axelrod, Paul Goldsmith, Hudson Marquez, Tom Morey, Allen Rucker, Michael Shamberg, Megan Williams.

* With: Lily Tomlin as Judy Beasley.

* Production: Rich Rosen, Wendy Apple, Calli Cerami, Megan Williams, Susan Martin, Allen Rucker, Paul Goldsmith, Hudson Marquez, Michael Shamberg, Steve Conant, Alison Cebaile, Karen Murphy, Ceil Gruessing, Jody Sibert, Michael Weselblatt, Cathy Buckley, Peter Kirby, Howard Campbell, Will Hoover, Mark Brown, Tom Baker, Tom Morey, Lisa Van Der Sluis, Mark Rosner, Eleanor Bingham, Bette Cohen, Harold Ramis, Billy Murray, David Axelrod, L.A. Johnson, Alida Davison, Elon Soltes.

* Camera: Wendy Apple, Baird Bryant, Steve Christiansen, Steve Conant, Tim Greenfield, Paul Goldsmith, Rich Rosen, Allen Rucker, David Sanderson, Elon Soltes.
* Sound: Bill Bradbury, Kent Gibson, L.A. Johnson, Hudson Marquez, Susan Martin.
* Editing: Wendy Apple, Petur Hliddal, Calli Cerami, Michael Shamberg.
* Additional Editing: Alida Davison, Susan Martin, Megan Williams.
* Super 8 Footage: Dale Castillo.
* 35mm Slides: Richard Lunn, Neil Fitzgerald.

* Thanks to: Harshe-Rotman & Druck Inc., Academy of Motion Picture Arts and Sciences, Chuck Allen, Larry Grossman, Mark Chavez, Harry Knierem, Andy Knierem, Joseph F. Escobosa, Betty Murrietta, Judy Francesconi, John Calentano, Judy Calentano, Howard Koch, Marty Pasetta, Maggie Abbott, Jim Songer, Gary Haber, Karen Danaher, Marya Small, Deborah Kavruck, Jerry Bick, Richard Chew, Ray Bolger, Brad Donrif, Sylvia Miles,

Richard Zanuck, David Brown, Bert Schneider, Maureen Orth, Optic Nerve.

- Special Thanks to: Ronee Blakely, Steve Blakely, Michael Douglas, Joseph Feury, Verna Fields, Louise Fletcher, Milos Foreman, Lee Grant, Goldie Hawn, Bill Hudson, Ken Kesey, Lucille, Ivan Passer, Steven Spielberg, Joe Spinell, Lily Tomlin, Ret Turner, Saul Zaentz.

Broadcast locally September 7, 1976 on KCET; national broadcast scheduled for spring 1977; reprised April 1983 on Channel Z in Las Angeles to good review in Los Angeles *Herald Examiner*

Hard Rain (1976) 60 min. color
Produced by TVTV in association with Screaming Eagle Productions Inc.

- Stage Director: Jacques Levy.
  For TVTV: Wendy Appel, David Axelrod, Steve Conant, Hudson Marquez, Allen Rucker, Michael Shamberg, Megan Williams.
- Cameramen: Howard Alk, Paul Goldsmith, L.A. Johnson, David Myers, Ron Sheldon.
- Supervising Engineer: John Godfrey
  Edited by Gangbusters.

Broadcast September 4, 1976, on NBC at 10 P.M. EST.

Super Vision (1976/77) 88 min. color & b/w
Consisted of 10 episodes:

1. It's Television (5:40)
2. Off Now (9:00)
3. Birth of an Industry (17:50)
4. Shoot Out (6:00)
5. '50s & '60s (10:00)
6. Talk Back (10:00)
7. Chroma Key Lane (3:30)
8. Opportunity Knocks (2:00)
9. The Video Asylum (17:00)
10. Top Value Television (7:00)

- A TVTV Production: Wendy Apple, David Axelrod, Paul Goldsmith, Tom Morey, Hudson Marquez, Allen Rucker, Michael Shamberg, Megan Williams.

- Written by: Frank Cavestany, Hudson Marquez, Harold Ramis, Michael Shamberg, Willie Walker.
- Executive Producer: Barbara Schultz.
- Produced by: Michael Shamberg.
- Directed by: Harold Ramis.
- Visual Concepts and Director of Photography: Paul Goldsmith.
- Associate Producers: Frank Cavestany, Allen Rucker, Megan Williams.
- Assistant Directors: Wendy Apple, Frank Cavestany.
- Audio: Leslie Shatz.
- Music composed by: Thaddeus Kosciusko.
- (Episodes 1–3) edited by : Wendy Apple, Frank Cavestany, Petur Hliddal, Michael Shamberg, Megan Williams.
- (Episodes 4-10) edited by: Wheeler Dixon.

Broadcast as fillers for the PBS dramatic anthology series "Visions" (beginning October 12, 1976).
First shown in its entirety at The Whitney Museum of American Art, May 31–June 5, 1977.

The TVTV Show (1977) 90 min. color
Cast:
Captain McNulty—Lewis Arquette
News Editor—Rene Auberjonois
2nd Man in Riot—Dan Barrows
WHAM Reporter—Ed Begley Jr.
Wilson—Robert Doqui
Father in Ad—Gary Combs
Tommy—Mike Darnell
Danny—Murphy Dunne
Billy "Bud" Herman—Gerrit Graham
Man Watching TV—Peter Elbling
Owner of Cleaners—Eugene Elman
Father—Garry Goodrow
Momo—Lloyd Kino
Mother—Mina Kolb
Boy in Ad—Sparkle Marcus
TV Repairman—Ira Miller
Jerry—Bill Murray
1st Woman in Riot—Barbara Minkus
Bartenders—Kate Murtagh
Nancy—Annie Potts

2nd Woman in Riot—Ann Shalla
1st Man in Riot—Dave Shelley
Clerk in Cleaners—Ann Weldon
3rd Man in Riot—Paul Wilson
Wilma "Dusty" Upstrum—Debra Winger
and with Carl Gotlieb as George Delardo
Howard Hesseman as Ralph Buckler
and Mary Frann as Mary Kay Foss

Directed by Allan Myerson.
Produced by Allen Rucker and Hudson Marquez.
Written by M.K. Brown, Peter Elbling, Brian McConnachie, Bill
Murray, Brian Doyle-Murray, Michael Shamberg.
Director of Photography—Paul Goldsmith.
Editor—Wheeler Dixon.
Assistant Director—Wendy Calloway.
Costumes—Ceil Gruessing and Susan Lyons.
Music—Thaddeus Kosciusko.
Sound—Leslie Shatz and Eleanor Bingham.
Lighting—John Lindley and Steve Conant.
Production Managers—Jeanie Field and John Thompson.
Associate Producer—David Axelrod and Tom Morey.
Associate Director—Wendy Appel.
Assistant Editors—Calli Cerami and Tom McGuire.
Video—Ron Stutzman, T.J. McHose, Ruxton Ltd.
Video Tape Editor—Robert Fisher.
Production Staff—Marsha Abrahams, Gloria Ashley, Jack Baran,
Rick Fee, Paulie Jenkins, Mike McHugh, Don Orlando, Bob Port,
Jodie Sibert.
Executive Producer—Michael Shamberg.

A TVTV Production
© TVTV Inc., 1977
A Robert Gimbel EMI Presentation

Broadcast April 30, 1977, on NBC as pilot.

Notes

1. Underground Video

1. Garth Jowett, "Dangling the Dream? The Presentation of Television to the American Public, 1928–1952," *Historical Journal of Film, Radio and Television* 14:2, 1994, p. 129.

2. Ibid., pp. 141–142.

3. Theodore Roszak is generally credited as having coined the term in his book, *The Making of a Counter Culture*, New York: Doubleday, 1969, in which he challenged the foundations of technocracy.

4. Fluxus artists like Nam June Paik, Wolf Vostell, and Joseph Beuys and Americans like Allen Kaprow, Robert Rauschenberg, and Claes Oldenberg produced "happenings" that incorporated media coverage as an integral element of their art work in the '60s. (David Ross, "Television: Bringing the Museum Home," *Televisions* 3:2, May 1975, pp. 6–7.)

5. The early portable video rigs cost about $1,000 and weighed about 20 pounds, which allowed women and children as well as burly men to wield the new communications technology.

6. Doug Davis, *Art and the Future*, New York: Praeger, 1973, p. 148.

7. See Martha Gever, "Pomp and Circumstances: The Coronation of Nam June Paik, *Afterimage* 10:3, October 1982: 12–16; Martha Rosler, "Video: Shedding the Utopian Moment," and Marita Sturken, "Paradox in the Evolution of an Art Form," in *Illuminating Video*, edited by Doug Hall and Sally Jo Fifer, New York: Aperture Press, 1990.

8. David Armstrong, *A Trumpet to Arms: Alternative Media in America*, Boston: South End, 1981, p. 21.

9. Michael Shamberg and Raindance Corporation, *Guerrilla Television*, New York: Holt, Rinehart and Winston, 1971.

10. Johanna Gill, *Video: State of the Art,* Rockefeller Foundation Working Papers, June 1976, pp. 7–8.

11. Jud Yalkut, "Frank Gillette and Ira Schneider: Part I and II of an Interview," *Radical Software*, 1:1, 1970, p. 9 (reprinted from *The East Village Other*, 4:35, July 30, 1969, p. 69).

12. This was not the first video art exhibition in the states. In 1963,

Nam June Paik, a Korean artist, and Wolf Vostell, a German artist, respectively exhibited *Electronic TV* and *TV De-Coll/age* in New York City.
(These works did not employ video per se since portable video equipment
had yet to appear on the American market.) In 1966 Billy Kluver organized
"9 Evenings: Theater and Engineering" at the 69th Regiment Armory, an
important show that included video projection of works by well-known artists
such as Robert Rauschenberg. Also in 1966 the New York Film Festival
featured *Selma Last Year*, a multichannel video installation by Bruce Davidson with music by Teri Riley. In 1968, a number of video exhibitions
began appearing. The Museum of Modern Art included Nam June Paik in
"The Machine as Seen at the End of the Mechanical Age"; at the Brooklyn
Museum Aldo Tambellini showed *Black: Video* in "Some More Beginnings";
and at the Corcoran Gallery in Washington, D.C. Paik's video was included
in "Cybernetic Serendipity: The Computer and the Arts." See Davidson
Gigliotti, "Video Art in the Sixties," *Abstract Painting: 1960–69*, P.S.1 catalog. New York: The Institute for Art and Urban Resource, 1982.

  13.   Yalkut, "Frank Gillette and Ira Schneider," p. 10.

  14.   Interview with Megan Williams, Los Angeles, California, October 4,
1984. Several women were key members of Raindance. Beryl Korot and
Phyllis Gershuny edited Raindance's publication, *Radical Software*, the chief
networking tool of the alternative video movement. Korot was also an innovative video artist whose installations rivalled those of her male colleagues.
The contributions of women were usually overshadowed by the preening dec-
larations of their outspoken male peers. Alternative video was no different
in its sexual politics than most Leftist organizations of the era, and the
women's movement was a reaction to just such paternalism.

  15.   Marco Vassi, "Zen Tubes," *Radical Software* 1:1, 1970, p. 18.

  16.   Pierre Teilhard de Chardin, *The Phenomenon of Man*, New York:
Harper, 1959, p. 31. A revised English language translation appeared in
1965, which coincided with the introduction of portable video.

  17.   R. Buckminster Fuller, *Operating Manual for Spaceship Earth*, New
York: Pocket Books, 1969, p. 113.

  18.   Marshall McLuhan, *Understanding Media: The Extensions of Man*,
New York: New American Library, 1964, p. 21.

  19.   Ibid., p. 292.

2. Subject to Change

  1.   G. Roy Levin, *Documentary Explorations, 15 Interviews with Filmmakers*, New York: Anchor Books, 1971, p. 393.

  2.   "The Smothers Brothers Comedy Hour" aired from February 1967
until June 1969. Brothers Tom and Dick Smothers battled the network for
two years over program content that featured open criticism of the Vietnam
War and the Johnson administration. The show was cancelled less than 100
days into the Nixon administration. Censorship problems began at the out-

set, involving not just lines or words but entire segments. Deleted from the show were segments with Harry Belafonte singing in front of a filmed montage of disturbances at the 1968 Democratic Convention and Pete Seeger's performance of "Waist Deep in the Big Muddy," with its antiwar overtones (Seeger had been blacklisted since the '50s, and this marked his return to network television). In spite of constant conflicts, CBS agreed to renew the show in March 1969, but the network was worried after Tom Smothers attended a National Broadcasters Association convention in Washington, where he sought support from liberal congressman and officials such as FCC Commissioner Nicholas Johnson. Two weeks later the show was cancelled on the pretext that Tom and Dick Smothers they had failed to deliver on time a tape for network review. *TV Guide* ran an editorial citing the network's responsibility to the American public and praising the decision as "wise, determined, and wholly justified." Although the Smothers Brothers produced several series during the '70s, none were as biting or as successful as their controversial "Comedy Hour." (See Bert Spector, "A Clash of Cultures: The Smothers Brothers vs. CBS Television," *American History/American Television*, ed. by John E. O'Connor, New York: Ungar, 1983.)

3. The Chicago 7 co-conspirators (Abbie Hoffman, John Froines, Lee Weiner, David Delligner, Rennie Davis, Jerry Rubin, Tom Hayden, and Bobby Seale) were accused of conspiracy to incite riot at the 1968 Democratic Convention. (Seale was tried separately.) The Chicago 7 trial was the most famous political trial of the decade. The seven defendants ultimately beat the charges but not without turning the court of U.S. Judge Julius Hoffman into a media circus.

4. Fred Hampton was killed while he lay in bed in a surprise raid by federal authorities and Chicago police. Evidence suggested the killing was unprovoked, but a grand jury dismissed it as justifiable homicide. Others viewed the murder of Hampton as part of a systematic program to destroy the Panther party.

The Panther Party was founded in 1966 in Oakland, CA, by Bobby Seale and Huey Newton, and it embodied the new militance of urban black youth. Dedicated to protecting the black community from harassment by white police, the Panthers won widespread support from the poor; with their "Breakfast for Children" program they reached nonviolent, nonmilitant blacks. J. Edgar Hoover, fearing the formation of a national black coalition around a "messiah" figure, claimed the Panthers represented "the greatest threat to internal security of this country." In 1967 the FBI initiated an enlarged Counterintelligence Program (COINTELPRO) to "expose, disrupt, misdirect, discredit, or otherwise neutralize the activities of black nationalists." Electronic surveillance of the Panther organization led to the indictment of Bobby Seale with the Chicago 7 for inciting riots at the 1968 Chicago convention. Between 1968 and 1969, 31 Panther headquarters were raided, with hundreds arrested on spurious charges. With 1,000 Panthers in prison, the focus of black militance shifted from ghetto streets to prisons.

Fred Hampton had been the likely successor to Black Panther chief of state David Hilliard, who had been arrested for threatening the life of President Nixon. (See Peter Carroll, *It Seemed Like Nothing Happened: The Tragedy and Promise of America in the 1970s*, New York: Holt, Rinehart and Winston, 1982.)

5. This version of The Now Project is based on interviews with the following participants: Skip Blumberg, New York, April 22, 1983; David Cort, Boston, November 9, 1983; Davidson Gigliotti, New York, April 20, 1983; Ira Schneider, New York, June 26, 1984; Parry Teasdale and Carol Vontobel, Phoenicia, New York, April 18, 1984; Megan Williams, Los Angeles, California, October 4, 1984; Don West, New York, May 21, 1984; and Ann Woodward, New York, April 10, 1984. See also Les Brown, *Television: The Business Behind the Box*, New York: Harcourt Brace Jovanovich, 1971, pp. 134–135.

3. Guerrilla versus Grassroots

1. Gene Youngblood, *Radical Software* 1:1, 1970, p.16.

2. Paul Ryan, "Cable Television: The Raw and the Overcooked," *Radical Software* 1:1, 1970, p. 12.

3. As Michael Murray wrote in his 1974 primer, cueing was the biggest problem in editing half-inch tape. "All cueing methods are ways of backing up the two machines so that . . . they will both hit the finish line—the simultaneous edit cue—at the same time. The counter on the face of the deck is one measure, but it is unreliable. . . . A similar procedure can be done with a stop watch instead of a counter." Murray noted that H. Allan Fredricksen in *Community Access Video* recommended the felt-tip pen method of marking tape.

> (1) Set up the tapes on both machines so that they are at the exact edit point. (2) Put a mark with a felt-tipped pen on the back of the tapes just past the audio record head. (3) Manually rewind each tape until the mark is even with the tension bar. (4) Then put *another* mark on each tape just past the audio record head. (5) Rewind again until *this* mark is even with the tension bar. (6) Start both machines at exactly the same moment. When the first mark passes the audio record head, push "Edit;" when the second mark passes, push "Record."

Murray concluded thus: "There is inevitable trial and error involved, and both patience and luck are necessary." (Michael Murray, *The Videotape Book*, New York: Bantam, 1974, pp. 165–166.)

4. Process art, earth art, conceptual art, and performance art all shared with process video a de-emphasis on the final work and an emphasis on how it came to be.

5. Chloe Aaron, "The Alternate-Media Guerrillas," *New York Magazine*, October 19, 1970, p. 50–53; "Guerrilla Television," *Newsweek*, December 7, 1970.

6. Chloe Aaron, "The Video Underground," *Art in America* May–June 1971, p. 78.

7. Marco Vassi, "Rappo: Why Aren't You Fucking," *Radical Software*, 1:2, 1970, p. 26.

8. Marco Vassi, "Zen Tubes," *Radical Software*, 1:1, 1970, p. 18.

9. Paul Ryan, "Cybernetic Strategy and Guerrilla Theory," *Radical Software*, 1:3, Spring 1971, p. 1

10. Ralph Engelman, "The Origins of Public Access Cable Television, 1966–1972," *Journalism Monographs*, no. 123, October 1990, p. 1–47.

11. See Hans Magnus Enzensberger, *The Consciousness Industry*, New York: Seabury Press, 1974; Raymond Williams, *Television: Technology & Cultural Form*, New York: Schocken Books, 1972; and Herbert Schiller, *Mass Communications and American Empire*, Boston: Beacon Press, 1969.

12. Bertolt Brecht, "The Radio as an Apparatus of Communication," *Brecht on Theater*, edited and translated by John Willet, New York: Hill and Wang, 1964. The essay first appeared in German in July 1932.

13. Todd Gitlin, "Sixteen Notes on Television and the Movement," in *Literature in Revolution*, edited by George Abbot White and Charles Newman, New York: Holt, Rinehart and Winston, 1972, pp. 335–336.

14. Michael Shamberg was a journalist and consolidator of other people's ideas. The contents of *Guerrilla Television* were the ideas, metaphors, and outright phraseology invented by Frank Gillette, Paul Ryan, Ira Schneider, and the other "brainiacs" around Raindance, according to Allen Rucker.

15. David Armstrong, *A Trumpet to Arms: Alternative Media in America*, 2nd ed., Boston: South End Press, 1983, pp. 72–73.

16. Michael Shamberg and Raindance Corporation, *Guerrilla Television*, New York: Holt Rinehart and Winston, 1971, p. 12.

17. Some underground video groups were more socially motivated, such as People's Video Theater, which produced tapes with the Puerto Rican Young Lords.

18. Armstrong, *A Trumpet to Arms*, p. 70.

19. Ibid., pp. 70–74.

20. Daniel Czitrom notes McLuhan's chapter on television in *Understanding Media* was a paean to American commercial television, a virtual apology for the corporate interests that controlled the medium. According to Czitrom, McLuhan's enduring legacy "may well be his role in legitimizing the status quo of American communications industries and their advertisers." (Daniel Czitrom, "Metahistory, Mythology and the Media: The American Thought of Harold Innis and Marshall McLuhan," in *Media and the American Mind from Morse to McLuhan*, Chapel Hill: University of North Carolina Press, 1982, pp. 147–182.)

21. If McLuhan was a guru for guerrilla television, Canadian media theorist Harold Innis provided inspiration for grassroots video activists. Innis' pioneering work posited a central relationship between mass media and economic development. He viewed Canada as embattled on the margins of

Western civilization, its cultural identity rooted in an oral tradition undermined by the penetration of international mass media, notably American
advertising and broadcasting. (Harold A. Innis, *Empire and Communications*, revised by Mary Q. Innis, 2nd ed. Foreword by Marshall McLuhan,
Toronto: University of Toronto Press, 1972, pp. 169–170.)

22. John Grierson, "Memo to Michelle about Decentralizing the Means
of Production," *Access* (Challenge for Change), Spring 1972, pp. 4–5.

23. George Stoney, "The Mirror Machine," *Sight and Sound*, 41:1, Winter 1971–72, p. 10.

24. Dorothy Todd Hénaut and Bonnie Klein, "In the Hands of Citizens," *Radical Software* 1:1, 1970, p. 11.

25. In 1969 the National Film Board of Canada produced a film titled
VTR St-Jacques (Opération Boule de Neige) that detailed the success of the
Challenge for Change's first videotape effort in Montréal. The film documents
the process of community organizing around health care, revealing how video
helped to break down boundaries between individuals and within them, drawing citizens together with a shared sense of purpose and new sense of power.
VTR St-Jacques is available on film and video from the NFBC.

26. Dorothy Todd Hénaut, "A Report from Canada: Television as Town
Meeting," *Radical Software* 1:2, 1970, p. 17.

27. Klein helped found Portable Channel, one of the first U.S. community video access centers, in Rochester, New York.

4. The World's Largest TV Studio

1. Interview with Michael Shamberg, Los Angeles, October 19, 1983.

2. Timothy Crouse, *The Boys on the Bus*, New York: Ballantine, 1973,
p. 181.

3. The "creepie-peepie" was a 45-pound Quad (two-inch) minicam. It
was the predecessor of the 1971 Ikegami, a one-inch broadcast camera commissioned by CBS.

4. Ant Farm gave TVTV a rock and roll animus that the more theo-
retically bound East Coasters badly needed, according to Allen Rucker.
"Chip Lord used to say that conversations with Frank Gillette and Ira
Schneider 'overheated his brain.'" The principal Ant Farmers vis-a-vis
TVTV were Hudson Marquez, Chip Lord, Doug Michels, and Curtis Schrier.
(Allen Rucker's letter to the author, April 25, 1995.)

5. The four principals in the Portolla Media Access Center were Pat
Crowley, Richard Kletter, Shelley Surpin, and Allen Rucker. Stewart Brand
(the man behind the Portolla Institute, *Whole Earth Catalog, Co-Evolution
Quarterly*, and the WELL computer network, among other things) was a
big supporter of video and helped TVTV financially. He introduced Rucker
to Obie Benz of the Vanguard Foundation who gave TVTV its first foundation dollar.

6. Dwight Whitney, "Irreverent, Questioning, Perhaps Unfair, But Undoubtedly Provocative," *TV Guide*, September 11, 1976, p. 23.

7. TVTV, "Top Value Television Coverage of 1972 Political Conventions," *Radical Software* 2:1, 1972, p. 12.

8. Obie Benz, head of the Vanguard Foundation, gave TVTV money when no one else would and guided TVTV to other foundations and "rich kids" who invested in TVTV Inc. According to Allen Rucker, socially active "rich kids" kick-started TVTV and many other fringe media and social do-good groups of the early '70s.

9. Maureen Orth, "Guerrilla Video: Days of Tape at the Conventions," *Rolling Stone*, July 20, 1972, p. 6.

10. Crouse, *The Boys on the Bus*, p. 181.

11. Orth, "Guerrilla Video," p. 6.

12. Ibid.

13. TVTV, "Top Value Television Coverage," p. 13.

14. The Yippies were media guerrillas who arose in late 1967 when antiwar activists Jerry Rubin, Abbie Hoffman, Keith Lampe, Paul Krassner, Bob Fass, and several other underground media activists formed YIP (Youth International Party) in a stoned, marathon brainstorming session. At one point, Krassner jumped out of his chair and shouted "Yippie! We're Yippies!" The party tried to join the theories of Che Guevara with those of Marshall McLuhan. Their strategy was to emerge from the underground media culture by staging media events so compelling and amusing that the mass media would have to cover them. Instead of guns, their revolutionary weapons were "the camera, the microphone, the tape recorder, the printing press, the put-on." This hybrid group of hippies and New Left activists used satire and calculated outrage to assault the electoral system itself.

15. TVTV, "Top Value Television Coverage," p. 12–13. (Note: TVTV prepared briefing instructions for crews on all their tapes.)

16. Ibid.

17. Interview with Megan Williams, Los Angeles, California, October 28, 1983.

18. Crouse, *The Boys on the Bus*, p. 165.

19. Hunter S. Thompson, *Fear and Loathing: On the Campaign Trail '72*, New York: Warner Books, 1973, p. 279.

20. Ibid., p. 285.

21. Ibid., p. 309.

22. Ibid., p. 285.

23. Renata Adler, "The Air: Who's Here? What Time Is It?," *The New Yorker*, September 16, 1972, pp. 115–120.

24. John J. O'Connor, "TV: A 'Scrapbook of the Democratic Convention,'" *New York Times*, August 17, 1972.

25. Anthony Monahan, "A Guerrilla Convention View," *Chicago Sun-Times*, August 24, 1972, p. 82.

26. Nancy Dickerson was the first woman to break through the all-male ranks at the networks, covering the conventions in 1960.

27. Missouri Senator Thomas Eagleton proved a serious liability to Mc-Govern when his medical history of depression propelled McGovern into a mid-course reversal of support, tarnishing McGovern's image as a man of principle.

28. O'Connor, "TV: A 'Scrapbook.' "

29. Suzanne Karen Singer, *TVTV*, unpublished thesis, University of California, Berkeley, December 1975.

30. Interview with Parry Teasdale, Phoenicia, New York, April 18, 1984.

31. Interview with Allen Rucker, Los Angeles, California, October 18, 1983.

32. Ibid.

33. Known for films like *The Cool World* and *Portrait of Jason*, Clarke was an important innovator of portable video and founder of a video group, TP Videospace.

34. Interview with Michael Shamberg, Los Angeles, California, October 19, 1983.

35. Singer, pp. 11–12.

36. Reeves, "Conventional Behavior," *New York Magazine*, August 28, 1972, p. 44.

37. Monahan, "A Guerrilla Cnvention View," p. 82.

5. Mountain Guerrilla

1. VISTA (Volunteers in Service to America) was created during the Johnson administration under the Economic Opportunity Act of 1964. Sargent Shriver, John F. Kennedy's brother-in-law, headed the task force that outlined the War on Poverty, including VISTA. VISTA combined the New Frontier's emphasis on voluntary service for youth with the antipoverty goals of the Great Society. Shriver, who headed the Peace Corps in 1960–61, helped design VISTA as "a domestic peace corps." Both were the only government programs that relied on fulltime volunteers. Each sought to liberate the poor from poverty through a strategy of planned interventions. VISTA volunteers lived in the community at a poverty level, subsisting on a minimal cost-of-living stipend while functioning as a change-agent resource for the community. They worked in a variety of programs managed by the Office of Economic Opportunity (OEO), such as Head Start, Job Corps, Community Action Program (CAP), Upward Bound, Foster Grandparents, and Legal Services. CAP was the heart of the War on Poverty effort, and by 1967 more than 87 percent of VISTA volunteers were assigned to local CAP projects.

Despite the shift from the liberal, activist politics of the '60s to the conservatism of the '80s, VISTA survived but the organization's understanding of poverty and its causes was redrawn to fit conservative ideology. For liberals of the '60s, poverty was caused by economic problems inherent in capitalism; conservatives believed it was caused by low individual self-esteem and low achievement goals. Under the Reagan administration, VISTA developed programmatic alternatives to traditional VISTA community organizing, focusing, for example, on the prevention of drug abuse. The poor no longer were VISTA's target clientele as its mandate shifted to motivating volunteers, not the poor. (T. Zane Reeves, *The Politics of the Peace Corps and VISTA*, Tuscaloosa: University of Alabama, 1988.)

2. "Homegrown Is Fresher: Broadside TV Pioneers in Regional Video Programming," *Appalachia*, April–May 1974, p. 13; and Ski Hilenski, "Mountain Guerrilla: The Life, Death, and Legacy of Broadside TV," undated draft of a paper in the possession of Ted Carpenter, pp. 1–2.

3. Ted Carpenter and Mike Clarke, "The Living Newsletter—Portable Videotape and a Regional Spirit," *Access* (Challenge for Change) no. 11, Spring 1973, p. 1.

4. Appalachia is not a group of states, but rather the mountainous area of several states. Southern Appalachia includes parts of Virginia, West Virginia, Kentucky, Tennessee, and North Carolina.

5. Hilenski, "Mountain Guerrilla," p. 1–2.

6. Ibid., p. 10.

7. Ted Carpenter, passage from the Alternate Media Center *Catalog*, as quoted in Michael Murray, *The Videotape Book*, New York: Bantam, 1975, p. 7.

8. Interview with Ted Carpenter, Virginia, May 23, 1984.

9. Ibid.

10. Hilenski, "Mountain Guerrilla," p. 3.

11. Interview with Ted Carpenter.

12. Ibid.

13. Carpenter participated as a resource person at a communications workshop held at Highlander in 1971. Participants proved enthusiastic about video and a number of tapes were made about people who had worked for basic change in the mountains during the past 50 years. ("Talk About Newspapers and Video Tape: Mountain People Attend Communications Workshop," *Highlander Reports*, September 1971, p. 4.) He also participated in a workshop on mountain movement music in which sections were videotaped and later shown to mountain community groups which were unable to send representatives (Carpenter and Clarke, "The Living Newsletter," p. 7). Richard Blaustein first became acquainted with Carpenter and video at a Highlander conference on Appalachian education in 1973, shortly before Carpenter moved to Johnson City to start Broadside. (Richard Blaustein, "Everyone Is History: Continuing Appalachian Culture," *Televisions* 3:4, 1975, p. 13) Clearly Carpenter's role as a video resource person was an important feature at Highlander, despite Miles Horton's reservations. According to Carpenter, John Giventa was able to integrate video into High-

lander, continuing the work Carpenter began in the early '70s. (Interview with Ted Carpenter.)

14. Hilenski, p. 5.

15. Interview with Ted Carpenter.

16. The only exception to this rule was when he had to travel to remote areas. Carrying his equipment in a backpack meant leaving the monitor behind. As a result, he played back the tape through the camera viewer and trusted his lapheld camera would not be too jerky. When Carpenter showed his tapes in George Stoney's classes, Stoney marvelled at his camera work, but Carpenter suspected Stoney was simply surprised his tapes had any visual sense at all, given his different motives and methods in shooting tape. (Interview with Carpenter.)

17. Charles W. Childs, "Portable Videotape and CATV in Appalachia: They Start People Thinking," *Educational & Industrial Television*, June 1973, pp. 16–17, 28–29.

18. Interview with Ted Carpenter.

19. "Homegrown is Fresher," *Appalachia*, p. 22. VideoMaker took out an ad in *Radical Software*, 2:4, 1973, p. 64:

> VideoMaker is an attempt to combine the need for universities, schools, cable TV stations and other groups to develop a greater insight into the Appalachian region and its people through Appalachian studies materials, and the great need for mountain people to communicate with and learn from their own experience. Through the Living Newsletter, portable, half-inch videotape equipment is used to motivate an educational dialogue or exchange among groups and individuals in the mountains. Mountain people who, past or present, have confronted problems and concerns central to Appalachian life record the experience that they [sic] as a group or community that shares the same vital concerns, and they in turn respond on tape to other mountain people. This problem-oriented, problem-centered technique expands on the oral learning tradition of the mountains and widens the constituency and framework for fundamental problem solving in Appalachia.

For further information and an annotated tape list, write to VideoMaker, 132 South Washington, Cookeville, TN 38501.

The next issue also listed VideoMaker's tapes for sale:

A Mountain Has No Seed	27 min.	$60
A Harlan Miner Speaks	30 min.	$45
I Would Have Gone Back	30 min.	$45
The Union Struggle	60 min.	$100
In These Hills	30 min	$60

20. Joe Farris, "He Starts People Thinking," *Herald–Citizen* (Cookeville, TN), July 6, 1972.

21. Carpenter and Clarke, "The Living Newsletter," pp. 3–4.

6. Four More Years

1. Timothy Crouse, *The Boys on the Bus*, New York: Ballantine, 1973, p. 182.

2. Interview with Allen Rucker, Los Angeles, California, October 18, 1983.

3. The Yippies were a hybrid group of hippies and New Left activists who used satire and calculated outrage to assault the electoral system itself (see also Note 14 in Chapter 4). They were major players during the bloody confrontations of the 1968 Chicago Democratic Convention, and among their demands was a call for "the open and full use of media," in particular, cable TV. They failed to exert significant impact at the subsequent conventions in 1972. (See David Armstrong, *A Trumpet to Arms: Alternative Media in America*, Boston: South End Press, 1981, p. 118.) A brief portrait of Jerry Rubin in *The World's Largest TV Studio* reveals him to be an opportunist, and John J. O'Connor, in his pivotal review, enthusiastically found his ego-stripping by TVTV to be "the most devastating moments" of the tape. Not surprisingly, Yippies Abbie Hoffman and Rennie Davis were starring figures in many alternate media tapes, and they figured prominently in later TVTV works.

The Zippies, led by "garbage analyst" A.J. Weberman and Tom Forcade, director of the Underground Press Syndicate, were media-grabbers without any serious political aspirations beyond a desire to discredit the Yippies, in particular, Jerry Rubin and Abbie Hoffman, whom they charged with having sold out the revolution.

After warring factions divided in 1969, little remained of the once coherent and formidable Students for Democratic Society (SDS), the standard-bearer for the New Left and, in particular, antiwar protest during the '60s. The very young SDSers at the 1972 Convention tried to catch up with the experiences of their elders, but they often sounded like an anachronism on issues that were still pressing. (See Nora Sayre, *Sixties Going on Seventies*, New York: Arbor House, 1973, pp. 382–383.)

4. Sayre, *Sixties Going on Seventies*, pp. 400–403.

5. Ibid., p. 405.

6. Hunter S. Thompson, *Fear and Loathing: On the Campaign Trail '72*, New York: Warner Books, 1973, p. 392.

7. *TVTV Scrapbook*, unpaged original document of TVTV at the Conventions, owned by Allen Rucker.

8. Thompson, *Fear and Loathing*, p. 388.

9. Ron Kovic later wrote the memoir, *Born on the Fourth of July*, which was turned into the popular movie by Oliver Stone.

10. Ibid., p. 392.

11. Sayre, *Sixties Going on Seventies*, p. 401.

12. Ibid., pp. 407, 410.

13. Ibid., p. 410.

14. Crouse, *The Boys on the Bus*, pp. 182–183.

15. Ibid., p. 181.

16. Cinema vérité in the United States was also called "direct cinema." Robert Drew and his associates shot the historic *vérité* classic of the John Kennedy–Hubert Humphrey contest for the Wisconsin Primary in 1960. *Primary*, made for network TV, was certainly an inspiration—whether conscious or unconscious—for TVTV's innovations on behind-the-scenes, narratorless campaign coverage.

17. Crouse, *The Boys on the Bus*, p. 180.

18. Suzanne Karen Singer, "TVTV," unpublished master's thesis, University of California, Berkeley, 1975, pp. 11–14.

19. *TV Guide*, October 28–November 3, 1972, p. A–38.

20. Charles E. Downie, "TV's Glimpse at the Floor of Two Conventions," *San Francisco Sunday Chronicle and Examiner*, October 29, 1972.

21. TVTV, *Prime Time*, pamphlet, circa 1973.

22. Herb Caen, "It Takes All Kinds," *San Francisco Chronicle*, late September 1972 (undated excerpt included in TVTV's *Prime Time*).

23. Crouse, *The Boys on the Bus*, p. 184. See also Chip Lord, "TVTV: Video Pioneers 10 Years Later," *SEND*, Summer 1983, pp. 18–23.

7. Communitube

1. "Cable TV: Democratizing the Airwaves?" *Many Corners* 1:9, November 1973.

2. Minneapolis hosted the First National Video Festival, sponsored by the Minneapolis College of Art and Design in August 1973. The national festival attracted 150 entries in four categories. A jury of "recognized professionals," including local experts and national figures such as George Stoney, Barbara Rose, and Gene Youngblood awarded prizes to the following:

Documentary: Fred Simon, *Bobby the Fife*
Video Art: Walter Wright, *31*
Student: Morris Brockman, *Cabbie Flyers*
Conceptual Art: Steina Vasulka, *Let It Be*
("1st National Video Festival," *Radical Software* 2:4, 1973, pp. 44–45.)

3. Barry Morrow, whom Kulczycki hired in 1973, was also involved in community video action. With Paul Gronseth he organized the Beltrami Ethnic History Project, using video to document the cultural and social history of a neighborhood in transition. He also worked with the Afro-American Cultural Arts Center on the "Video Involvement Project" training elementary, junior-high, and senior-high school students in studio and portable video recording and editing techniques. Their objective was to develop cultural and educational tapes for distribution to public schools and community centers. (Barry Morrow, Tacoumba Aitken, and Bruce Doepke, "Video In-

volvement Project," and Barry Morrow and Paul Gronseth, "Beltrami Ethnic History Project," *Radical Software*, 2:4, 1973, pp. 38–39.)

4. The tape, *Demonstrations: University of Minnesota, Spring 1972*, was a 55-minute rough edit of student tapes, including interviews with West Bank residents, University officials, bystanders, a medic, some off-air news footage, and "lots of on-the-scene rough shots." UCV produced a number of tapes on the Vietnam War. Mogulescu was responsible for a later tape titled *Viet, Vietnam, Vietnamization*, a 45-minute overview of "some of the horrors and atrocities carried out by the U.S. in Vietnam, few of which are known by the American public." "Changing Channels" included a special program on the "End of the Vietnam War" in 1975; it presented "leftist views on the fall of Saigon" and included excerpts from *Introduction to the Enemy*, a film shot by Jane Fonda, Tom Hayden, and Haskell Wexler in South Vietnam, as well as comments by three local people who had spent time in both North and South Vietnam. (*Catalog of Videotapes*, UCV, 1982)

5. Interview with Stephen Kulczycki, Los Angeles, California, October 14, 1983.

6. Cynthia Hanson, "Video Center Adds 'Commercials' to CCTV programming," *Minnesota Daily*, October 9, 1973.

7. "Cable TV: Democratizing The Airwaves?," *Many Corners* 1:9, November 1973.

8. Hanson, "Video Center."

9. Interview with Ron McCoy, Minneapolis, Minnesota, June 9, 1983.

10. Interview with Stephen Kulczycki.

11. Ibid.

12. Ibid.

13. Interview with Jim Mulligan, Minneapolis, Minnesota, June 14, 1983. Both Mulligan and UCV staffer Greg Pratt agreed that it was Shell Goldstein, working for the university, who was the "godfather" of the program. It was Goldstein who sold them the half-hour airtime and defended their right to do so both to station and university bigwigs.

14. Jim Mulligan and Stephen Kulczycki, "Changing Channels," *Televisions* 4:2, Summer 1976, p. 23.

15. Ann Baker, "Video Tape: A New Way to Express Yourself," *St. Paul Pioneer Press*, February 13, 1974.

16. The first season an Emmy was given for achievement in "magazine type" programming was 1969–1970. Winners included NET's "Black Journal" and NBC's "First Tuesday"; in succeeding years awards went to CBS's "60 Minutes" and PBS's "The Great American Dream Machine," "Behind the Lines," and "Bill Moyers' Journal."

Greg Pratt recalled writing a paper for a grad course at the time in which he predicted video technology would give birth to a new era of magazine-format television. He reasoned that with the availability of inexpensive, portable video equipment and training centers like UCV to teach people the skills to use video, people would seize the tools, produce tapes, and want new programming outlets—magazine-format shows. For evidence, he noted the same rise in production had occurred when 35mm cameras were first developed and people started taking snapshots, or when 16mm film cameras and later 8mm cameras were made available and the public began making home movies. "Changing Channels" was way ahead of its time, Pratt concluded. But people laughed at his idea at the time. That was before the era of "PM Magazine," "Entertainment Tonight," and "Real People" proved him correct. Along with these more commercial ventures came a resurgence of programming like "Changing Channels," such as the PBS national series, "The Nineties," a direct descendant of early video activism (occasionally produced by aging pioneers) and the satellite-distributed public access sampler show, "Deep Dish Television."

17. In 1974 a Roper poll indicated that for the first time a majority of Americans were relying more on television than on newspapers for their news.

18. Baker, "Video Tape."

19. Ibid.

20. Pat Aufderheide, "The Movies," *Minnesota Daily*, January 25, 1974.

21. Carl Griffin Jr. and Irv Letofsky, "Do-It-Yourself TV: A Story of the Expanding Use of Video Tape," *Minneapolis Tribune*, January 27, 1974, pp. 1D, 6D.

22. Interview with Stephen Kulczycki. Schwartzwalder continued to complain about UCV and its programming, although he mellowed as critical response and viewership for "Changing Channels" proved how successful a program it was. In 1977 he invited Kulczycki to his office and suggested that KTCA and UCV start working together. This was not fated to happen because within two months, Schwartzwalder had resigned.

23. For example, in early 1971, Walter Cronkite's "Evening News" on CBS broadcast a half-inch videotape of Eldridge Cleaver in Algiers shot by video activist Bill Stephens, founder of the Revolutionary People's Communication Network. ("Time Scan," *Televisions* 4:2, Summer 1976, p. 6.)

24. Interview with Stephen Kulczycki.

25. Interview with Ron McCoy.

26. Baker, "Video Tape."

27. "Minneapolis: Student-Based Video Work—Interview with Ron McCoy," *Community Video Report* 1:4, Spring 1974, p. 9.

8. GaGa Over Guru

1. Suzanne Karen Singer, "TVTV," unpublished master's thesis, University of California, Berkeley, 1975, p. 14.

2. Ibid.

3. Credits for the show are not listed, but women's presence is notably lacking in this tape.

4. As David Armstrong notes in *A Trumpet to Arms* (p. 178), the magazine had betrayed its early ambitions: "In its pursuit of profit—and its promotion of the star system, competition, hedonism, and, above all, a kind of sated passivity—[*Rolling Stone*] became the antithesis of what cultural and political radicals intended when they launched the underground media."

5. Jack Newfield, "The 'Truth' About Objectivity and the New Journalism" in *Liberating the Media: The New Journalism*, ed. Charles C. Flippen, Washington, D.C.: Acropolis Books, 1974, pp. 64–67.

6. Jay Jensen, "The New Journalism in Historical Perspective" in Flippen, *Liberating the Media*, pp. 18–28.

7. Newfield, "The 'Truth' About Objectivity," p.15.

8. TVTV, *Prime Time*, pamphlet, circa 1973, p.1.

9. The Point Foundation was the money-giving arm of Stewart Brand's *Whole Earth Catalog* and its related enterprises. In addition to help from Brand, TVTV was also assisted by Point board member Michael Phillips, author of *The Seven Laws of Money*, and a big fan of TVTV.

10. Singer, "TVTV," p. 15.

11. Richard Casey, "TVTV Illuminates the Ji," *Berkeley Barb*, March 22–28, 1974, p. 18.

12. Interview with David Loxton, New York, April 2, 1984. See also Leendert Drukker, "Broadcast TV Opens up for Portapak Tapes," *Popular Photography*, 76:6, June 1975, pp. 100, 118–119; and "Conversation with John Godfrey," *Videography*, August 1983, pp. 48–50, 55–66.

13. Interview with David Loxton.

14. Interview with Michael Shamberg, Los Angeles, California, October 19, 1983.

15. TVTV, *The Prime Time Survey*, self-published, 1974, pp. 13–14.

16. Interview with David Loxton.

17. Interview with Elon Soltes, Los Angeles, California, October 1983. See also John Godfrey, "Getting Technical: The Lord of the Universe," *Vision News* 1:2, May 1974, p. 8.

18. *The Prime Time Survey*, p. 20.

19. Paul Goldsmith, " 'Lord of the Universe': An Eclairman in Videoland," *Filmmakers Newsletter*, Summer 1974, pp. 25–27.

20. Interview with Paul Goldsmith, Los Angeles, California, October 13, 1983. See also TVTV, " 'Lord of the Universe': A Technical Report," *Filmmakers Newsletter*, Summer 1974, p. 28.

21. *The Prime Time Survey*, pp.18–20. See also TVTV, " 'Lord of the Universe,' " pp. 28–29.

22. Interview with David Loxton.

23. Goldsmith, " 'Lord of the Universe,' " pp. 25–27.

24. Ibid.

25. *The Prime Time Survey*, pp. 22–23.

26. Todd Gitlin, *The Whole World Is Watching: Mass Media in the Mak-

ing and Unmaking of the New Left, Berkeley: University of California Press, 1980, pp. 167–170.

27. Goldsmith, " 'Lord of the Universe,' " p. 25.

28. *The Prime Time Survey*, p. 24.

29. Ibid., pp. 24–25.

30. Ibid., p. 26.

31. Ibid., pp. 14–15.

32. Ibid., pp. 15–17.

33. Ron Powers, "Participatory TV Goes to Guru Gala," *Chicago Sun-Times*, March 16, 1974.

34. John J. O'Connor, "TV: Meditating on Young Guru and His Followers," *The New York Times*, February 25, 1974.

35. Arthur Unger, "Weekend Trio of Documentaries," *The Christian Science Monitor*, February 22, 1974.

36. Kay Butler, "Dissecting the Guru on the Tube," *The San Francisco Bay Guardian*, February 28, 1974.

37. Interview with Michael Shamberg.

38. Interview with Elon Soltes.

39. Peter Caranicas, "Conversation with TVTV," *Videography*, May 1977, p. 37. TVTV later acquired an Angenieux lens that cost several thousand dollars, compared with its original $30 attachment.

40. Drukker, "Broadcast TV Opens Up," pp. 100, 118–119.

41. Bob Williams, "On the Air," *New York Post*, February 25, 1974.

42. Casey, "TVTV Illuminates the Ji."

43. Interview with Parry Teasdale, Phoenicia, New York, April 18, 1984.

44. Interview with Elon Soltes. Chapter is also based on interviews with Wendy Appel, Los Angeles, California, October 1983, and Megan Williams, Los Angeles, California, October 18, 1983, and on "Guru Show a Breakthrough," *Vision News* 1:3, May 1974, p. 1, 7.

9. Prime Time TVTV

1. Powers, "A Merciless Look at TV-ad Makers," *Chicago Sun-Times*, April 8, 1974, p. 60.

2. Suzanne Karen Singer, "TVTV," unpublished master's thesis, University of California at Berkeley, 1975, p. 19.

3. TVTV, *The Prime Time Survey*, self-published, 1974, p. 27.

4. Ibid.

5. Ibid., pp. 29–30.

6. Ibid., p. 30.

7. TVTV, "The TVTV Story," *Vision News* 1:2, October 1973, p. 2.

8. Powers, "A Merciless Look," p. 60.

9. Terence O'Flaherty, "A Source of Ignorance," *San Francisco Examiner*, August 31, 1974, p. 32.

10. TVTV, "The TVTV Story," p. 7.

11. Ron Powers, "What You'll Watch in the Year 2000," *Chicago Sun–Times*, July 31, 1974, p. 52.

12. TVTV, *The Prime Time Survey*, p. 4.

13. Ibid., pp. 8–9.

14. Michael Shamberg and Raindance Corporation, *Guerrilla Television*, New York: Holt, Rinehart and Winston, 1971, p. 32.

15. Powers, "A Merciless Look," p. 60.

10. Broadside TV

1. *Kingsport (Tennessee) News*, October 24, 1973.

2. Participating companies and the cable systems they operated were: Warner Cable (which had systems in Kingsport, Greeneville, and Erwin, Tennessee, and Abingdon, Virginia); Sammons Communications (Bristol, Johnson City, and Elizabethton, Tennessee); PGR Enterprises (Appalachia, Wise, Norton, and Big Stone Gap, Virginia); and the Washington County Utility District, a private utility that had cable systems in Jonesboro, Tennessee, and surrounding areas in Washington County. ("Homegrown is Fresher: Broadside TV Pioneers in Regional Video Programming," *Appalachia* [an ARC publication], April–May 1974, p. 17.)

3. A forerunner of Broadside TV's local origination programming was DCTV of Dale City, Virginia. Dale City was located about 25 miles south of Washington, D.C. in northern Virginia. The cable system rented its local origination channel to the community between 1968 and 1970. They cablecast one hour every Tuesday evening plus a weekend special once a month. As its equipment deteriorated, DCTV disintegrated, despite popular support for its programming from a young (average age 19 years) viewing population (see N.E. Feldman, *Cable Television: Opportunities and Problems in Local Program Origination,* Santa Monica, California: Rand, 1970).

4. Interview with Ted Carpenter, Virginia, May 23, 1984.

5. Ibid.

6. Ibid.

7. Ibid.

8. Ski Hilenski, "Mountain Guerrilla: The Life, Death, and Legacy of Broadside TV," undated draft of a paper in the possession of Ted Carpenter, p. 8.

9. Interview with Ted Carpenter.

10. "Broadside T.V. and Videomaker: An Appalachian Video Network," brochure circa 1973. At that time, Broadside's address in the Tri-Cities was 204 E. Watauga Ave., Johnson City, Tennessee.

11. Hilenski, "Mountain Guerrilla," p. 6.

12. Ted Carpenter and Mike Clarke, "The Living Newsletter—Portable Videotape and a Regional Spirit," *Access* (Challenge for Change), no. 11, Spring 1973, p. 5.

13. Charles W. Childs, "Portable Videotape and CATV in Appalachia: They Start People Thinking," *Educational & Industrial Television*, June 1973, p. 29.

14. "Homegrown Is Fresher," *Appalachia*, p. 14.

15. Ibid., pp. 19–21.

16. Hilenski, "Mountain Guerrilla," p. 13. A Broadside brochure (circa 1975) says they were providing four to six hours per week of Appalachian studies, mountain music, bluegrass music, and mountain history, plus regional news, entertainment, and sports.

17. Interview with Ted Carpenter.

18. Interview with Blaine Dunlap, Atlanta, Georgia, April 17, 1983.

19. Broadside worked with local colleges and universities such as Appalachian State University, East Tennessee State University, the University of Tennessee, Mountain Empire Community College, Stone Gap, Clinch Valley College, and Mountain People's Photo Center.

20. Richard Blaustein, "Everyone Is History: Continuing Appalachian Culture," *Televisions* 3:4, 1975, p. 13.

21. Tape annotations in SAVES Catalog, June 1975.

22. Blaustein, "Everyone Is History," p. 13.

23. Blaustein worked with a number of ETSU students during the SAVES project, such as Bob Williams, Jim Meadows, Dan Blevins, Larry Nave, and Dick Handshaw. Credits for the tapes in the 1975 SAVES catalog suggest that many of the tapes then in distribution had been made by Broadside producers and friends. Prominent names included Paul Congo, Phyllis Scalf, Margaret McClellan, and Ted Carpenter.

24. Broadside's brochure (circa 1975) lists the following goal under the SAVES project: "The creation of new channels of communication and sources of income for regional folk artists via the cable TV medium, and the encouragement of a positive Appalachian cultural image." Sharing information with other mountain people had dropped out of the list entirely. Priority is given to establishing an archive of tapes to be distributed to teachers of anthropology, sociology, folklore, and Appalachian studies.

25. Childs, "Portable Videotape," p. 28.

11. Impeaching Evidence

1. The Rockefeller Foundation awarded the TV Lab a one-year grant of $340,000 in 1974. It was the Foundation's third grant to the Lab in support of "pure research into the nature of television and exploration of its artistic limits and its effect on human perception." Loxton noted at the time, "This generous increase in the level of support provided . . . will enable us to consolidate the experience and knowledge we have gained in the past. . . . And we hope to embark on a year of major activity, concentrating our efforts primarily on the production of several innovative experimental broadcast projects" (WNET press release, June 12, 1974).

2. Suzanne Karen Singer, "TVTV," unpublished master's thesis, University of California, Berkeley, 1975, p. 35.

3. "They Found a New Guru," *Vision News* 2:2, December 1974, pp. 1, 7.

4. Singer, "TVTV," p. 22.

5. TVTV, *The Prime Time Survey*, self-published, 1974, pp. 56–68.

6. Geraldine Wurzburg, "Top Value Television Hits DeeCee with Video," *Community Video Report* 2:2, Autumn 1974, pp. 1, 6.

7. Ibid., p. 58.

8. "They Found a New Guru," p. 7.

9. Interview with Allen Rucker, Los Angeles, California, October 18, 1983.

10. Wurzburg, "Top Value Television," p. 6.

11. Ibid.

12. Ann Crutcher, "A Jarring Look at 'Gerald Ford's America,'" *Washington Star-News*, January 10, 1975.

13. Harry Waters, "Candid Camera," *Newsweek*, January 27, 1975, p. 59.

14. "Gerald Ford's America," *Variety*, January 15, 1975.

15. John J. O'Connor, "TV: View of 'Gerald Ford's America,'" *The New York Times*, February 6, 1975.

16. Renee Epstein, "TVTV," *Film Comment*, September–October 1975, p. 35.

17. Tom Shales and Donnie Radcliffe, "'Chic to Sheik,'" *The Washington Post*, January 17, 1975.

18. Peter Caranicas, "Conversation with TVTV," *Videography*, May 1977, pp. 37–38.

19. Interview with Megan Williams, Los Angeles, California, October 28, 1983.

20. Crutcher, "A Jarring Look.".

21. Frank Swertlow, "'Ford's America' Will Be Aired," UPI syndicated review, January 8, 1975.

22. Marvin Kitman, "'Chic to Sheik' Is Almost Better Than Being There," *Newsday*, January 17, 1975.

23. Haynes Johnson, "Focusing on the Widest, Easiest Target in Town," *The Washington Post*, January 24, 1975.

24. Benjamin DeMott, "Culture Watch," *The Atlantic* 235:6, June 1975, pp. 87–92.

25. "'Gerald Ford's America,'" *The Washington Post*, January 10, 1975.

26. Waters, "Candid Camera."

27. Since 1960, commercial networks had a policy of accepting virtually no independent productions of news or public affairs, following the debacle of the quiz scandals which so damaged network credibility. But, according to broadcast historian Erik Barnouw, the real reason for their refusal of the

test case—a documentary on the space race—was that each network had their own crews working on similar projects and did not want the competition. ("Television Has an All-electronic Future," *Televisions* 4:2, June 1976, p. 9.)

28. Les Brown, "Channel 13 to Aid Group Trying to Expand Videotape Programs," *The New York Times*, November 15, 1974.

29. Catherine Twohill, "TVTV: Tomorrow's Television Today?," *Image*, April 1975.

30. Interview with David Loxton, New York, New York, April 2, 1984.

31. Wurzburg, "Candid Camera." See also Val Adams, "Channel 13 Eying New Uses for Portable TV Cameras," *New York Daily News*, January 2, 1975, and Gary Deeb, "Documentaries on D.C.," *Chicago Tribune*, February 3, 1975.

12. Changing Channels

1. Will Jones, "After Last Night," *Minneapolis Tribune*, October 5, 1974.

2. Aron Kahn, "New Idea for TV series," *St. Paul Dispatch*, October 2, 1974. In early 1974 in Rochester, New York, a video group named Portable Channel began regular programming of its series, "Homemade TV," over the local PBS affiliate. ("Video Shots," *Televisions*, 3:1, 1975, p. 16)

3. Interview with Jim Mulligan, Minneapolis, Minnesota, June 14, 1983.

4. Jones, "After Last Night."

5. Barb Volp, "Disgruntled TV Viewers Offered Chance to Air Own Shows," *Minnesota Daily*, October 21, 1974. Barb Volp later worked as a student producer at UCV and was coproducer of episode 10 of "Changing Channels," a half-hour devoted to four women's media collectives in the Twin Cities, broadcast February 12, 1975.

6. "Favorable Response Received to Circle Pines Utilities Segment on TV program," *Circulating Pines*, October 17, 1974.

7. Interview with Jim Mulligan.

8. Interview with Greg Pratt, Minneapolis, Minnesota, June 14, 1983.

9. Ibid.

10. Interview with Stephen Kulczycki, Los Angeles, California, October 14, 1983; and interview with Jim Mulligan.

11. Interview with Jim Mulligan.

12. Interview with Stephen Kulczycki.

13. A UCV distribution catalog (circa 1975) provided this annotation for *Art and Politics*:

Many critics say that good art and good politics just don't mix. Others maintain that all art is political whether it wants to admit it or not. This special one-hour "Changing Channels" program, aired over the local PBS station, documents three cultural groups that try to combine good artistic expression and good political expression: Singer Holly Near, The Alive and Trucking Theater Company, and filmmakers Julia Reichert and James Klein of New Day Films. Included is a singing performance by Holly Near, excerpts from the play "Battered Homes and Gardens," and clips from the Reichert/Klein film, "Methadone: An American Way of Dealing." This tape is especially appropriate for English, Art, Theatre, Filmmaking, and Music classes.

14. UCV's segments outstripped existing network time conventions for public affairs and news reporting. In 1973 "The CBS Evening News" devoted what was for them an unprecedented 11 minutes to a segment on who benefitted from the grain deal with the Russians.

15. UCV served as an access facility and video archive for many tapes produced by Native American groups in the upper Midwest. Some of the better known tapes, all of which aired on "Changing Channels," include: *Sara Badheart Bull* (produced by Miles Mogulescu and American Indian Movement, Rapid City, South Dakota, 1974); *We Are Evidence of This Western Hemisphere* and *Born To Be a Nation* (produced by the Second International Indian Treaty Council, Yankton, South Dakota, 1976); and *The Trial of Leonard Peltier* (produced by Paul Burtness and American Indian Students in Communication, Fargo, North Dakota, 1977).

16. The half-hour, black-and-white tape was entitled *The Minnesota Citizens Review Commission on the F.B.I.*

17. Interviews with Stephen Kulczycki and Jim Mulligan. Mulligan's memory contradicts Kulczycki's impression that they received only 1 ratings. According to Mulligan, when KTCA started being counted in the Nielsen ratings, "Changing Channels" received a 3 rating and 7 share, especially at the beginning of a new season. This was a respectable number for a market that size, especially back when few people were watching public television.

18. "Video Jobs Offered," *Televisions* 3:3, August–September 1975, p. 15.

19. Abortion was not considered an appropriate subject for television programming in the early '70s, despite the liberal Supreme Court ruling that made abortions legal. In 1973 20 percent of CBS local affiliates refused to carry a repeat showing of a "Maude" episode dealing with her decision to have an abortion.

20. Interview with Stephen Kulczycki.

21. In a further odd wrinkle to this story, Tony Bouza, the police captain who effectively served as the narrator in *The Police Tapes*, was subsequently fired from his job for his outspoken views about being "the commander of an army of occupation in the ghetto." After the police department, Bouza worked briefly for the New York City Transit Department before again being fired for independent thinking. He eventually wound up as Chief of Police in Minneapolis, a controversial figure who had at last

found a city that could respect his unconventional views and independent spirit.

22. Interview with Ron McCoy, Minneapolis, Minnesota, June 14, 1983. McCoy left UCV and the University Student Telecommunications Corporation in 1977 to set up his own video ventures, eventually establishing two corporate-sector multi-image and video production houses, Associated Images and Video Resources.

23. Interview with Jim Mulligan.

24. Interview with Stephen Kulczycki.

25. Interview with Jim Mulligan.

26. UCV's portrait of Bly preceded a profile done by Bill Moyers. In fact, the Moyers crew screened the tape before embarking on their own production, and this precluded *A Man Writes to a Part of Himself* from a national broadcast for years, following the logic of television that says: "we've already done that story." (Interview with Mike Hazard, Minneapolis, Minnesota, June 17, 1983.)

13. Furor Over Fugitive

1. Betsy Ross, "TVTV Bids a Not-So-Reluctant Farewell," *San Francisco Examiner*, March 7, 1975.

2. Ibid.

3. Ibid.

4. Patty Hearst, granddaughter of William Randolph Hearst and daughter of the publisher of *The San Francisco Examiner*, was taken prisoner by the Symbionese Liberation Army in February 1974. The 19-year-old heiress initially served as a hostage to force her family to provide $2 million worth of food to needy people. Hearst later denounced the food program and joined the SLA in a bank robbery, having adopted the nom de guerre of "Tania." She was captured after 591 days in the underground, describing herself as an urban guerrilla and radical feminist. Basing her legal defense on the grounds of brainwashing, she failed to persuade a jury of her innocence. Her ordeal ended with a presidential pardon in 1978.

5. Todd Gitlin, *The Sixties: Years of Hope, Days of Rage*, New York: Bantam, 1987, p. 233.

6. Todd Gitlin, *The Whole World Is Watching: Mass Media in the Making and Unmaking of the Left*, Berkeley: University of California Press, 1980, p. 156.

7. Abbie Hoffman, *Soon To Be a Major Motion Picture*, New York: Perigee, 1980, p. 116.

8. Ibid., p. 114.

9. Gitlin, *The Sixties*, p. 237.

10. David Armstrong, *A Trumpet to Arms: Alternative Media in America*, Boston: South End Press, 1981, p. 133.

11. *New Times* (1973–1978) was the creation of former Time-Life ex-

ecutive George Hirsch, who bankrolled the magazine with money from Chase Manhattan, the Bank of America, and American Express—"a sign that investigative reporting had arrived—and was considered harmless by its proper targets." (Armstrong, *A Trumpet to Arms*, p. 309.)

12. Interview with Megan Williams, Los Angeles, California, October 28, 1983.

13. Interview with Michael Shamberg, Los Angeles, California, October 19, 1983.

14. Ron Rosenbaum, "What Makes Abbie Run?" *New Times*, June 13, 1975, p. 40.

15. Interview with Megan Williams.

16. Interview with Michael Shamberg.

17. Ingrid Wiegand, "At Home with Abbie Hoffman: The Soft-Sell Savvy of the Underground," *Soho Weekly News*, May 29, 1975, p. 12.

18. Abbie Hoffman was six years underground. Facing 15 years to life for arranging the sale of three pounds of cocaine to undercover cops, he skipped bail and went underground. He settled in Fineview, New York, on the St. Lawrence River, and in 1976 he took the name Barry Freed, becoming the respected leader of the Save the River movement, which successfully opposed a dredging project. His environmental work was cited by 400 luminaries who wrote on his behalf when he surfaced in 1980, and he served only 11 months in prison. Hoffman began his activist career in the civil rights movement, ferrying volunteers into Mississippi and Georgia. "I have never seen myself as anything more than a good community organizer," Hoffman wrote in his 1980 autobiography, *Soon To Be a Major Motion Picture*. "It was just the Vietnam War that made the community bigger, that's all." Diagnosed in the early '80s as a manic-depressive, the self-styled "Groucho Marxist" of the Woodstock Nation committed suicide in April 1989.

19. Interview with David Loxton, New York, April 2, 1984.

20. "Abbie Hoffman Says He Could Find Patty," *Post-Dispatch* (Pittsburgh, California), May 19, 1975.

21. "Abbie Hoffman on TV in Hiding," *Washington Star-News*, May 19, 1975.

22. Paul L. Montgomery, "Abbie Hoffman Speaks of Life in 'Underground,' " *The New York Times*, May 19, 1975.

23. John J. O'Connor, "TV: On Abbie Hoffman," *The New York Times*, May 19, 1975.

24. Interview with David Loxton.

25. Les Brown, "Ford Fund, WNET Decry Hoffman Fee," *The New York Times*, May 19, 1975.

26. "Fred is Unfriendly with WNET After 'Checkbook' Hoffman Gab," *Variety*, May 28, 1975, p. 71.

27. Brown, "Ford Fund, WNET Decry Hoffman Fee."

28. Les Brown, "TV Interview Payments," *The New York Times*, May 24, 1975.

29. Ibid.

30. Ibid.

31. "Buckley Asks Inquiry on Hoffman Payment," *The New York Times*, May 19, 1975.

32. "Paid Interview of Abbie Hoffman on WNET arouses Ire of Ford Foundation," *Broadcasting*, May 26, 1975, p. 35.

33. Ibid.

34. "Fred is Unfriendly."

35. "Paid Interview on Abbie Hoffman on WNET."

36. "PBS Statement of Policy on Program Standards and Document of Journalism Standards and Guidelines," April 15, 1971.

37. Brown, "TV Interview Payments."

38. Wiegand, "At Home with Abbie Hoffman."

39. Ibid.

40. Interviews with Michael Shamberg and David Loxton.

14. Living Newsletter?

1. "Cable Policy Changing: Deregulation Push, FCC Eliminates Mandatory Origination," *Community Video Report* 2:2, 1974, pp. 1, 4.

2. Ski Hilenski, "Mountain Guerrilla: The Life, Death, and Legacy of Broadside TV," undated draft of a paper in the possession of Ted Carpenter, p. 16.

3. Neil Goldstein and Nick DeMartino, "FCC Weighing Crucial Access, Origination Regs," *Community Video Report* 2:1, 1974, p. 3.

4. "Homegrown Is Fresher: Broadside TV Pioneers in Regional Video Programming," *Appalachia*, April–May 1974, p. 21.

5. Audiotape of Broadside TV's First Board Meeting, 1975, housed at the Archives of Appalachia, Eastern Tennessee State University, Johnson City, Tennessee.

6. Interview with Ted Carpenter, Virginia, May 23, 1984.

7. Nicholas Johnson moved The National Citizens Committee for Broadcasting to Washington, D.C., in 1974 and began the magazine, *Access*, pressuring broadcasters on behalf of various public interest groups.

8. Carpenter was equally critical of the plight-of-the-week trendiness of some foundations that often would only fund an organization if its needs could fit into what they were supporting that year. "Ecology is in, so if you can tailor your proposal to emphasize it. . . ." This approach forced cash-poor nonprofit organizations to constantly reorient themselves in order to fit the funders' whims. Not only did they risk losing sight of their central goals, but nonprofits stretched themselves thinner and thinner to accommodate the dictates of different funders.

9. Lynn Bennett and Marge Gregg both served as directors after Ted Carpenter left. They each tried to keep Broadside running, securing some

funding from CETA and the Legal Enforcement Administration. With NEA funds and a grant from the Southern Arts Foundation, Gregg succeeded in organizing Video South, a three-day conference for Southeastern video artists, held in the spring of 1977. This event brought in outside resource people like Michael Shamberg and Gene Youngblood to discuss the technical, creative, and organizational aspects of alternative media. The conference also included a juried festival of independent video at Vanderbilt University. Unfortunately, garnering prestige for a regional meeting was not enough to rescue a dying organization. Gregg was director when Broadside eventually went bankrupt in 1978.

10. Interview with Jo Carson, Johnson City, Tennessee, January 27, 1984.

11. Interview with Ray Moore, Whitesburg, Kentucky, January 25, 1984.

12. Interview with Ted Carpenter.

13. Interview with Ray Moore.

14. Hilenski, "Mountain Guerrilla," p. 18–24.

15. At the very least, Ted Carpenter's ideas had an influence on the future of public broadcasting. The second Carnegie Commission report on public broadcasting contained a key recommendation derived directly from Broadside TV. Carpenter, who helped draft the report, urged that public radio and television stations need whole blocks of discretionary money for use particularly in the development of public affairs programming, thereby freeing stations from tieing programs to funding dollars. Broadside TV was the only working model for this idea.

15. The Good Times Are Killing Me

1. Paul Goldsmith and Megan Williams, "The Good Times Are Killing Me: TVTV Debriefing," *Filmmakers Newsletter*, October 1975, pp. 25–26.

2. Interview with Paul Goldsmith, Los Angeles, California, October 13, 1983.

3. Revon Reed, "Comme Çi, Comme Ça," *The Mamou Acadian Press*, January 30, 1975.

4. Goldsmith and Williams, "The Good Times," p. 26.

5. Victoria Costello, Nick DeMartino and Larry Kirkman, "Small Format Video Broadcast," *Televisions* 4:2, 1976, p. 8.

6. Goldsmith and Williams, p. 26.

7. *The Good Times Are Killing Me* was criticized, among other things, for excluding black Cajuns. (See " 'Good Times' Misses," *New York Daily News*, June 23, 1975.) TVTV taped Black Mardi Gras, White Mardi Gras, and Women's Mardi Gras and planned to include all three in the final tape, but when they had to cut the 80 hours into a one-hour program, they decided to drop all the black material. Since the crew that shot Black Mardi Gras

got drunk on tequila and then got their car stuck in the mud, it is not entirely clear whether the material was usable, as reported. (See Goldsmith and Williams, "The Good Times," p. 29.) According to Paul Goldsmith, plans to produce a second program on Black Cajuns failed to materialized.

8. Ibid, p. 26.

9. Suzanne Karen Singer, *TVTV*, unpublished thesis, University of California at Berkeley, December 1975, p. 29.

10. "TV Filming Planned of Mardi Gras Event," *The Eunice News*, February 6, 1975.

11. Reed, "Comme Çi, Comme Ça."

12. "TV Filming Planned."

13. " 'The Good Times Are Killing Me' Documents a Two-Hundred-Year-Old Culture in Danger of Being Lost," WNET/13 Press Release, June 9, 1975.

14. Goldsmith and Williams, "The Good Times," pp. 28–29.

15. Ibid.

16. Phil Perlman, "TVTV in Cajun Country," *Millimeter*, 3:6, June 1975, pp. 27–28.

17. Goldsmith and Williams, "The Good Times," pp. 28.

18. Perlman, "TVTV in Cajun Country."

19. Judy Flander, "Everywhere You Turn," *The Washington Star*, June 25, 1975.

20. Tom Shales, "Close-Ups on Cajuns: Fresh Air for TV," *The Washington Post*, June 25, 1975.

21. Goldsmith and Williams, "The Good Times," pp. 27–28.

22. Ibid., pp. 28–29.

23. Flander, "Everywhere You Turn."

24. Perlman, "TVTV in Cajun Country."

25. Goldsmith and Williams, "The Good Times," pp. 27–28.

26. Ibid., p. 30.

27. John J. O'Connor, "Young Film Makers, Video Documentarians," *The New York Times*, June 23, 1975.

28. Arthur Unger, "Cajun Special, or How to Picture a Culture," *The Christian Science Monitor*, June 23, 1975.

29. Interview with Paul Goldsmith.

30. Perlman, "TVTV in Cajun Country." See also Robert McLean, "Bittersweet Look at the Dying Cajun Culture," *The Boston Globe*, June 24, 1975.

31. Shales, "Close-Ups on Cajuns."

32. Ibid.

33. Perlman, "TVTV in Cajun Country."

34. Singer, "TVTV," p. 28. (Note: Singer refers reader to "TVTV Debriefing" in *Filmmakers Newsletter*; she probably was referring to the manuscript for this article, since the wording as such did not appear in the magazine.)

35. Renee Epstein, "TVTV," *Film Comment*, September–October 1975, p. 35.

36. Perlman, "TVTV in Cajun Country."

37. Ibid.

38. Dwight Whitney, "Irreverent, Questioning, Perhaps Unfair, but Undoubtedly Provocative," *TV Guide*, September 11, 1976, p. 23.

39. Interview with Paul Goldsmith.

40. Interview with David Loxton, New York, New York, April 2, 1984.

41. Ibid.

42. Carey Winfrey hired TVTV to do the tape on *Rolling Stone* for WNET. (Interview with Michael Shamberg, Los Angeles, California, October 1983.)

43. John J. O'Connor, "Technology is Reshaping Documentaries," *The New York Times*, June 29, 1975.

44. Benjamin Stein, "We Need It Now More Than Ever," *TV Guide*, December 27, 1975, p. 30.

45. Leendert Drukker, "Broadcast TV Opens up for Portapak Tapes," *Popular Photography*, 76:6, June 1975, pp. 100, 118–119.

46. Nick DeMartino, "Getting into PBS: Independents Make Inroads on National Programming," *Televisions* 3:3, August–September 1975, p. 13.

47. Ibid.

48. "Time Scan," *Televisions* 4:2, Summer 1976, p. 8.

49. Les Brown, "Independent TV News Films Face Dim Prospects," *The New York Times*, March 11, 1975.

50. Catherine Twohill, "TVTV: Tomorrow's Television Today?" *Image*, April 1975.

51. Years later former TVTV member Tom Weinberg, a producer for Chicago public television station WTTW, became executive producer of a PBS series titled "The Nineties," which briefly realized TVTV's idea of using portable video as an alternative news-and-information service for public television.

52. DeMartino, "Getting Into PBS," p. 13.

16. Super Video

1. Suzanne Karen Singer, "TVTV," unpublished master's thesis, University of California, Berkeley, December 1975, p. 35.

2. Ibid.

3. Ibid., p. 37.

4. Ibid., pp. 31–32.

5. Richard Levine, "The Cameraman Comes Out of the Ocean, See?" *The New York Times*, October 5, 1975, p. 27.

6. Singer, "TVTV," p. 37.

7. Interview with Megan Williams, Los Angeles, California, October 28, 1983.

8. Interview with David Loxton, New York, April 2, 1984.

9. Letter to author from Allen Rucker, August 24, 1983.

10. Levine, "The Cameraman."

11. Singer, "TVTV," p. 33.

12. Ibid., p. 33.

13. Ibid., p. 34.

14. Benjamin Stein, "We Need It Now More Than Ever," *TV Guide*, December 27, 1975, p. 30.

15. Skip Blumberg, " 'The TVTV Show': Behind the Scenes and Between the Lines," *Televisions* 5:2, 1977, p. 4.

16. "Video Documentary, 'Super Bowl,' Takes an Irreverent, Behind-the-Scenes Look at Pro Football and Its Ultimate Event—Super Bowl X," WNET/13 press release, February 25, 1976.

17. Interview with David Loxton.

18. Jay Sharbutt, "Super Bowl X: Game Is Not The Thing," Associated Press story, *Asbury Park Press*, January 16, 1976.

19. "Video Documentary, 'SuperBowl,' " WNET/13 Press Release.

20. Sharbutt, "Super Bowl X."

21. Dwight Whitney, "Irreverent, Questioning, Perhaps Unfair, But Undoubtedly Provocative," *TV Guide*, September 11, 1976, p. 22.

22. Ingrid Wiegand, "TVTV Turns Its Camera on the Rest of Us," *The Village Voice*, May 17, 1976.

23. Tom Shales, " 'Superbowl': Bringing Video Vérité Closer to Art," *The Washington Post*, March 10, 1976.

24. Interview with David Loxton.

25. Shales, " 'Superbowl.' "

26. Ibid.

27. John J. O'Connor, "Ebullient 'Superbowl' Is on Channel 13," *The New York Times*, March 15, 1976.

28. Ann Hodges, "Documentary on Super Bowl Teed Up," *Houston Chronicle*, March 19, 1976, p. 22.

29. Marvin Kitman, "The Real Super Bowl," *Newsday*, March 15, 1976.

30. O'Connor, "Ebullient 'Superbowl,' " and Shales, " 'Superbowl.' "

31. Benjamin Stein, "A Syrupy Soaper and Two Winners," *Wall Street Journal*, March 9, 1975.

32. Wiegand, "TVTV Turns Its Camera on the Rest of Us."

33. Kitman, "The Real Super Bowl."

34. Shales, " 'Superbowl.' "

35. Stein, "A Syrupy Soaper."

36. Shales, " 'Superbowl.' "

17. Intermedia

1. The half-hour tape in question was titled *Smoke*, which was described in the UCV catalogue as "an impressionistic piece by independent filmmaker

Tom Compa of a young woman savoring a cigarette." Kulczycki's antipathy to the tape may have had as much to do with its arty pretensions as its apparent boredom.

2. Interview with Stephen Kulczycki, Los Angeles, California, October 14, 1983.

3. Sallie Fischer, "UCV Serves University, Minneapolis Community," *Community Television Review*, circa 1979, pp.10–11.

4. Ibid., p.11.

5. Interview with Ron McCoy, Minneapolis, Minnesota, June 9, 1983.

6. Fisher, "UCV serves University," p. 11.

7. Interview with Tom Borrup, Minneapolis, Minnesota, June 17, 1983.

8. *University Community Video: Annual Report 1981* and *University Community Video: Annual Report 1981–1982*.

18. Hooray for Hollywood?

1. Ingrid Wiegand, "TVTV Turns Its Camera on the Rest of Us," *The Village Voice*, May 17, 1976.

2. Ibid.

3. Interview with Elon Soltes, Los Angeles, California, October 12, 1983.

4. Interview with Megan Williams, Los Angeles, California, October 28, 1983.

5. Interview with Allen Rucker, Los Angeles, California, October 18, 1983.

6. Lee Margulies, "A Late or Early Look at Oscars," *Los Angeles Times*, September 7, 1976.

7. Peter Caranicas, "Conversation with TVTV," *Videography,* May 1977, p. 60.

8. Wiegand, "TVTV Turns Its Camera on the Rest of Us."

9. Ibid.

10. Ibid.

11. Charlie McCollum, "Tonight: A Startling Dylan," *The Washington Star*, September 14, 1976, p. C–3.

12. Interview with Paul Goldsmith, Los Angeles, California, October 13, 1983.

13. Caranicas, "Conversation with TVTV," pp. 39–40.

14. Ebersol was executive producer of "NBC's Saturday Night," which debuted in October 1975.

15. Interview with Paul Goldsmith.

16. McCollum, "Tonight: A Startling Dylan."

17. Eliot Wald, "Bob Dylan Emerges for a Refreshing Hour," *Chicago Daily News*, September 14, 1976.

18. James Brown, "Dylan Dominates 'Hard Rain,' " *Los Angeles Times*, September 14, 1976.

19. Morna Murphy, "Hard Rain," *The Hollywood Reporter.*

20. Caranicas, "Conversation With TVTV," p. 39.

21. Dwight Whitney, "Irreverent, Questioning, Perhaps Unfair, But Undoubtedly Provocative," *TV Guide,* September 11, 1976. p. 22.

22. Ibid., pp. 22, 24.

23. "An American Family" was a controversial documentary series produced for public television and originally aired in early 1973. The 12 hour-long segments of the series chronicled the lives of the Loud family of Santa Barbara, California. Producer Craig Gilbert spent seven months living with the Louds, and the filmmaking team of Alan and Susan Raymond shot some 300 hours of film.

24. Whitney,"Irreverent, Questioning, Perhaps Unfair," p. 24.

25. Interview with Megan Williams.

26. It is hard not to see this as a send-up of the rhetoric of early guerrilla video, best expressed in Gene Youngblood's proclamation in the first issue of *Radical Software*:

> The media must be liberated, must be removed from private ownership and commercial sponsorship, must be placed in the service of all humanity. We must make the media believable. We must assume conscious control over the videosphere. We must wrench the intermedia network free from the archaic and corrupt intelligence that now dominates it.

27. Interview with Megan Williams.

28. Because of their placement as fillers to the highly acclaimed "Visions" series, *Super Vision* did not receive any critical mention until it was screened in its entirety in the spring of 1977 at the Whitney Museum of American Art. John J. O'Connor, who had witnessed and commented upon TVTV's magnum opus, wrote a brief acknowledgement for "TV Weekend" in *The New York Times.* Suggesting that energetic viewers bored by summer TV repeats might want to see the Whitney exhibition, O'Connor noted: "Using solid facts and selective dramatic recreations, TVTV . . . traces broadcasting from marvelous toy to incredible money-making machine. In some cases, the names of major characters have been changed to demolish the guilty and avoid harassing lawsuits." (*The New York Times,* June 3, 1977, p. 23.) The brevity of O'Connor's remarks is provocative. He wrote eleven feature-length reviews of the plays in the "Visions" series, dubbing it a "crucially important" series with "breakthrough" productions, yet nowhere commented on TVTV's fillers.

29. Interview with Michael Shamberg, Los Angeles, California, October 19, 1983.

30. Caranicas, "Conversation with TVTV," p. 34.

31. Interview with Elon Soltes.

32. Interview with Michael Shamberg.

33. John J. O'Connor, "TV Weekend," *The New York Times,* April 29, 1977, p. 31.

34. Ibid.
35. Allen Rucker in letter to author, April 25, 1995.
36. Skip Blumberg, " 'The TVTV Show': Behind the Scenes and Between the Lines," *Televisions*, 5:2 1977, pp. 4–5.
37. Caranicas, "Conversation with TVTV," p. 61.
38. Ibid.
39. Interview with Allen Rucker.
40. Interview with Michael Shamberg.
41. Ibid.
42. Blumberg, " 'The TVTV Show,' " pp. 4–5.
43. Ibid.

19. The Big Chill

1. Interview with Wendy Appel, Topanga Canyon, California, October 17, 1983.
2. Interview with Allen Rucker, Los Angeles, California, March 8, 1992.
3. Ibid.
4. In an anonymous note dappled with coffee stains and tucked into one of TVTV's Umatic cassette cases of the program, the following warning was typewritten:

> Here's another item . . . for your own edification: DIARY OF THE VIDEO GUERRILLAS, KCET's masterful recreation and summation of TVTV's legacy.
> WARNING: This material has been known to cause nausea, cramps, and occasional breathing difficulty among certain segments of the viewing audience. This program is recommended only for those people with a strong constitution and little sense of reality or good taste.
> VIEW AT YOUR OWN RISK.
> After viewing, immediately degauss and rerecord with some other material.

5. Interview with Megan Williams, Los Angeles, California, October 28, 1983.
6. Ibid.
7. Interview with Elon Soltes, Los Angeles, California, October 12, 1983.
8. Interview with Michael Shamberg, Los Angeles, California, October 19, 1983.
9. Shamberg had sent Schlatter, who also produced "Laugh-In," tapes of all of TVTV's work shortly after they arrived in Los Angeles; Schlatter never returned them. Whether he was directly inspired by TVTV's work—as Steven Bochco was by the Raymonds' *Police Tapes* when creating "Hill Street Blues"—is anyone's guess. TVTV's work had been broadcast and

widely written about, so their influences were in the air for anyone to borrow. "NBC's Saturday Night Live" had taken some of TVTV's work for its inspiration, and some of their regular players—John Belushi, Bill Murray, and Dan Ackroyd—had worked with TVTV.

10. Interview with Shamberg.

11. "Dialogue on Film: Michael Shamberg," *American Film*, January–February 1989, p. 18.

12. Interview with Allen Rucker, Los Angeles, California, August 23, 1994. Rucker admits to being a member of SDS, but claimed "the day Bobby Kennedy died was like a kick in the gonads for anyone who really thought you could create change in American politics." He admits that he never really knew much about politics and still doesn't understand the South Carolina challenge.

13. Interview with Wendy Appel.

14. Interview with Shamberg.

20. Epilogue

1. Nora Sayre, *Running Time*, New York: Dial Press, 1982, p. 5.

2. David Moberg, "Experimenting with the Future: Alternative Institutions and American Socialism," in *Co-Ops, Communes & Collectives: Experiments in Social Change in the 1960s and 1970s*, edited by John Case and Rosemary C.R. Taylor, New York: Pantheon, 1979, pp. 276–278.

3. Ibid., pp. 276–281.

4. Todd Gitlin, *The Whole World Is Watching: Mass Media in the Making and Unmaking of the New Left*, Berkeley: University of California Press, 1980, pp. 2–3, 11.

5. Paul Starr, "The Phantom Community" in Case and Taylor, *Co-Ops, Communes & Collectives*, pp. 252–253.

6. Ibid.

7. The essay, "The Wired Nation," appeared in the May 18, 1970 issue of *The Nation*. Two years later Harper & Row published an expanded, book-length version, *The Wired Nation—Cable TV: The Electronic Communications Highway*.

8. Harry J. Skornia in *Television and Society* as quoted by Smith in *The Wired Nation*, p. 38.

9. Ibid., p. 8.

10. Ralph Engelman, "The Origins of Public Access Cable Television, 1966–1972," *Journalism Monographs*, no. 123, October 1990, pp. 1–47.

11. Thomas Whiteside, "Cable—I," *The New Yorker*, May 20, 1985, pp. 44–87; and "Cable—II," May 27, 1985, pp. 43–73.

12. Thomas Whiteside, "Cable—III," *The New Yorker*, June 3, 1985, pp. 82–105.

13. Ibid.

14. As Joel Levitch pointed up, PBS reluctance to commit scare resources to independent productions

has been aggravated in recent years by the development of low-cost ¾-inch portable video technology. For many independents who now specialize in this type of production, there is virtually no place to turn for exposure except television because commercial distribution systems using video have been slow to develop and, at least thus far, the quality of image . . . does not allow for satisfactory conversion to 16mm film. Furthermore, video producers who work in the ¾-inch format are entirely dependent on local stations to provide more sophisticated and exorbitantly expensive video systems to "boost" their signal up to the 2-inch format which is required for broadcast.

(Joel Levitch, "The Independent Producer and Public Broadcasting," *Public Telecommunications Review*, November–December 1977, p. 3.)

15. The term "access" was ambiguous, as Zimmermann notes. Independents argued that entry into broadcasting's "marketplace of ideas" should not be controlled by corporate or governmental interests alone, viewing public television as an outlet insuring the free flow of information. Others contended that access also included public representation on station boards, arguing that access implies the public has a constitutional right to hear a variety of viewpoints. (See Patricia Zimmermann, "Public Television, Independent Documentary Producer and Public Policy," *Journal of the University Film and Video Association* 34:3, 1982.)

16. Nick DeMartino, "Independent Producers in Public TV," *Televisions* 6:4, 1979, pp. 2–17. Concern over independent documentary production spilled over into the '80s. In 1980 a task force report to the National News Council on "Independent Documentarians and Public Television" was issued, reaffirming the importance of independent producers and the documentary for public television. And in the spring of 1983 the CPB and the American Film Institute sponsored a conference titled "The Independent Documentary: The Implications of Diversity," also publishing a report. For more on this conference, see "Does Documentary Have a Future?" *American Film*, April 1982, pp. 57–64, and Susan Linfield, "Documentary Conference: Sidestepping the Issue," *The Independent*, April 1982, pp. 12, 14.

17. David C. Stewart, "Corporation for Public Broadcasting Support for Independent Producers, 1969–1978," January 1978, a document prepared by CPB staffer Stewart for the Carnegie Commission on the Future of Public Broadcasting.

18. The Center for New Public Affairs Programming was coordinated by Nick DeMartino, former editor of *Televisions* magazine and consultant to the new Carnegie Commission on the Future of Public Broadcasting. The coalition included the following: Broadside TV (Johnson City, Tennesee), Center for Understanding Media (New York), Downtown Community Television Center (New York), Global Village (New York), Marin Community

Video (Marin County, California), Media Bus, Inc. (Lanesville, New York), Optic Nerve (San Francisco, California), Pacific Coast Community Video (Santa Barbara, California), Portable Channel (Rochester, New York), State-of-the-Art, Inc. (Washington, D.C.), *Televisions* (Washington, D.C.), TVTV (Los Angeles, California), University Community Video (Minneapolis, Minnesota), Videopolis (Chicago, Illinois), and Videoworks Inc. (Santa Monica, California.)

19. Carnegie Commission, *A Public Trust: The Report of the Carnegie Commission on the Future of Public Broadcasting,* New York: Bantam, 1979, p. 296.

20. Support for the circulation of a variety of ideas is far more problematic because legal interpretations of the First Amendment have not supported ideas that challenge the American political system or policies the system generates during times of crisis. Patricia Zimmermann points up the contradiction between the philosophical position that advocates the public discussion of competing ideas and legal practice (such as the Sedition Act) which excludes socialists, labor unions, or antiwar agitators from First Amendment protections. (Patricia R. Zimmermann, "Public Television, Independent Documentary Producer, and Public Policy.")

21. Carnegie Commission, *A Public Trust*, pp. 300–301.

22. David Loxton speaking on "Journalistic Integrity and the Tradition of the Television Documentary" panel in *The Independent Documentary: The Implications of Diversity—A Conference Report*, American Film Institute and the Corporation for Public Broadcasting, 1983.

23. Whiteside, "Cable–III."

24. William Hoynes, *Public Television for Sale: Media, the Market, and the Public Sphere*, Boulder, Colorado: Westview Press, 1994, pp. 1–5.

25. John Culhane, "Where TV Documentaries Don't Dare to Tread," *The New York Times*, February 20, 1977.

26. Patricia R. Zimmermann, "Independent Documentary Producers and the American Television Networks," *American Screen* 22:4, 1981, pp. 43–53.

27. During the '70s a few community video centers formed alliances with their local network affiliates or commercial independent TV stations, providing documentaries that helped the broadcasters meet their FCC licensing requirements to provide local public affairs programming. The New Orleans Video Access Center (NOVAC), for example, had an arrangement with the city's commercial independent TV station WGNO. As part of their series on "Being Poor in New Orleans," WGNO aired a tape by NOVAC's Andy Kolker and Louis Alvarez titled *The Clarks* (1978), a sensitive video vérité study of the everyday lives of a family of ten in the St. Thomas housing project. Such relationships were local and such programming did not have the impact of national programming on PBS.

28. John J. O'Connor, "ABC Is the Most Active News Game in Town," *The New York Times,* April 9, 1978, pp. 31–32.

29. Patricia Thomson, "Under Fire on the Home Front," *Afterimage*, April 1987, pp. 8–10. See also Jane Hall, "Filming a Philippine Ambush, Lone Reporter Jon Alpert Scores Another Journalistic Coup," *People*, March 24, 1986, pp. 79–80; Jonathan Alter, "Taking Chances," *Newsweek*, March 24, 1986, pp. 59–60; and Mark Christensen, "His Aim Is True: Jon Alpert Is Television's Most Controversial Newsman," *Rolling Stone*, April 10, 1986, pp. 33, 36.

30. Michael Hoyt, "Jon Alpert: NBC's Odd Man Out," *Columbia Journalism Review*, September–October 1991, pp. 44–47.

31. Alpert now produces documentaries on a freelance basis for HBO as one of a few well-known documentary independents who have found limited support from commercial cable.

32. Todd Gitlin, "Make It Look Messy: Striking a New Note with 'Hill Street Blues,'" *American Film*, September 1983, pp. 45–49.

33. Walter Goodman, "Seeking the Truth Amid a Chorus of Video Voices," *The New York Times*, September 26, 1989, pp. C13, C18.

34. Daniel Marcus, editor, *Roar: The Paper Tiger Television Guide to Media Activism*, New York: Paper Tiger Television Collective, 1991. The four-part series was broadcast on public television as well as over local public-access channels.

35. Marlon T. Riggs, "Meet the New Willie Horton," *The New York Times*, March 6, 1991, p. A33.

Bibliography

Aaron, Chloe. "The Alternate-Media Guerrillas." *New York Magazine,* October 19, 1970.

———. "The Video Underground." *Art in America,* May–June 1971.

"Abbie Hoffman on TV in Hiding." *Washington Star-News,* May 19, 1975.

"Abbie Hoffman Says He Could Find Patty." *Post-Dispatch* (Pittsburgh, California), May 19, 1975.

Adams, Val. "Channel 13 Eyeing New Uses for Portable TV Cameras." *New York Daily News,* January 2, 1975.

Adler, Renata. "The Air: Who's Here? What Time Is It?" *The New Yorker,* September 16, 1972.

Adler, Richard, and Walter S. Baer, editors. *The Electronic Box Office: Humanities and Arts on the Cable.* New York: Praeger, 1974.

Alter, Jonathan. "Taking Chances." *Newsweek,* March 24, 1986.

Antin, David. "Television: Video's Frightful Parent." *Artforum* 14, December 1975.

Armstrong, David. *A Trumpet to Arms: Alternative Media in America.* Boston: South End Press, 1981.

Aufderheide, Pat. "The Movies." *Minnesota Daily,* January 25, 1974.

Baker, Ann. "Video Tape: A New Way to Express Yourself." *St. Paul Pioneer Press,* February 13, 1974.

Barnouw, Erik. *Documentary, A History of Non-Fiction Film.* New York: Oxford University Press, 1974.

———. *Tube of Plenty.* New York: Oxford University Press, 1978.

Bateson, Gregory. *Steps to an Ecology of Mind.* New York: Ballantine Books, 1972.

Battcock, Gregory, editor. *New Artists Video.* New York: Dutton, 1978.

Blaustein, Richard. "Everyone Is History: Continuing Appalachian Culture." *Televisions* 3:4, 1975.

Blumberg, Skip. " 'The TVTV Show': Behind the Scenes and Between the Lines." *Televisions* 5:2, 1977.

Boyle, Deirdre. "American Documentary Video: Subject to Change." Catalog. New York: The American Federation of Arts and The Museum of Modern Art, 1988.

————. "A Brief History of American Documentary Video." In *Illuminating Video*, edited by Doug Hall and Sally Jo Fifer. New York: Aperture Press, 1991.

————. "Documentary Video Classics: A Core Collection." *Sightlines,* Spring 1983.

————. "From Portapak to Camcorder: A Brief History of Guerrilla Television." *Journal of Film and Video* 44:1–2, Spring/Summer 1992.

————. "Guerrilla Television." In *Transmissions,* edited by Peter D'Agostino. New York: Tanam Press, 1985; rev. ed. Sage Publications, 1994.

————. "Home Video Review: Paper Tiger Television." *Cineaste* 14:2, 1985.

————. *Parallel Realities, Northern Dreams: Some Thoughts on the National Film Board of Canada.* Montreal and New York: National Film Board of Canada. 1993.

————. "Return of Guerrilla Television: A TVTV Retrospective." Video Feature Program Notes, November 14, 1986–February 22, 1987. New York: International Center for Photography, 1986.

————. "Skip Blumberg Warms Up TV." *Sightlines,* Spring 1982.

————. "Subject to Change: Guerrilla Television Revisited." *College Art Journal,* Fall 1985.

————. "Survival Information Television: Turning Watching into Waiting—and Learning." *Televisions* 8:1–2, 1981.

————. "Top Value TV & Guerrilla Television—Pioneering the Vast Wasteland." *Sightlines,* Fall/Winter 1984/85.

————. "Truth or Verisimilitude? Evolution of the Raymonds." *Sightlines,* Winter 1981.

————. "Video." In *International Encyclopedia of Communications.* edited by Erik Barnouw. New York: The Annenberg School of Communications, University of Pennsylvania, and Oxford University Press, 1989.

————. *Video Classics: A Guide to Video Art and Documentary Tapes.* Phoenix: Oryx Press, 1986.

————. "Video Documentary: The New Wave." *American Film,* May 1981.

————. "Video from the Global Village." *Sightlines,* Summer 1980.

————. "Video From the Heartlands." *Sightlines,* Fall/Winter 1983/84.

————. *Video Preservation: Securing the Future of the Past.* New York: Media Alliance, 1993.

————. "Whatever Happened to Guerrilla TV?" *Videography,* December 1984.

————. "Who's Who in Video: Jon Alpert." *Sightlines,* Spring 1980.

Brecht, Bertolt. "The Radio as an Apparatus of Communication." *Brecht on Theater,* edited and translated by John Willet. New York: Hill and Wang, 1964.

"Broadside TV and Videomaker: An Appalachian Video Network." Brochure circa 1973.

Brown, James. "Dylan Dominates 'Hard Rain.' " *Los Angeles Times,* September 14, 1976.

Brown, Les. "Channel 13 to Aid Group Trying to Expand Videotape Programs." *The New York Times*, November 15, 1974.

———. "Ford Fund, WNET Decry Hoffman Fee." *The New York Times*, May 19, 1975.

———. "Independent TV News Films Face Dim Prospects." *The New York Times*, March 11, 1975.

———. "TV Interview Payments." *The New York Times*, May 24, 1975.

———. *Television: The Business Behind the Box*. New York: Harcourt Brace Jovanovich, 1971.

"Buckley Asks Inquiry on Hoffman Payment." *The New York Times*, May 19, 1975.

Butler, Katy. "Dissecting the Guru on the Tube." *The San Francisco Bay Guardian*, February 28, 1974.

"Cable TV: Democratizing the Airwaves?" *Many Corners* (Cedar/Riverside Community Newspaper) 1:9, November 1973.

"Cable Policy Changing: Deregulation Push, FCC Eliminates Mandatory Origination." *Community Video Report* 2:2, 1974.

Caen, Herb. "It Takes All Kinds." *San Francisco Chronicle*, circa September 1972.

Caranicas, Peter. "Conversation with TVTV." *Videography*, May 1977.

Carnegie Commission. *A Public Trust: The Report of the Carnegie Commission on the Future of Public Broadcasting* New York: Bantam, 1979.

Carpenter, Ted, and Mike Clarke. "The Living Newsletter—Portable Videotape and a Regional Spirit." *Access* (Challenge for Change), no. 11, Spring 1973.

Carroll, Peter. *It Seemed Like Nothing Happened: The Tragedy and Promise of America in the 1970s*. New York: Holt, Rinehart and Winston, 1982.

Case, John, and Rosemary C.R. Taylor, editors. *Co-Ops, Communes & Collectives: Experiments in Social Change in the 1960s and 1970s*. New York: Pantheon, 1979.

Casey, Richard. "TVTV Illuminates the Ji." *Berkeley Barb*, March 22–28, 1974.

Cater, Douglas, and Richard Adler. *Television as a Social Force: New Approaches to TV Criticism*. Palo Alto, California: Aspen Institute, 1975.

Childs, Charles W. "Portable Videotape and CATV in Appalachia: They Start People Thinking." *Educational & Industrial Television*, June 1973.

Christensen, Mark. "His Aim is True: Jon Alpert is Television's Most Controversial Newsman." *Rolling Stone*, April 10, 1986.

"Conversation with John Godfrey." *Videography*, August 1983.

Costello, Victoria, Nick DeMartino, and Larry Kirkman. "Small Format Video Broadcast." *Televisions* 4:2, 1976.

Crouse, Timothy. *The Boys on the Bus*. New York: Ballantine, 1973.

Crutcher, Ann. "A Jarring Look at 'Gerald Ford's America.' " *Washington Star-News*, January 10, 1975.

Culhane, John. "Where TV Documentaries Don't Dare to Tread." *The New York Times*, February 20, 1977.

Czitrom, Daniel. *Media and the American Mind from Morse to McLuhan.* Chapel Hill: University of North Carolina Press, 1982.

D'Agostino, Peter, editor. *Transmission.* New York: Tanam Press, 1985.

Davis, Douglas. *Art and the Future.* New York: Praeger, 1973.

————, "Television's Avant-Garde." *Newsweek*, February 9, 1970.

Davis, Douglas, and Allison Simmons, editors. *The New Television: A Public/ Private Art.* Cambridge, Massachusetts: The MIT Press, 1977.

Deeb, Gary. "Documentaries on D.C." *Chicago Tribune*, February 3, 1975.

DeMartino, Nick. "Getting into PBS: Independents Make Inroads on National Programming." *Televisions* 3:3, August–September 1975.

————. "Independent Producers in Public TV." *Televisions* 6:4, 1979.

DeMott, Benjamin. "Culture Watch." *The Atlantic* 235:6, June 1975.

"Dialog on Film: Michael Shamberg." *American Film*, January-February; 1989.

"Does Documentary Have a Future?" *American Film*, April 1982.

Downie, Charles E. "TV's Glimpse at the Floor of Two Conventions." *San Francisco Sunday Chronicle and Examiner*, October 29, 1972.

Drukker, Leendert. "Broadcast TV Opens Up for Portapak Tapes." *Popular Photography* 76:6, June 1975.

Engelman, Ralph. *Public Radio and Television in America: A Political History.* Thousand Oaks, California: Sage Publications, 1996.

————, "The Origins of Public Access Cable Television, 1966–1972." *Journalism Monographs*, no. 123, October 1990.

Enzensberger, Hans Magnus. *The Consciousness Industry.* New York: Seabury Press, 1974.

Epstein, Renee. "TVTV." *Film Comment*, September–October 1975.

Farris, Joe. "He Starts People Thinking." *Herald*-Citizen (Cookville, Tennessee), July 6, 1972.

"Favorable Response Received to Circle Pines Utilities Segment on TV Program." *Circulating Pines*, October 17, 1974.

Feldman, N.E. *Cable Television: Opportunities and Problems in Local Program Origination.* Santa Monica California: Rand, 1970.

"1st National Video Festival." *Radical Software* 2:4, 1973.

Fischer, Sallie. "UCV Serves University, Minneapolis Community." *Community Television Review*, circa 1979.

Flander, Judy. "Everywhere You Turn." *The Washington Star*, June 25, 1975.

Flippen, Charles C. editor. *Liberating the Media: The New Journalism.* Washington, D.C.: Acropolis Books, 1974.

"Fred Is Unfriendly with WNET After 'Checkbook' Hoffman Gab." *Variety*, May 28, 1975.

Fuller, R. Buckminster. *Operating Manual for Spaceship Earth.* New York: Pocket Books, 1969.

" 'Gerald Ford's America.' " *Washington Post*, January 15, 1975.

"Gerald Ford's America." *Variety*, January 15, 1974.

"Getting Technical: The Lord of the Universe." *Vision News* 1:2, May 1974.

Gever, Martha. "Meet the Press: On Paper Tiger Television." *Afterimage*, 11:4, November 1983.

———. "Pomp and Circumstances: The Coronation of Nam June Paik." *Afterimage* 10:3, October 1982.

———. "Video Politics: Early Feminist Projects." *Afterimage* 11:1–2, Summer 1983.

Gigliotti, Davidson. "Video Art in the Sixties." In *Abstract Painting: 1960-69.* P.S. 1 catalog. New York: The Institute for Art and Urban Resources, 1982.

Gill, Johanna. *Video: State of the Art*. New York: Rockefeller Foundation Working Papers, June 1976.

Gitlin, Todd. *Inside Prime Time*. New York: Pantheon, 1983.

———. "Make It Look Messy: Striking a New Note with 'Hill Street Blues.' " *American Film*, September 1983.

———. "Sixteen Notes on Television and The Movement." In *Literature in Revolution*, edited by George Abbot White and Charles Newman. New York: Holt, Rinehart and Winston, 1972.

———. *The Sixties: Years of Hope, Days of Rage*. New York: Bantam, 1987.

———. *The Whole World Is Watching: Mass Media in the Making and Unmaking of the New Left*. Berkeley: University of California Press, 1980.

Godfrey, John. "Getting Technical: The Lord of the Universe." *Vision News* 1:3, May 1974.

Goldsmith, Paul. " 'Lord of the Universe': An Eclairman in Videoland." *Filmmakers Newsletter*, Summer 1974.

Goldsmith, Paul, and Megan Williams, "The Good Times are Killing Me: TVTV Debriefing." *Filmmakers Newsletter*, October 1975.

Goldstein, Neil, and Nick DeMartino. "FCC Weighing Crucial Access, Origination Regs." *Community Video Report* 2:1, 1974.

" 'Good Times' Misses." *New York Daily News*, June 23, 1975.

" 'The Good Times Are Killing Me' Documents a Two-Hundred-Year-Old Culture in Danger of Being Lost." WNET/13 Press Release, June 9, 1975.

Goodman, Walter. "Seeking the Truth Amid a Chorus of Video Voices." *The New York Times*, September 26, 1989.

Grierson, John. "Memo to Michelle about Decentralizing the Means of Production." *Access* (Challenge for Change), Spring 1972.

Griffin, Carl, Jr., and Irv Letofsky. "Do-It-Yourself TV: A Story of the Expanding Use of Video Tape." *Minneapolis Tribune*, January 27, 1974.

"Guerrilla Television." *Newsweek*, December 7, 1970.

"Guru Show a Breakthrough." *Vision News* 1:3, May 1974.

Hall, Doug, and Sally Jo Fifer, editors. *Illuminating Video*. New York: Aperture Press, 1991.

Hall, Jane. "Filming a Philippine Ambush, Lone Reporter Jon Alpert Scores Another Journalistic Coup." *People*, March 24, 1986.

Hanhardt, John, editor. *Video Culture: A Critical Investigation*. Layton, Utah: Peregrine Smith Books, 1986.

Hanson, Cynthia. "Video Center Adds 'Commercials' to CCTV Programming." *Minnesota Daily*, October 9, 1973.

Hénaut, Dorothy Todd. "A Report from Canada: Television as Town Meeting." *Radical Software* 1:2, 1970.

Hénaut, Dorothy Todd, and Bonnie Klein. "In the Hands of Citizens." *Radical Software*, 1:1, 1970.

Hickey, Neil. "From Broadcasting to Narrowcasting." *TV Guide*, December 16, 1972.

―――. "Notes From the Video Underground." *TV Guide*, December 9, 1972.

Hilenski, Ski. "Mountain Guerrilla: The Life, Death, and Legacy of Broadside TV." Undated draft of a paper in the possession of Ted Carpenter.

Hodges, Ann. "Documentary on Super Bowl Teed Up." *Houston Chronicle*, March 19, 1976.

Hoffman, Abbie. *Soon To Be a Major Motion Picture*. New York: Perigee, 1980.

―――. *Steal This Book*. Worcester, MA: Abbie Yo-Yo Productions, Inc., 1772 [*sic*].

"Homegrown Is Fresher: Broadside TV Pioneers in Regional Video Programming." *Appalachia*, April–May 1974.

Hoynes, William. *Public Television for Sale: Media, the Market, and the Public Sphere*. Boulder, Colorado: Westview Press, 1994.

Hoyt, Michael. "Jon Alpert: NBC's Odd Man Out." *Columbia Journalism Review*, September–October 1991.

Huffman, Kathy Rae, editor. *Video: A Retrospective*. Long Beach, California: Long Beach Museum of Art, 1984.

The Independent Documentary: The Implications of Diversity—A Conference Report. Washington, D.C.: American Film Institute and the Corporation for Public Broadcasting, 1983.

Innis, Harold A. *The Bias of Communication*, 2nd ed. Toronto: University of Toronto Press, 1971.

―――. *Empire and Communications*, revised by Mary Q. Innis, 2nd ed. Toronto: University of Toronto Press, 1972.

Jensen, Jay. "The New Journalism in Historical Perspective." In *Liberating the Media: The New Journalism*, edited by Charles C. Flippen. Washington, D.C.: Acropolis Books, 1974.

Johnson, Haynes. "Focusing on the Widest, Easiest Target in Town." *The Washington Post*, January 24, 1975.

Johnson, Nicholas. *How to Talk Back to Your TV Set*. New York: Bantam, 1972.

Jones, Will. "After Last Night." *Minneapolis Tribune*, October 5, 1974.

Jowett, Garth. "Dangling the Dream? The Presentation of Television to the American Public, 1928–1952." *Historical Journal of Film, Radio and Television*, 14:2, 1994.

Kahn, Aron. "New Idea for TV Series." *St. Paul Dispatch*, October 2, 1974.

Kalba, Kas. "The Video Implosion: Models for Reinventing Television." In *The Electronic Box Office*, edited by Richard Adler and Walter S. Baer. New York: Praeger Publishers, 1974.

Kitman, Marvin. " 'Chic to Sheik' Is Almost Better Than Being There." *Newsday*, January 17, 1975.

———. "The Real Super Bowl." *Newsday*, March 15, 1976.

Levin, G. Roy. *Documentary Explorations, 15 Interviews with Filmmakers*. New York: Anchor Books, 1971.

Levine, Faye. *The Culture Barons: An Analysis of Power and Money in the Arts*. New York: Crowell, 1976.

Levine, Richard. "The Cameraman Comes Out of the Ocean, See?" *The New York Times*, October 5, 1975.

Levitch, Joel. "The Independent Producer and Public Broadcasting." *Public Telecommunications Review*, November–December 1977.

Linfield, Susan. "Documentary Conference: Sidestepping the Issue." *The Independent*, April 1982.

London, Barbara. "Independent Video: The First Fifteen Years."*Artforum* 9, September 1980.

London, Barbara, and Lorraine Zippay. "A Chronology of Video Activity in the United States: 1965–1980." *Artforum* 9, September 1980.

Lord, Chip. "TVTV: Video Pioneers 10 Years Later." *SEND*, Summer 1983.

Lyons, Nick. *The SONY Vision*. New York: Crown, 1976.

Marcus, Daniel, editor. *Roar: The Paper Tiger Television Guide to Media Activism*. New York: Paper Tiger Television Collective, 1991.

Margulies, Lee. "A Late or Early Look at the Oscars." *Los Angeles Times*, September 7, 1976.

McCollum, Charlie. "Tonight: A Startling Bob Dylan." *The Washington Star*, September 14, 1976.

McLean, Robert. "Bittersweet Look at the Dying Cajun Culture." *The Boston Globe*, June 24, 1975.

McLuhan, Marshall. *The Gutenberg Galaxy*. New York: New American Library, 1962.

———. *Understanding Media: The Extensions of Man*. New York: McGraw-Hill, 1964.

McLuhan, Marshall, and Quentin Fiore. *The Medium is the Massage: An Inventory of Effects*. New York: Bantam, 1967.

Mellencamp, Patricia. "Video Politics: *Guerrilla TV*, Ant Farm, *Eternal Frame*." *Discourse*, Spring–Summer 1988.

"Minneapolis: Student-Based Video Work—Interview with Ron McCoy." *Community Video Report* 1:4, Spring 1974.

Moberg, David. "Experimenting with the Future: Alternative Institutions and American Socialism." In *Co-Ops, Communes & Collectives: Experiments in Social Change in the 1960s and 1970s*, edited by John Case and Rosemary C.R. Taylor. New York: Pantheon, 1979.

Monahan, Anthony. "A Guerrilla Convention View." *Chicago Sun-Times*, August 24, 1972.

Montgomery, Paul L. "Abbie Hoffman Speaks of Life in 'Underground.'" *The New York Times*, May 19, 1975.

Morrow, Barry and Paul Gronseth. "Beltrami Ethnic History Project." *Radical Software* 2:4, 1973.

Morrow, Barry, Tacoumba Aitken, and Bruce Doepke. "Video Involvement Project." *Radical Software* 2:4, 1973.

Mulligan, Jim, and Stephen Kulczycik. "Changing Channels." *Televisions* 4: 2, Summer 1976.

Murphy, Mona. "Hard Rain." *The Hollywood Reporter*.

Murray, Michael. *The Videotape Book*. New York: Bantam, 1975.

Newfield, Jack. "The 'Truth' about Objectivity and the New Journalism." In *Liberating the Media: The New Journalism*, edited by Charles C. Flippen. Washington, D.C.: Acropolis Books, 1974.

O'Connor, John J. "ABC is the Most Active News Game in Town." *The New York Times*, April 9, 1978.

―――. "Ebullient 'Superbowl' Is On Channel 13." *The New York Times*, March 15, 1976.

―――. "Technology is Reshaping Documentaries." *The New York Times*, June 29, 1975.

―――. "TV: Meditating on Young Guru and His Followers." *The New York Times*, February 25, 1974.

―――. "TV: On Abbie Hoffman." *The New York Times*, May 19, 1975.

―――. "TV: A 'Scrapbook of the Democratic Convention.'" *The New York Times*, August 17, 1972.

―――. "TV: View of 'Gerald Ford's America.'" *The New York Times*, February 6, 1975.

―――. "TV Weekend." *The New York Times*, April 29, 1977.

―――, "TV Weekend." *The New York Times*, June 3, 1977.

―――. "Young Film Makers, Video Documentarians." *The New York Times*, June 23, 1975.

O'Flaherty, Terence. "A Source of Ignorance." *San Francisco Examiner*, August 31, 1974.

O'Neill, William L. *Coming Apart: An Informal History of America in the 1960's*. New York: Times Books, 1971.

Orth, Maureen. "Guerrilla Video: Days of Tape at the Conventions." *Rolling Stone*, July 20, 1972.

"Paid Interview of Abbie Hoffman on WNET Arouses Ire of Ford Foundation." *Broadcasting*, May 26, 1975.

"PBS Statement of Policy on Program Standards and Document of Journalism Standards and Guidelines." April 15, 1971.

Peck, Abe. *Uncovering the Sixties: The Life and Times of the Underground Press.* New York: Pantheon, 1985.

Perlman, Phil. "TVTV in Cajun Country." *Millimeter* 3:6, June 1975.

Porter, William E. *Assault on the Media: The Nixon Years.* Ann Arbor: University of Michigan Press, 1976.

Powers, Ron. "A Merciless Look at TV-ad Makers." *Chicago Sun-Times,* April 8, 1974.

———. "Participatory TV Goes to Guru Gala." *Chicago Sun-Times,* March 16, 1974.

———. "What You'll Watch in the Year 2000." *Chicago Sun-Times,* July 31, 1974.

Price, Jonathan. *Video Visions: A Medium Discovers Itself.* New York: New American Library, 1972.

Reed, Revon. "Comme Çi, Comme Ça." *The Mamou Acadian Press,* January 30, 1975.

Reeves, Richard. "Conventional Behavior." *New York Magazine,* August 28, 1972.

Reeves, T. Zane. *The Politics of the Peace Corps and VISTA.* Tuscaloosa: University of Alabama, 1988.

Riggs, Marlon. "Meet the New Willie Horton." *The New York Times,* March 6, 1991.

Rosenbaum, Ron. "What Makes Abbie Run?" *New Times,* June 13, 1975.

Rosler, Martha. "Video: Shedding the Utopian Moment." In *Illuminating Video,* edited by Doug Hall and Sally Jo Fifer. New York: Aperture Press, 1990.

Ross, Betsy. "TVTV Bids a Not-So-Reluctant Farewell." *San Francisco Examiner,* March 7, 1975.

Ross, David. "Television: Bringing the Museum Home." *Televisions* 3:2, May 1975.

Roszak, Theodore. *The Making of a Counter Culture.* New York: Doubleday, 1969.

Ryan, Paul. "Cable Television: The Raw and the Overcooked." *Radical Software,* 1:1, 1970.

———. "Cybernetic Strategy and Guerrilla Theory." *Radical Software* 1:3, Spring 1971.

———. *Cybernetics of the Sacred.* New York: Doubleday, 1974.

———. "A Genealogy of Video." *Leonardo: Journal of the International Society for the Arts and Technology,* 21:1, 1988.

Sayre, Nora. *Running Time.* New York: Dial Press, 1982.

———. *Sixties Going on Seventies.* New York: Arbor House, 1973.

Schiller, Herbert. *Mass Communications and American Empire.* Boston: Beacon Press, 1969.

———. *The Mind Managers.* Boston: Beacon Press, 1973.

Schneider, Ira, and Beryl Korot, editors. *Video Art: An Anthology.* New York: Harcourt Brace Jovanovich, 1976.

Shales, Tom. "Close-Ups on Cajuns: Fresh Air for TV." *The Washington Post*, June 25, 1975.

———. " 'Superbowl': Bringing Video Verite Closer to Art." *The Washington Post*, March 10, 1976.

Shales, Tom, and Donnie Radcliffe. " 'Chic to Sheik.' " *The Washington Post*, January 17, 1975.

Shamberg, Michael, and Raindance Corporation. *Guerrilla Television*. New York: Holt, Rinehart and Winston, 1971.

Sharbutt, Jay. "Super Bowl X: Game Is Not the Thing." Associated Press story. *Asbury Park Press*, January 16, 1976.

Sinard, Craig Paul. "Television and Video Access." Unpublished master's thesis, Iowa State University, 1979.

Singer, Suzanne Karen. "TVTV." Unpublished master's thesis, University of California, Berkeley, December 1975.

Sloan, Alfred P., Foundation. *On the Cable: The Television of Abundance*. New York: McGraw Hill, 1972.

Smith, Ralph Lee. "The Wired Nation." *The Nation* 210:19, May 18, 1970.

———. *The Wired Nation—Cable TV: The Electronic Communications Highway*. New York: Harper Books, 1972.

Spector, Bert. "A Clash of Cultures: The Smothers Brothers vs. CBS Television." *American History/American Television*, edited by John E. O'Connor. New York: Ungar, 1983.

Starr, Paul. "The Phantom Community." In *Co-Ops, Communes & Collectives: Experiments in Social Change in the 1960s and 1970s*, edited by John Case and Rosemary C.R. Taylor. New York: Pantheon, 1979.

Stein, Benjamin. "A Syrupy Soaper and Two Winners." *Wall Street Journal*, March 9, 1975.

———. "We Need It Now More Than Ever." *TV Guide*, December 27, 1975.

Stewart, David C. "Corporation for Public Broadcasting Support for Independent Producers, 1969–1978." A document for the Carnegie Commission on the Future of Public Television, January 1978.

Stoney, George. "The Mirror Machine." *Sight and Sound*, 41:1, Winter 1971–72.

Sturken, Marita. "An Interview with George Stoney." *Afterimage* 9: 9, April 1982.

———. "Paradox in the Evolution of an Art Form." In *Illuminating Video*, edited by Doug Hall and Sally Jo Fifer. New York: Aperture Press, 1990.

———. "Private Money and Personal Influence: Howard Klein and The Rockefeller Foundation's Funding of the Media Arts." *Afterimage* 14:6, January 1987.

Swertlow, Frank. " 'Ford's America' Will be Aired." UPI syndicated review, January 8, 1975.

"Talk About Newspapers and Videotape: Mountain People Attend Communications Workshop." *Highlander Reports*, September 1971.

Teilhard de Chardin, Pierre. *The Phenomenon of Man*. New York: Harper, 1959.

"Television Has an All–Electronic Future." *Televisions* 4:2, June 1976.

"They Found a New Guru." *Vision News* 2:2, December 1974.

"Time Scans." *Televisions* 4:2, Summer 1976.

Thompson, Hunter S. *Fear and Loathing: On the Campaign Trail '72*. New York: Warner Books, 1973.

Thomson, Patricia. "Under Fire on the Home Front." *Afterimage*, April 1987.

Twohill, Catherine. "TVTV: Tomorrow's Television Today?" *Image*, April 1975.

"TV Filming Planned of Mardi Gras Event." *The Eunice News*, February 6, 1975.

TVTV, " 'Lord of the Universe': A Technical Report." *Filmmakers Newsletter*, Summer 1974.

———. *Prime Time*. Circa 1973. Pamphlet.

———. *The Prime Time Survey*. Self-published, 1974.

———. "The TVTV Story." *Vision News* 1:2, October 1973.

———."Top Value Television Coverage of 1972 Political Conventions." *Radical Software* 2:1, 1972.

———. *TVTV Scrapbook*. Unpaged original document of TVTV at the conventions, owned by Allen Rucker.

Unger, Arthur. "Cajun Special, or How to Picture a Culture." *The Christian Science Monitor*, June 23, 1975.

———. "Weekend Trio of Documentaries." *The Christian Science Monitor*, February 22, 1974.

University Community Video. *Annual Report 1981*.

———. *Annual Report 1981–1982*.

Vassi, Marco. "Rappo: Why Aren't You Fucking." *Radical Software* 1:2, 1970.

———. "Zen Tubes." *Radical Software* 1: 1, 1970.

"Video Documentary, 'Superbowl,' Takes an Irrelevant, Behind-the-Scenes Look at Pro Football and Its Ultimate Event—Super Bowl X." WNET/13 Press Release, February 25, 1976.

"Video Jobs Offered." *Televisions* 3:3, August–September 1975.

Videofreex. *Spaghetti City Video Manual*. New York: Praeger Publishers, 1973.

"Video Shots." *Televisions* 3:1, 1975.

Volp, Barbara. "Disgruntled TV Viewers Offered Chance to Air Own Shows." *Minnesota Daily*, October 21, 1974.

Wald, Eliot. "Bob Dylan Emerges for a Refreshing Hour." *Chicago Daily News*, September 14, 1976.

Waters, Harry. "Candid Camera." *Newsweek*, January 27, 1975.

Whiteside, Thomas. "Cable." Three-part article in *The New Yorker*, May 20, 27, June 3, 1985.

Whitney, Dwight. "Irreverent, Questioning, Perhaps Unfair, but Undoubtedly Provocative." *TV Guide*, September 11, 1976.

Wiegand, Ingrid. "At Home with Abbie Hoffman: The Soft-Sell Story of the
Underground." *Soho Weekly News*, May 29, 1975.

———. "TVTV Turns its Camera on the Rest of Us." *The Village Voice*,
May 17, 1976.

Williams, Bob. "On the Air." *New York Post*, February 25, 1974.

Williams, Raymond. *Television: Technology and Cultural Form*. New York:
Schocken Books, 1974.

Wolfe, Tom. *The New Journalism*. New York: Harper & Row, 1973.

Wurzburg, Geraldine. "Top Value Television Hits DeeCee with Video." *Community Video Report*, 2:2, Autumn 1974.

Yalkut, Jud. "Frank Gillette and Ira Schneider: Part I and II of an Interview." *Radical Software* 1: 1, 1970.

Youngblood, Gene. *Expanded Cinema*. New York: Dutton, 1970.

Zimmerman, Patricia. "Independent Documentary Producers and the American Television Networks." *American Screen* 22:4, 1981.

———. "Public Television, Independent Documentary Producer and Public
Policy." *Journal of the University Film and Video Association* 34:3,
1982.

Index

271